Discovering Geography of North America with Books Kids Love

Discovering Geography of North America with Books Kids Love

Carol J. Fuhler

Illustrated by Audra Loyal

fulcrum resources
Golden, Colorado

To my dad who was there to celebrate the beginning of this book
but didn't get to see its completion, and to my mom
whose concern and encouragement
have been a blessing when I needed them most.

—C. J. F.

Text copyright © 1998 Carol J. Fuhler
Illustrations copyright © 1998 Audra Loyal, except those on pages 191–195, 199–201, 207, 208, and 209
    (Grandmother's Fan Pattern)
Book design by Bill Spahr

Library of Congress Cataloging-in-Publication Data

Fuhler, Carol J.
        Discovering geography of North America with books kids love /
Carol J. Fuhler ; illustrated by Audra Loyal.
            p.   cm.
        Includes bibliographical references and index.
        ISBN 1-55591-954-5 (paperback)
        1. North America—Geography—Study and teaching (Elementary)—
Activity programs.   2. North America—Geography—Juvenile
literature—Bibliography.   I. Title.
CURR E40.5.F84   1998
        917.0071'2—dc21   97-43816
                                                                        CIP

Printed in United States of America

0 9 8 7 6 5 4 3 2 1

Fulcrum Publishing
350 Indiana Street, Suite 350
Golden, Colorado 80401-5093
(800) 992-2908 • (303) 277-1623
website: www.fulcrum-resources.com
e-mail: fulcrum@fulcrum-resources.com

Contents

Acknowledgments

No one writes a book alone and this one is no exception. I certainly appreciate the help of my friends and colleagues who would drop by my office from time to time with a book they had discovered that might fit one of the geography lessons. I would especially like to thank the owners of The Book Nest, Linda and Fred Salazar, for their friendly support, for letting me browse through their books time and time again, for their genuine interest, and for keeping their eyes open for just one more current title for my book. I would also like to thank my husband, Richard, for his probing questions and keen eye when it came to the first editing of my chapters. A heartfelt thanks for his incredible patience during this lengthy creative process as well. Finally, my gratitude goes to the following publishers for sharing review copies: Candlewick Press, The Putnam & Grosset Group, and William Morrow Children's Books.

Preface

I love books. I can't remember a time when that wasn't true. One of my favorite places to spend inordinate amounts of time in is a bookstore, most often in the children's section. There is something so tantalizing about a brand new book that my eager fingers anticipate opening it. I delight in the feel of the crisp pages, in the fabulous illustrations of picture books, and in the promise of making new friends and visiting intriguing places within novels. If you are reading this preface, there is a good chance we share similar feelings.

I have vivid memories of sitting in front of the bookcase filled with well-read books at my grandmother's house in Seattle as an early teen. I would pour over the titles and leaf through books once enjoyed by my aunts and mother when they were younger. Eventually I would settle on a title that would carry me away into worlds of possibilities and imagination. I can also distinctly remember reading Nancy Drew by flashlight under a tent of covers, when I was supposed to be sound asleep, and worrying with Nancy about how to get out of her particular predicament. Then, too, I loved reading to my two sons at a time when they could barely understand what a book was all about. I was still reading aloud some years later when I taught reading, language arts, and social studies to seventh and eighth graders. It seems that the extraordinary world of literature, both for children and adults, has long been a part of my life.

The most exciting thing about this love of books is that I know I am not alone as I work alongside teachers who read to their classes and infuse their curriculums with timely fiction and nonfiction. I have learned that a thing loved and shared is something that grows. For example, in my education courses I see this excitement again with college students who are getting caught up in the world of children's books, some of them for the first time. It is one of those good news/bad news situations when those students groan about how much it is costing them for children's books after taking my classes. They frequently explain how their Christmas wish lists are expanding as they add longed-for books. The fascination with children's literature is an expensive habit, I'll agree, but it certainly is a healthy one, and I can guarantee that it is nearly impossible to break!

In this particular book I have the opportunity to share my enthusiasm for well-wrought children's literature starting with picture books and expanding to novels. I elaborate on the potential for weaving these books into the once dry subject of geography. I share the concern with a growing number of educators that learners of all ages are almost ignorant of the geographic world around them. I worry that each child's world is shrinking to a minuscule size rather than expanding to encompass our global society. You see, I know that geography is exciting. I want teachers and students to understand that, too. It just makes sense to me to use dynamite children's picture books as a jumping-off place for building geographic concepts, and for learning about the five key themes, in an effort to make the quest for geographic knowledge personal and memorable.

Enjoy becoming familiar with the suggested titles used in the upcoming lessons. Go on a geographic investigation of your own and add or exchange books that work better for you. There is something so satisfying in discovering just the right book to help get a concept across. Mold and adapt the lessons and ideas to fit your child or your classroom. Send your learners off across the continent of North America on a journey of geographic discovery that begins within the pages of a picture book and ends with the creation of a geographically informed adult. I simply don't believe there is a better way to accomplish such a goal than through the world of children's and adult literature.

Carol J. Fuhler
Northern Arizona University
Flagstaff, Arizona

This Is My Right
by Sigmund A. Boloz

Give me the vast–unveiled universe,
Let loose my inquisitive mind
For I was born to wonder
And to contemplate what I find.

Give me this magnificent world to ponder,
Intriguing cultures and tongues
And I shall devour their mysteries
Frolic as their songs are sung.

Give me the rolling, open waters,
The salt breezes upon my face
For I was born to stroll their crests
And to exult the windward chase.

Give me the wide western skies,
The wealth of fresh, mountain air
And I shall dance with eagles
In the dazzling sunsets there.

Give me the open fields
For I was born to run free,
To scale grand rocks
And to climb the wisdom tree.

Give me the dirty hands of discovery,
The eyes of enterprising youth.
Give me gales of ruckus laughter
And a heart filled with childhood truth.

Respect my right to be a child
For children are not born to be still.
Help to lead me out of myself
For I have a splendid mind to fill.

Used with permission by Sigmund A. Boloz. Originally published in *Odious Mud: A Collection of Poems* by Sigmund A. Boloz. Illustrated by Preston A. Boloz. Ganado, Ariz.: Wooded Hill Productions, 1995.

Introduction

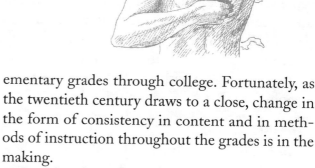

A Backward Glance

In a time long past, a man stoops to grasp a stick then begins to scratch a simple map into the dust showing a route to the nearest water supply. At another time and in a separate location, an early Native American mixes natural dyes and painstakingly paints rudimentary directions on a massive stone showing the migrations of his tribe. Years slip by. In yet another distant spot, a member of the Anasazi tribe deftly chisels symbols into a wall with a sharp rock as he relates the story of the lives and travels of his people.

Time moves on. The Greek and Roman scholars begin to record topographical accounts of the world as they know it. Records in various forms indicate that humans have long been aware of place, of their own personal geography, and have mapped their existence either on cave walls or later, on charts created by early explorers, and more recently via contemporary satellite photographs of the earth.

Geography is a subject with an interesting history of its own, isn't it? It was pursued as long as 2,000 years ago and has been an integral part of most children's education ever since. However, the subject has not received uniform attention from year to year, classroom to classroom, or school to school. Over the years geography has either been taught separately or integrated into the social studies curriculum in our nation's classrooms. Unfortunately, it has received less attention in some schools than in others. Traditionally, very little geography was taught in the primary grades as instruction was typically targeted at middle elementary grades through college. Fortunately, as the twentieth century draws to a close, change in the form of consistency in content and in methods of instruction throughout the grades is in the making.

Evolving from such fascinating roots, the exciting news for our nation's teachers and learners today is that geography is still an intriguing topic. It is much more than a mundane course as many have thought in the past. Its content can bring the people and places within our nation and our world into the classroom. Once there they can be examined with delight, not dread. Topics can be scrutinized in depth rather than in a perfunctory manner. Armed with pertinent geographic information, students can realize the potential for developing into critically thinking future citizens cognizant of the realities of global awareness rather than becoming complacent, self-absorbed American citizens.

One way to begin thinking about this subject is to consider a few pieces of fact and fiction wrapped up in the word "geography."

Fact: When concentrating on the United States, geography includes such aspects as the study of maps, globes, landforms, and locations, such as of states and their capitals.

Fiction: In order to master the content of geography, a learner must rely heavily on memorization skills.

Fact: Beyond the topic of location, geography also includes learning more about place as one studies, in particular physical and human characteristics that make a certain place unique. In addition, geography asks questions about human and environmental interactions, how one affects the other. Furthermore, it investigates the movement of people across the face of the earth, examining, in the process, how and why various places are related to one another. Finally, geography investigates regions of the earth, comparing and contrasting one region with another. As you see, geography is so much more than simple identification of place via maps and memorization.

Fiction: The basic content of social studies is best taught through a good atlas and a standard textbook. The truth is that both of these items are sensible tools to have at the learners' disposal, but both fact and fiction in another form, that of quality children's literature can breathe life into a subject many feel has been neglected over the last fifty years. There is room for "Once upon a time …" in the study of geography. Facts are the backbone of geography, to be sure, but fiction, whether picture book or novel, can take children across the United States and the continent. In the process, they will be introduced to higher-level thinking skills and real problem solving that will infuse the curriculum with a vitality it has long been lacking. As students move beyond the rote memorization to the asking of relevant geographic questions, they will enter a content area that is fascinating as well as informative.

What Has Happened to Geography?

While the study of geography can turn into an adventure in learning, it hasn't always been that way. In particular, during the last fifty years attention to geography in our nation's classrooms has declined. Perhaps this was due to the fact that some teachers felt ill prepared to teach the subject. Others felt they were teaching geography but relied primarily on rote memorization to learn factual trivia rather than the who's, how's, and why's within the subject. Perhaps, too, the situation was augmented by a feeling of complacency within a country that has long been dominant as a world power. Because it was not adequately addressed in the classroom, the question, Why should I learn about relationships within our country and with other countries? did not dispel potentially harmful attitudes. Whatever the reason, the situation eventually resulted in lower national test scores in geography in the 1980s, students graduating with backgrounds deficient in basic geographic knowledge, and the concern of some educators that the nation was flirting seriously with geographic illiteracy.

A turnaround is imperative. In reality, a sound understanding of geography is indispensable if our nation is to remain a strong contender in global affairs. Therefore, geographic content is essential for every child as he or she grows into a thoughtful, intelligent, problem-solving adult. In an era where communications and air travel make cities within North America and across the world readily accessible, a solid understanding of people and place is a necessity. Armed with adequate knowledge, issues from where the next school in town should be built to understanding pertinent political policies that connect countries of the world can be dealt with intelligently. In short, geographic knowledge is the foundation upon which responsible citizens can build skills useful in developing or evaluating policies and decisions that will impact the neighborhood, the country, and the world.

Just What Is Geography?

According to *Geography for Life: National Geography Standards* (1994), geography is "an integrative discipline that brings together the physical and human dimensions of the world in the study of people, places, and environments. Its subject matter is earth's surface and the processes that shape it, the relationships between people and environments, and the connections between people and places" (p. 18). A growing cadre of educators feels that the subject should be taught through five interrelated themes as outlined in *Guidelines for Geographic Education: Elementary and Secondary Schools* (1984). This volume discusses the scope and sequence in geography giving suggested learning outcomes for grades K–12. Its most far-reaching contribution, however, is the five fundamental themes, which provide a blueprint for teachers to follow as they develop and organize their curriculum. The themes are as follows:

Location: Position on the Earth's Surface. Absolute and relative location are the two ways of describing the positions of people and places on the earth, which students should understand. Absolute location is identified by using latitude and longitude. It gives a place a specific global address. Relative location is more general and is decided by examining the relationship of one place to another. The basic question to be addressed is, Where is it?

Place: Physical and Human Characteristics. All places on the earth have both tangible and intangible characteristics that give them meaning and character, setting them apart from other places. Questions to be asked are, Where? Why there? and What is it like there? Answers to these questions require looking at the physical characteristics of a place (landforms, bodies of water, climate, soils, natural vegetation, and animal life), the impact of human characteristics to the place (population density, social traits, cultural traditions, and political institutions), and the image or emotional response that people have to the place. Both historical and cultural features can be studied when learning more about place.

Human/Environmental Interactions: Humans and Environments. All places on the earth have advantages and disadvantages for human settlement. How people interact with, adapt to, and change the physical environment to meet their basic needs is a part of this study. The question to investigate is, What is the relationship between people and the area in which they live?

Movement: Humans Interacting on the Earth. No matter where they live, people interact with each other. They travel from farms to cities, from towns to small villages, to communicate. In addition, goods are transported from one place to another to meet people's needs. People migrate, ship their products, and share their ideas. A question to promote thinking about movement is, How and why is this place changing?

Region: A basic unit of geographic study is the region, an area that has similar characteristics. Questions to ask when looking at regions are, How and why is one area similar to another? How are these areas different? How would it feel to live in this place? Regions might be defined in a variety of ways such as by human or physical criteria or by political power, by a language group or a landform type, depending on the need of the learners.

Based on its definition and five supporting themes, it is easy to see that geography poses titillating questions that can stimulate engrossing research and study on the part of the students. For starters, students can look at a map of the United States. Why are some state boundaries straight while others ripple and curve? Why are some cities brimming with people and industry while others remain small and nondescript? When studying a state map, what kinds of information can be obtained by an interested sleuth? Why did some of our ancestors choose to live in desert regions and what was the impact of their choice upon their lives and the area's geography? Geography has answers to a myriad of questions beyond what has long been taught. The prospect of seeking those answers spurred on by the impetus of children's literature promises to be challenging indeed.

Rationale for Incorporating Children's Literature

Our lives are wrapped up in the world of stories. The history of this country and our personal histories come alive through story, the local news or the latest gossip is in story form, and daily events are recounted to family and friends as stories. Geography has stories to tell as well. Discovering those stories through fine children's books is one way to make the issues in geography lively enough to interest children to learn more about this compelling subject. Thus, integrating fiction, biographies, autobiographies, picture books, and informational titles can make people, places, and events pulse with life within the realm of geography. Obviously, the titles chosen must demonstrate scholarly integrity through the accurate portrayal of people and places, past and present. Then the selections can help the learner to more easily grasp concepts within selected time periods, places, and cultures, as well as to learn to appreciate relationships between the five themes as students construct geographic knowledge.

Children's books can accomplish a variety of tasks within the geography curriculum. One vital link between children's literature and learning is that these books can provide background information for learners who need to fill in the gaps where their knowledge is still weak. Learning theory supports the fact that additional learning "sticks" better when a child can attach it to something concrete. Next, quality children's literature, whether fiction or nonfiction, picture book or novel, is motivating. The probability of capturing the interests of students is high when using a stirring book to draw them into a content area. Furthermore, engrossed readers live side by side with the book's characters unconsciously absorbing memorable characteristics of a different time and place. Caught up in a story, readers problem solve right along with a main character.

After children live vicariously in another time and place, they come back to reality with a broadened understanding of a part of the world previously unknown, expanding their life space, so to speak. Then, carefully selected literature develops children's imaginations and helps them to consider nature, people, experiences, and ideas in new ways. Finally, literature moves beyond facts to consider feelings, the quality of someone else's life. From this perspective readers can see and understand relationships they have not personally experienced. All of these attributes soundly support the integration of children's literature into the curriculum as a means of revitalizing geography. Now more than ever is the time to approach the teaching and learning of geography from a different direction aside from the standard textbook instruction.

The focus of this book will be on integrating some of today's exceptional picture books into the elementary geography curriculum as students from third through sixth grades study the continent of North America. When carefully crafted text and finely wrought illustrations are coupled into an appealing picture book, that book becomes a viable tool for learning as well as for pure aesthetic enjoyment. These books are not to be short-changed today. They present a visual context for learning by older students as well as by younger readers. Consider, for example, how relying on picture books can motivate, interest, and provide a meaningful context for practicing such skills as interpreting maps or other geographic information. Readers can study closely related text and illustrations for clues that reveal interrelationships between people and their environment. Depending on the book, they can also examine climate, farm practices, foods eaten, types of buildings, clothing, and even methods of transportation. Picture books have a rich potential. In the geography classroom they can become the impetus for delving further into a subject to broaden knowledge about areas throughout our country.

One picture book is never enough. There are advantages for using a number of books about a theme or state being studied. First, a variety of books means there is a book for every student regardless of individual reading levels. Secondly, a student reading one book can share the information and perspectives gained from reading their chosen title with others. Thirdly, the topic under study becomes clearer as students learn that there is more than one story to consider. And finally, readers can begin to develop the insight that conditions in a place today evolved as a part of a complex web of past events. Imagine the critical thinking being fostered as students compare their personal

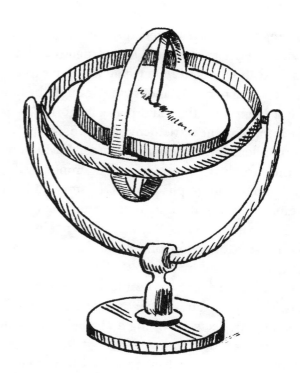

interpretations and points of view on issues under study. A picture book can be a powerful teaching tool, indeed.

A Quick Preview of This Book

This book will be organized around ten geographic regions as designated by the National Geographic Society in their filmstrip and video materials covering the study of the United States. In order to get a complete picture of North America, the countries of Canada and Mexico will also be included. The five themes of geography will be integrated into the study of the specific regions in all three countries. Within the United States, for example, a picture book will be the catalyst for studying particular states within the regions. In addition, the suggested activities will encourage learning across disciplines whenever reasonable connections can be made.

The book follows the premise that it makes sense to integrate geographic learning across the curriculum. In doing so, students then have more opportunities to use their new information, skills, and concepts as they are acquired. For instance, learning will be strengthened in language arts as students write to share the knowledge they have acquired about a state. They may write an expository report, a narrative about what it might be like to live in another time and place, a short play or skit describing the settlement of a town, or a poem that condenses their learning. Students will draw on their math skills as maps are examined, mileage figured, and graphs created. History and geography are natural companions. Students will be caught up in history as they discover what life was like in a state or region long ago and how the state has been affected by people's actions in the past. Art, music, and drama can be integrated into lessons as cultures are examined, or as a part of student-generated projects providing a change of pace in the learning routine. How exciting to see the numerous ways in which geography can permeate the curriculum!

As often as possible, skills in reading, writing, thinking, listening, and speaking will be reinforced in an effort to strengthen literacy in general and geographic literacy in particular. Specific attention will be given to geographic skills also. This means that students will be taught to ask geographic questions, acquire geographic information using a variety of resources, analyze the information as it is acquired, present that information to classmates, and finally, develop and test any geographic generalizations that develop. It is also important to note that while a picture book may be focused in the study of one theme, it may overlap with another theme as well. The five themes are closely interrelated and it would be doing them

and the study of geography a disservice to try to segregate them.

At the end of each lesson additional titles of picture books will be recommended for student use in the pursuit of further information. A list of useful teacher resources can be found in Appendix I. An annotated bibliography of pertinent chapter books will appear in Appendix II. These will be listed by region for readers who wish to spend more time in a particular part of the country. Finally, directions for specific projects are included in Appendix III.

While the content of the lessons in each chapter will be geared toward grades 3–6, it is expected that these materials will be adapted to or used interchangeably within a variety of grade levels. Some of the lessons may be catalysts for additional rewarding learning experiences for students. However it is used, it is fervently hoped that through the use of these materials both students and teachers will become more and more eager to embark upon an absorbing geographic journey across North America, visiting each part of the United States, Canada, and Mexico.

References

Geography Education Standards Project. *Geography for Life: National Geography Standards.* Washington, D.C.: National Geographic Research and Exploration, 1994.

Joint Committee on Geographic Education. *Guidelines for Geographic Education: Elementary and Secondary Schools.* Washington, D.C.: Association of American Geographers and the National Council for Geographic Education, 1984.

1

Starting with the Whole

The focus of this initial chapter is to present a variety of ways in which teachers and students can get a perspective of the United States as a whole before breaking it into pieces for closer study. This same process also applies to the study of Mexico and Canada. Having a sense of the big picture—United States, Mexico, Canada, and the whole North American continent—will build a strong foundation for later investigation of each country's fascinating intricate parts. Put another way, an overview will provide essential cognitive hooks upon which learners can later place new knowledge.

Take the United States, for example. Begin with books like *America the Beautiful* or *O Beautiful for Spacious Skies* to give the students a sweeping view of the United States. A third choice could be *Oregon's Journey*, a thoughtful story about a circus bear's trek across the United States from Pittsburgh to the lush woods of Oregon in search of his home. Yet another book that might pique interest in the study of the United States is *Stringbean's Trip to the Shining Sea* by Vera Williams. The book is sure to spark conversations about vacations spent with family and relatives in various parts of the United States. A natural extension of this book is to have students create their own postcards from a favorite vacation spot, complete with colorful stamps, and share them with the class. Attach the postcards to a large map of the United States with yarn and thumbtacks, connecting the postcard and the specific spot. A language arts reminder: Be sure the postcards are properly addressed.

An additional activity spurred on by this book would be to have students act as travel agents. They can introduce their favorite vacation spot, giving specifics about the area and the state it is in. They can discuss how to get to this spot as well. Photographs, postcards, a brief snippet of video, and other mementos could enhance the presentation. Willing parents could be invited to help with slide shows as could other interested members of the community. An option for children who are fascinated with the rail system in the United States is to research the development of the railroads as they linked the country from the east to the west. Reinforce the idea of growth of the United States by looking at it from east to west when organizing presentations. Of course, teachers should be a part of this activity, sharing their memorable vacations along with the class.

The Language of Geography

When undertaking a new unit of study, one of the first activities a teacher usually engages in is to explain the unfamiliar vocabulary to students to aid in their comprehension of the material. In learning about the geography of the United States, Canada, and Mexico, a common understanding

of terms used in lessons and projects is important to establish. An interesting way to accomplish this task is to put the students to work with terms that describe the landforms across the United States, for example, learning the terms by creating a "Landform Dictionary." Each student could pick a term or two from a collection placed in a box or a basket. It would then be their task to work individually or in pairs to define the term and then illustrate it attractively on a page. After teaching their term or terms to the class and locating an example on a landform map, each completed dictionary page could be laminated and compiled into a book. A book like *Geography from A to Z: A Picture Book Glossary* by Jack Knowlton would serve as a great starting point. The glossaries in a textbook and other geography references would also be additional helpful sources of terms. This work could be repeated for the study of Canada and Mexico at a later time.

To make this project more interesting, students could use alliteration in the sentences that define their terms. Not only will students be learning that alliteration is a device often used in poetry, when numerous words in the poem begin with the same letter, but they will be involved in an imaginative learning experience. A spectacular example of the alphabet done this way is *Animalia* by Graeme Base. Share several copies of the book in class, giving students time to examine the sentences and illustrations, and then turn them loose with their own creativity. One way to describe Arizona patterned after this book is: An appealing Arizona arroyo attracted agile antelope, active ants, and arresting arachnids.

Provide plenty of dictionaries and thesauruses as students play with language and expand their vocabularies at the same time. Students could practice with their names first. Encourage them to describe themselves by writing a sensible sentence in which nearly every word begins with the first letter of their name. Then have them apply their newfound skills to geography. Teachers might want to work through one or two word samples with the class that are particularly pertinent to the state in which the students live.

Here are some suggestions that might go into the basket of vocabulary words:

- aquifer
- arroyo
- barrier island
- basin
- bay
- bayou
- bluff
- border
- canyon
- coast
- continent
- Continental Divide
- continental shelf
- dam
- delta

desert
Everglades
geography
grasslands
gulf
hill
lake
lowlands
marsh
mountain
mountain range
mouth
natural resource
oasis
ocean
panhandle
peak
peninsula
plains
plateau
prairie
rainforest
reservation
reservoir
river
river valley
sea level
temperate zone
terrace
tributary
volcano

A Way to Begin

As you begin the study of geography, introduce the states divided into their regions. Have the students predict why the states are grouped as they are. These geographic predictions can be recorded on the chalkboard, with a student recorder also writing them down to be saved for future reference. Reexamine the predictions as study moves from region to region, confirming or replacing predictions based upon the students' new knowledge.

Variations on a Quilt Theme

Large projects that will eventually tie the pieces of geographic studies back together again might carry through your entire study of the United States, Mexico, or Canada. For example, a fabric quilt could be made of one of the countries. If the United States were used, the quilt would include a square from each state designed and contributed by a classroom from that state. Teachers could contact the superintendent's office in each state, requesting addresses of schools to contact. Correspondence by both teacher and students with an interested classroom would be the groundwork. Then, a premeasured square of light-colored fabric, like muslin, and an explanation of the project could be sent to the classrooms as that region of the United States is under study. Perhaps two squares could be sent to each state, one to an urban school and another to a rural setting. Children there would decorate the square with a design that symbolizes their area and write an explanation to accompany it. Once the squares are completed and returned, volunteers could help the students stitch and stuff the quilt for display at the end of the unit of study. The students' explanations could be compiled into a companion book. Picture books that might inspire the project are *My Grandmother's Patchwork Quilt: A Book and Pocketful of Patchwork Quilts* by Janet Bolton, *Kids Making Quilts for Kids* by Quilt Digest Press, or *Eight Hands Round: A Patchwork Alphabet* by Ann Whitford Paul.

Another approach is a paper quilt of the regions under study made by using the individual states or provinces as "squares." Students could work individually or in groups, depending on the country, to create an informative colorful quilt piece. Done on sturdy brightly colored paper shaped like the state, each piece might include key cities, important tourist attractions, major landmarks, natural resources, ethnic diversity, and even famous people. The completed pieces could be stitched together using large needles and brightly colored yarn and displayed on the classroom wall, in a hallway, or in the school's learning center where the work could both inform and be enjoyed by the whole school.

Additional Projects

Students could work in groups to make books based on and in the shape of the state under study. Once a group is assigned a state, they design the cover and shape of the pages, eventually compiling an intriguing book with as much pertinent information and as creaatively as they deem appropriate. Sturdy covers could be cut out of tagboard and decorated with items that symbolize the state. If another group is studying a specific aspect of the state, pthose results would be incorporated into the state book. Upon completion, the books could be displayed in the reading or learning center for other students to peruse.

Travels with Poetry

In order to develop a comfort level with poetry, it needs to be an integral part of a student's day. One way to make it so is to weave poetry throughout the curriculum. A suggestion for using poetry as an activity to introduce the United States, Mexico, and Canada to learners is through the following poem by Sigmund Boloz. Invite listeners to imagine where a penny has been after reading this poem with the students. Then, each student should pick a penny out of a collection passed around the room. As creatively as they can, they are to describe where on this continent that penny might have been. Final masterpieces might be "published" by creating a student-designed bulletin board, presented to another class during a poetry reading session, or shared with the poet, Sigmund A. Boloz.

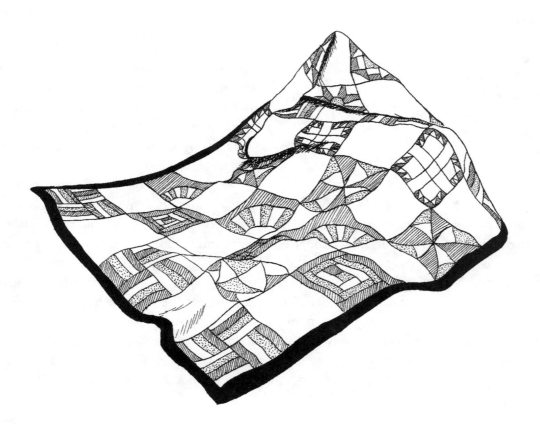

I Ride the Backs of Pennies
by Sigmund A. Boloz

Have you ever considered where a penny has wandered,
Where that small coin may have been?
Have you ever wondered about the places it has travelled
Again, and again, and again?

Have you ever thought about whom else may have touched it,
Ever wondered to whom that penny did belong,
Ever thought that pennies sit in pockets,
And that travellers take their money along?

Well, I ride the backs of pennies
And I've travelled just about everywhere,
Because I ride the backs of pennies
As my imagination takes me there.

Because when I'm alone and bored,
When I don't have much to do,
I find all the pennies I own
And start searching my way on through

Until I find an interesting one,
A penny, brown and thin,
Then I close my eyes and imagine …
Where that old penny has been.

And so, I have travelled just about everywhere,
Everywhere that I have heard of or I know,
For I have travelled on backs of pennies,
Wherever my mind and pennies can go.

Used with permission by Sigmund A. Boloz. Originally published in *Prairie Dog Dreams: A Collection of Poems* by Sigmund A. Boloz. Illustrated by Abraham Jones. Ganado, Ariz.: Wooded Hill Productions, 1995.

Riddles and Guessing Games

Set the tone for this activity by sharing a number of riddles from *Geographunny: A Book of Global Riddles* by Mort Gerberg. The listeners will be challenged and amused by the riddles and their answers. Students can be encouraged to devise their own riddles at the end of this activity. Give each student a sheet of riddles and an atlas or map of the United States. This activity will help the class familiarize themselves with the states and their locations in the country. You might give the students a specific time limit to work on their own, and then let them pair up to compare answers and solve some of the more difficult riddles.

Suggested Riddles
Specifically for the United States

Where are you if you can stand in four states at the same time?
(Four Corners: Utah, Arizona, New Mexico, and Colorado)

Which states are divided in two with one part attached to another state?
(Virginia and Michigan. The Eastern Shore of Virginia is joined to Maryland while Michigan's popular Upper Peninsula connects to Wisconsin.)

Where are you if you are in two states that border eight other states?
(Tennessee and Missouri, which border each other as well)

If you only touch one other state, what is your name and who is your neighbor?
(Maine, which borders New Hampshire)

I am a lonely state because I am so out of touch. I don't touch any other state or country.
(Hawaii)

Travel from coast to coast to find the four states that border only two others.

(Washington, Florida, South Carolina, and Rhode Island)

You'll need the proper perspective to look carefully for the hidden man who reaches from south to north, border to border.
(Louisiana: feet; Arkansas: pants; Missouri: upper body; Iowa: head and nose; Minnesota: large hat)

I am a straight state that borders seven other states.
(Colorado)

I am well known because of Dorothy, Toto, tornadoes, and a major river that is one of my boundaries. Centrally located, I touch four other states.
(Kansas)

Maps and Their Key Features

Maps and globes are essential tools to better understand location in geography. Globes are but small models of the earth. Despite their size, globes give learners the most accurate representation of the earth. While they are not shaped like globes, the maps most of us carry around in our heads are used daily to get us to school, work, favorite restaurant, or friend's house. Students will be pleased to learn that they are already cartographers, or mapmakers, as they use their personal maps day after day. When thinking about maps and how they are used, students might be interested to know that maps have been around for hundreds and hundreds of years. In fact, the oldest known map is a clay tablet made in Mesopotamia around 2500 B.C. It showed a valley settlement surrounded by mountains. In order to understand how maps work, students need to understand the language of maps, a language of symbols and numbers. One possible resource to use is *Using and Understanding Maps* by Scott Morris.

In learning map language, students will benefit most from practical experience. Expose learners to a variety of maps explaining that each map has a theme. A map might be generated by a computer, be used to navigate out at sea, depict political boundaries between people and countries, be a Mercator projection, show population or precipitation in a region, or illustrate the topography of an area. Bring a selection of local city and/or state maps into the classroom for student use and practice. Examine the key features of these maps with the whole group.

You might begin with the grid system that allows readers to locate specific points of interest on the map. Explain that the black lines on the map are arranged in a grid system to help readers find exact locations within the town or state. The grid lines cross each other to form boxes. The boxes are marked with letters and numbers along the side of the map. By using these letters and numbers, specific places can be located. Start with a map of the city in which you live and work together to locate the school, a park, several popular restaurants, other particular places of interest, and the streets on which the children live. Then students might practice on each other by listing several grid locations for a classmate to find.

Next, locate and discuss the uses of the legend or key to the symbols that are used on the map. Students might like to know that the legend is so named because it tells the story of a particular map by explaining what the colors and symbols mean. Thus, specific features on the map will be represented by symbols that are listed in the legend box on the map. Give the students time to locate the symbols on various parts of the map.

The use of scale, a way of showing size or distance on a map, also deserves attention. Give the students time to figure the mileage between several cities using the scale on the map.

Finally, have the students locate the compass rose on the map. It shows the four cardinal directions: north, south, east, and west. Intermediate directions might also be shown: northeast, southeast, northwest, and southwest. Students might like to research the designs of compass roses on other maps, referring to some older maps as well,

and then create their own designs to be displayed on a map they are working on or somewhere appropriate in the classroom. Tell the learners that a compass rose may be at an angle on a map rather than straight up and down. This occurs so it is properly oriented toward the north and south.

One creative and practical application of skills at this point might be the creation of a neighborhood of graham cracker homes and buildings that reflects the neighborhood around the school. Eliciting the help of parents and bus drivers, students can learn the mileage between their homes and school, decide as a group what the appropriate scale should be, and then sketch the neighborhood on thin board or heavy cardboard that won't curl as the children build their homes. Graham cracker houses and the school can be held together with canned cake frosting and decorated with other appropriate candies and materials. What an appealing way to apply map skills! Older students can get quite creative with an activity like this. This might also be a good time to stress the importance of a germfree construction zone, urging children to wash their hands in warm, soapy water before beginning to build, keeping fingers out of mouths, and washing up again after the work has been completed.

Once the language of maps is understood, have the students practice applying the skills to a map of the school, a map from school to home, a treasure map using the school playground as an area to investigate, or a map of an imaginary country. A stimulating mapping activity might be based on mapping the travels of Johnny Appleseed in *Johnny Appleseed,* a tall tale retold by Steven Kellogg, or the ingenious *Oh, the Places You'll Go!* by Dr. Seuss. Using the book *Roxaboxen* by Alice McLerran, students can work in groups of three or four to draw maps of their version of the town of Roxaboxen. They should include a scale for distance, some symbols for buildings in town, and a compass rose.

By using projects like those described in this chapter, threads of continuity and understanding are developed as each country is examined as a whole, separated for closer scrutiny, and then re-assembled again by more knowledgeable students.

Some Thoughts on Evaluation

In order to chart students' progress during the study of geography, each student could have a personal folder or a three-pronged, two-pocket folder in which to keep work in progress. Folders could be stored in milk crates in the room. Students and teacher can confer about which materials should be transferred to a more permanent, ongoing personal portfolio demonstrating the student's progress through process and products as the study of each region is completed.

In addition, teacher observation and anecdotal records will add further information. For example, use teacher-developed checklists to target specific learning behaviors or to aid in assessing whether district curriculum guidelines are being met.

Watch interactions between students as they work in groups and take notes for use with the students as well as with parents at conference time. Brief notes can be kept on Post-it™ Notes or peel-and-stick labels with each student's name on them, to be tacked later into a folder or notebook page designated for that learner. If the teacher zeros in on four or five learners a week, quality information on each student will be gleaned over time.

Then, too, one might assess acquisition of knowledge through noting how each learner grasps concepts as projects are worked through and completed. How does the student understand what has been taught about a state as evidenced during presentations? If students keep content area journals, how does the student express growing knowledge within the pages of that journal? Finally, at designated times during the year, students are to review their portfolios with the teacher, personally evaluating their progress as they review their work. Obviously, this is a valuable time for feedback from the teacher. When evaluating progress during the study of geography, strive for a balance between the process of learning itself and the final product. Such a strategy will produce a well-rounded picture of the student as he or she masters the fascinating subject matter within the realm of geography.

Suggested Companion Titles

ABC Quilts Staff. *Kids Making Quilts for Kids.* Lincolnwood, Ill.: Quilt Digest Press, 1992.

Base, Graeme. *Animalia.* New York: Abrams, 1987.

Bates, Katherine Lee. *O Beautiful for Spacious Skies.* Illus. by Wayne Thiebaud. San Francisco: Chronicle Books, 1994.

———. *America the Beautiful.* Illus. by Neil Waldman. New York: Atheneum, 1993.

Bolton, Janet. *My Grandmother's Patchwork Quilt: A Book and Pocketful of Patchwork Quilts.* New York: Doubleday, 1994.

Gerberg, Mort. *Geographunny: A Book of Global Riddles.* Illus. by author. New York: Clarion Books, 1991.

Hausman, Gerald. *Turtle Island ABC: A Gathering of Native American Symbols.* Illus. by Cara Moser and Barry Moser. New York: HarperCollins, 1994.

Hopkins, Lee Bennett. *Hand in Hand: An American History Through Poetry.* Illus. by Peter M. Fiore. New York: Simon & Schuster, 1994.

Kellogg, Steven. *Johnny Appleseed.* Illus. by author. New York: Morrow Junior Books, 1988.

Knowlton, Jack. *Geography from A to Z: A Picture Book Glossary.* Illus. by Harriett Barton. New York: HarperCollins, 1988.

Lauber, Patricia. *How We Learned the Earth Is Round.* Illus. by Megan Lloyd. New York: HarperTrophy, 1990.

———. *Seeing Earth from Space.* New York: Orchard Books, 1990.

Lyle, Keith. *Measuring and Maps.* New York: Gloucester Press, 1991.

McLerran, Alice. *Roxaboxen.* Illus. by Barbara Cooney. New York: Lothrop, Lee & Shepard, 1991.

Morris, Scott E. *Using and Understanding Maps: How to Read a Map.* New York: Chelsea House, 1993.

National Geographic Society. *National Geographic Picture Atlas of Our Fifty States.* Washington, D.C.: National Geographic Society, 1991.

Nebenzahl, Kenneth. *Atlas of Columbus and the Great Discoveries.* New York: Rand McNally, 1990.

Paul, Ann Whitford. *Eight Hands Round: A Patchwork Alphabet.* Illus. by Jeanette Winter. New York: HarperCollins, 1991.

Perl, L. *It Happened in America: True Stories from the Fifty States.* Illus. by I. Ohlsson. New York: Henry Holt, 1992.

Porter, Malcolm. *The Dillon Press Children's Atlas.* New York: Dillon Press, 1993.

Rascal. *Oregon's Journey.* Illus. by Louis Joos. New York: Troll Medallion, 1993.

Rosenthal, Paul. *Where on Earth: A Geografunny Guide to the Globe.* Illus. by Marc Rosenthal. New York: Alfred A. Knopf, 1992.

Saul, Carol P. *Someplace Else.* Illus. by Barry Root. New York: Simon & Schuster, 1995.

Seuss, Dr. *Oh, the Places You'll Go!* New York: Random House, 1990.

Simon, Seymour. *Spring Across America.* New York: Hyperion, 1996.

———. *Earth: Our Planet in Space.* New York: Four Winds Press, 1984.

Taylor, C. J. *Bones in the Basket: Native American Stories of the Origin of People.* Montreal, Que.: Tundra Books, 1994.

Time-Life Books for Children. *Geography: Understanding Science and Nature.* New York: Time-Life, 1993.

Weiss, Harvey. *Maps: Getting from Here to There.* Chicago: Houghton Mifflin, 1991.

Williams, Vera B. *Stringbean's Trip to the Shining Sea.* Illus. by Vera Williams and Jennifer Williams. New York: Greenwillow, 1988.

2

The Pacific Coast States:
Washington, Oregon, and California

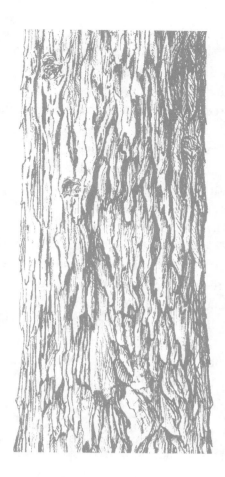

When studying these three states along the West Coast, one is struck by their amazing diversity. Such topographical features as rugged mountains, snow-capped peaks, lush rainforests, surprisingly arid high deserts, and fertile valleys prolific with a wide variety of produce characterize this region of the United States. In considering California alone, the variety of goods and services produced there generates tremendous wealth. No other state ships more manufactured goods; canned, frozen, and dried fruits; or nuts and vegetables than this geographically appealing state. Of course, there are similarities and differences that make these three states a dynamic region as well. During the course of study have the students polish their inductive reasoning skills, moving from numerous details to some general threads that hold these states together as a region.

As the study of each geographic region begins, a student can volunteer to write to the tourism department, one student per state to be studied. Initially, work as a class to create a general letter that explains the geography unit under study and requests further information about the state. Later, students can adapt their individual letters to their state in particular. Addresses for each state's department of tourism are located in Appendix I. Mail is exciting to receive so students will find this activity an enjoyable way to practice letter-writing skills in anticipation of a response to their queries. Once each student's letter has been answered, let that student highlight the information. Store the accumulating materials in a milk crate with dividers organized by state so that all of the students can use pertinent information for future projects.

Initiating Activity

Encourage students to draw on what they already know through a brainstorming activity. Explain that the image of a place is part of the study of geography that most people don't think about. One question for students to answer is, Just what is it that makes one place feel different or evoke a different image from another?

Experiment with the three Pacific Coast states and see what images emerge. Give the students a piece of notebook paper and ask them to fold it into thirds lengthwise, forming three columns. Write one state's name at the top of each column. Then tell the students to brainstorm as many words, images, and impressions of the state as they can working on one state at a time. For example, images for the state of Washington might include: rain, foggy beaches, Mount Rainier, Mount St. Helens, steep hills in Seattle, fresh salmon and crab, blackberries, the Space Needle, ferryboats, trees, trees, and more trees. After students have worked for what the teacher deems an appropriate amount of time, ask them to share their images, recording them on the chalkboard or overhead as they are contributed. Teachers might add their own personal images to those on each list after the students are finished. A volunteer can copy words from the chalkboard or overhead as the teacher writes them. Post the completed lists where students can review them from time to time during the ensuing study.

Discuss the similarities and differences in the images students have of each state. Ask the learners why they have the impressions that they do. Just what is it that creates a state's image? One answer that the teacher could suggest is that the history of a state plays a part in its image. Consider the settlement of California, for example. First, Native Americans inhabited the lands alone until the Spanish explorers arrived. The gold rush brought eager forty-niners and thousands of Chinese people who not only took part in the gold rush but slaved away to build the transcontinental railroad. Later, many African Americans migrated from the South because of available jobs during World War II. The largest percentage of recent arrivals include those of Asian and Hispanic descent. All of these nationalities have stayed, put down roots, and are sharing their cultures. Thus, people and unique events have contributed to the state that makes up California.

Tell students to keep a copy of their image sheets in their personal folder. Check sheets periodically during the course of studying the three states to see how these preconceived images alter, jotting down changing perceptions.

Motivator

Introduce this region by reading the amusing *No Dear, Not Here: The Marbled Murrelets' Quest for a Nest in the Pacific Northwest.* The personable pair of birds travels from Canada, up and down the coast, and finally settles in an old-growth forest. This is a delightful book to quickly highlight aspects of Washington, Oregon, and California as well as a northern neighbor, British Columbia.

Lesson 1

Discovering Washington Through the Themes of Location, Place, and Region

Objectives

- to examine the natural phenomena that change the geography of an area
- to learn about the region of old-growth forests
- to glean an understanding of the geography of Washington through Native American Indian tales
- to review how people affect the environment and examine the results of their presence

Materials

- *The Wave of the Sea-Wolf* by David Wisniewski
- *Volcano: The Eruption and Healing of Mount St. Helens* by Patricia Lauber
- *Ancient Ones: The World of the Old-Growth Douglas Fir* by Barbara Bash

Motivator

Show the cover of the book *The Wave of the Sea-Wolf* by David Wisniewski to the students. Ask them to predict what they think the story might be about. What is the Sea-Wolf or what might it symbolize? Briefly discuss the answers before reading the story of Kchokeen, a wise Tlingit princess.

After reading the story, discuss why the author might have written this book. Were the worries of the princess and her father well founded? How has humans' greed destroyed many lush or prolific areas of the United States, and in the Pacific Northwest in particular? Once that destruction occurs, what is the geographic change? After the students recognize the power of an earthquake in this tale, ask them what other natural disasters have occurred in this state. Share the information in the Author's Note section of *The Wave of the Sea-Wolf* and let it become the impetus for further research by the students.

Activities

A Look at Change

Use the companion nonfiction book *Volcano: The Eruption and Healing of Mount St. Helens* by Patricia Lauber to move the group into investigating how the geographical features of a place can change. One group of students may wish to investigate volcanoes. What activities are going on under the earth's crust that may precipitate another eruption of Mount St. Helens or of California's active Lassen Peak? Students might gather information from newspaper articles about the May 18, 1980, eruption of Mount St. Helens, seek out other informational books such as those listed in chapter 3, or interview an expert on volcanoes if there is one available in their locale. One resource for a such a person might be the geology department of a nearby university or a docent from a local natural history or science museum. Some students may want to conduct an experiment to understand the forces behind a volcano before pre-

senting their findings to the class. Other students may choose to examine the rest of the Cascade Range. What created these mountains? Suggestions for eye-opening experiments can be found in Robert Wood's *Science for Kids: 39 Easy Geography Activities*.

Another question to investigate might be, "How does the existence of the mountains influence life to the west and to the east of this majestic range?" Encourage students to investigate why nearly two-thirds of Washington's citizens live within an hour's drive of the city of Seattle. Why is the theme of location important in this instance? Students can carefully examine a topographical map to understand the terrain of this area. At the conclusion of their study, learners will see how geography asserts itself as it influences where and how people live.

Letter Writing for Information

Read the beautifully illustrated, informative *Ancient Ones: The World of the Old-Growth Douglas Fir* by Barbara Bash to build upon the image of the forested world presented in *The Wave of the Sea-Wolf*. Locate the old-growth forests on the state map. After discussing the abundant wildlife that depends on this environment to live, have students contact their local library or chamber of commerce for the address of a logging company. Write to the logging industry and the Sierra Club to learn more about both the logging industry and how to preserve the beauty of the wilderness.

Sierra Club
730 Polk Street
San Francisco, CA 94109

Present newly acquired information using student-created colorful posters as props. Learners may even want to try their hand at writing a rap song or putting words to a familiar tune as a creative way to express what they have learned.

Make a Time Line

Show the destruction of the old-growth forests using an illustrated time line. Indicate when the movement of people began to change the Washington area, plus show what other key events were occurring in the United States as the trees grew and later when they began to be harvested. Students may want to add to this information when Oregon is studied. What geological factors aid the growth of these forests? What will happen if these forests are eventually destroyed? Author Barbara Bash has said that one can replant trees, but one cannot plant the magnificent forests that are being destroyed. Since it can take a thousand years or more to regrow such a forest, if it can ever be replaced at all, what might be a realistic solution to preserving these ancient trees?

Students can express their carefully researched opinions in letters to the editor in a local newspaper or via a lively classroom debate. Another topic to discuss might be what kind of industry could replace the jobs lost if logging doesn't continue. What other kinds of jobs are tied to logging that also will be affected? Is job retraining feasible? Interested students might write for information about an organization called Children for Old Growth.

Children for Old Growth
P.O. Box 1090
Redway, CA 95560

If students choose to join this organization, they will receive a poster of large forests and a newsletter written by children.

A Focus on Native American Tales from the Region

Suggestions follow in the titles of additional books to read. What characteristics of the region emerge? Such answers might include the dependence on the ocean as a food source, abundant wildlife, salmon, many uses of cedar, variety of berries, foothills, bays, beaches, and rain-soaked forests. List these characteristics to be compared with those that emerge when learning about Oregon and California. What universal message comes from these wise Native Americans through their myths and legends? A carefully planned collage might be a perfect way to share the group's findings.

Closure

Highlight what has been learned about the state of Washington. Allow time for students to fill in pertinent information on the blank outline maps of the United States, beginning with Washington. Students should have noted any changes in their impressions of this state on their three-column paper. Ask students to share one thing they learned about this state that surprised them or most interested them.

Books Used in This Lesson

Bash, Barbara. *Ancient Ones: The World of the Old-Growth Douglas Fir.* Illus. by author. San Francisco: Sierra Club Books for Children, 1994.

Lauber, Patricia. *Volcano: The Eruption and Healing of Mount St. Helens.* New York: Bradbury Press, 1986.

Okimoto, Jean Davies. *No Dear, Not Here: The Marbled Murrelets' Quest for a Nest in the Pacific Northwest.* Illus. by Celeste Henriquez. Seattle, Wash.: Sasquatch Books, 1995.

Wisniewski, David. *The Wave of the Sea-Wolf.* Illus. by author. New York: Clarion Books, 1994.

Suggested Companion Titles

Cherry, Lynne. *The Dragon and the Unicorn*. Illus. by author. New York: Harcourt Brace, 1995.

Cole, Joanna. *The Magic School Bus: Inside the Earth*. Illus. by Bruce Degen. New York: Scholastic, 1987.

Cone, M. *Come Back, Salmon: How a Group of Dedicated Kids Adopted Pigeon Creek and Brought it Back to Life*. Photographs by Sidnee Wheelwright. New York: Sierra Club, 1992.

Fradin, Dennis, and Judith Fradin. *From Sea to Shining Sea: Washington*. Chicago: Children's Press, 1994.

George, Jean Craighead. *The Moon of the Mountain Lions*. Illus. by Ron Parker. New York: HarperCollins, 1991.

Grabowski, John, and Patricia Grabowski. *The Northwest: Alaska, Idaho, Oregon, Washington*. New York: Chelsea House, 1992.

Herda, D. J. *Environmental America: The Northwestern States*. Brookfield, Conn.: Millbrook Press, 1991.

Hirschi, Ron. *Seya's Song*. Illus. by Constance R. Bergum. Seattle, Wash.: Sasquatch Books, 1992.

Jeffers, Susan. *Brother Eagle, Sister Sky: A Message from Chief Seattle*. Illus. by author. New York: Dial, 1991.

Luenn, Nancy. *Squish! A Wetland Walk*. Illus. by Ronald Himler. New York: Atheneum, 1994.

McDermott, Gerald. *Raven: A Trickster Tale from the Pacific Northwest*. Illus. by author. New York: Scholastic, 1993.

Martin, Rafe. *The Boy Who Lived with the Seals*. Illus. by David Shannon. New York: Putnam, 1993.

Morgan, Pierr. *Supper for Crow: A Northwest Coast Indian Tale*. Illus. by author. New York: Crown, 1995.

Powell, E. S. *Washington*. Minneapolis, Minn.: Lerner, 1993.

Rodanas, Kristina. *The Eagle's Song: A Tale from the Pacific Northwest*. Illus. by author. Boston: Little, Brown, 1995.

Simon, Seymour. *Mountains*. New York: Morrow Junior Books, 1994.

———. *Volcanoes*. New York: William Morrow, 1988.

Seuss, Dr. *The Lorax*. Illus. by author. New York: Random House, 1971.

Wood, Robert W. *Science for Kids: 39 Easy Geography Activities*. Illus. by John D. Wood. Blue Ridge Summit, Pa.: Tab Books, 1992.

Lesson 2

Discovering Oregon Through the Themes of Location, Place, Movement, and Region

Objectives
- to learn about Oregon from the past to the present
- to examine the lumber industry as it relates to geography
- to learn to understand and appreciate different points of view regarding the various uses of the environment
- to appreciate the challenges that geography posed as people migrated across the United States
- to note the varying coastline of the Pacific Coast and its potential uses

Materials
- *Only Opal: The Dairy of a Young Girl* by Barbara Cooney
- *The Way West: Journal of a Pioneer Woman* by Amelia Stewart Knight
- *Daily Life in a Covered Wagon* by Paul Erickson
- lined paper to serve as a temporary journal
- maps of Oregon

Motivator

Read a page or two from *The Way West*, an interesting journal written by a pioneer on the Oregon Trail or from *Diary: Josh's Journal* by Tom Novak. Show students a few of the detailed pages revealing a typical day of life in a wagon train as revealed in the fabulous *Daily Life in a Covered Wagon* by Paul Erickson. In this book, Mrs. Larkin's diary records day-to-day events. Next, have the students record daily events on sheets of paper as if it were their diary, covering recent events in their lives or just in the last several days. Tell them once they are finished writing, they will compare their diary entries to those of young Opal, a real child who lived with her stepparents in nineteen lumber camps during her lifetime. Finally, read the story aloud, giving students plenty of time to enjoy the beautiful illustrations of the Oregon countryside in the early 1900s.

Ask the students for reactions to the book and the Author's Note at the end. Specifically, seek responses on aspects of Opal's life that stood out for the listeners. Then have them compare a typical day in their lives according to their diaries to a typical day in Opal's life. Students might evaluate lifestyles explaining what they might prefer in each one and why.

Activities

Life in a Lumber Town

Working in pairs, have students research life in logging towns. Based upon the information they are able to glean from the library or from writing to lumber industries, each pair is to create their own logging town. Pick an absolute location after studying a map of Oregon, and record it on their maps. These budding cartographers are to name the camp and to place buildings, tents, sawmill, and roads on a map, carefully labeling key features. Indicate how logs are to be transported to a large city or port and where their destination will be. A scale of miles, compass rose, and legend should also be a part of the map. Upon completion of the project, finished products can be displayed and discussed. Some students may choose to make a three-dimensional map using a variety of materials in the construction of their town.

A statement of the students' views on logging could accompany the map. In concluding the activity students might discuss where logging is being done presently, locating the places on the map and highlighting issues that are still of concern.

Oregon from a Pioneer's Perspective

How people have or have not altered the geography of Oregon with their presence can be investigated by either large or small groups. Begin with learning about Oregon as the pioneers found it by reading excerpts from a diary of Amelia Stewart Knight in *The Way West: Journal of a Pioneer Woman*. Return again to Erickson's *Daily Life in a Covered Wagon*. Anyone who harbored the idea that it would be fun and exciting to lead the life of a pioneer will certainly look at the experience differently after reading this picture book. Study a topographical map of the United States to determine how the geography of the land hampered the progress of pioneers as they traveled the famous Oregon Trail.

There are some wonderful opportunities for studying the topography of the land between a town on the Missouri River and a final destination in Oregon. One popular destination for more than 50,000 emigrants was the fertile Willamette Valley. Locate it on the map. Students may want to draw before and after pictures of the valley, either in words or as sketches, as it once looked and what it looks like today. How many people live in this area today? How is the land used by current residents?

Closure

Before filling in important features on the students' personal outline maps of Oregon, ask the students to discuss similarities between this state and its northern neighbor, Washington. Begin to draw conclusions as to what might link these states as part of the same region. Take time to write down changing images or impressions as well.

Books Used in This Lesson

Cooney, Barbara. *Only Opal: The Diary of a Young Girl.* Illus. by author. New York: Philomel, 1994.

Erickson, Paul. *Daily Life in a Covered Wagon.* Illus. by author. Washington, D.C.: The Preservation Press, 1994.

Knight, Amelia Stewart. *The Way West: Journal of a Pioneer Woman.* Illus. by Michael McCurdy. New York: Simon & Schuster, 1993.

Suggested Companion Titles

Bratvold, Gretchen. *Oregon.* Minneapolis, Minn.: Lerner, 1991.

Fisher, Leonard E. *The Oregon Trail.* Illus. by author. New York: Holiday House, 1990.

Fradin, Dennis, and Judith Fradin. *From Sea to Shining Sea: Oregon.* Chicago: Children's Press, 1995.

Guiberson, Brenda Z. *Spotted Owl: Bird of the Ancient Forest.* New York: Henry Holt, 1994.

Novak, Tom. *Diary: Josh's Journal.* Baker City, Ore.: The Paper Shop, 1993.

Russell, Marion. *Along the Santa Fe Trail: Marion Russell's Own Story.* Illus. by James Watling. New York: Albert Whitman, 1993.

Shetterly, Susan. *Raven's Light: A Myth from the People of the Northwest Coast.* Illus. by Robert Shetterly. New York: Macmillan, 1991.

Silverstein, Alvin, Virginia Silverstein, and Robert Silverstein. *The Spotted Owl.* Brookfield, Conn.: Millbrook Press, 1994.

Steber, Rick. *Oregon Trail: Volume 1—Tales of the Old West.* Illus. by Don Gray. Prinville, Ore.: Bonanza Publishing, 1986.

Stein, R. Conrad. *Oregon.* Chicago: Children's Press, 1989.

Lesson 3

Discovering California Through the Themes of Location, Place, and Movement

Objectives

- to discover the role that migrant workers play in California's economy
- to locate areas where large crops are grown and require the help of migrant workers to harvest
- to study what the environment is like in the produce regions and compare/contrast that with similar regions in both Washington and Oregon
- to compare/contrast images of life in a rural migrant camp to life in urban Los Angeles or other large cities
- to further investigate the variety of cultures that make up Los Angeles and other large cities in an effort to support cultural awareness

Materials

- *Amelia's Road* by Linda J. Altman
- *Smoky Night* by Eve Bunting
- paper and pencil for jotting down notes
- a variety of fiction and nonfiction titles for research

Motivator

Ask the students to do some reflective thinking. Invite them to think about a place that is particularly special to them or to invent an ideal place. Describe it by writing in a few sentences and sketching it quickly. Students can share ideas on a volunteer basis. Read *Amelia's Road.* Ask the students to listen for specific crops that are grown in

California, to scrutinize the illustrations looking for clues to the geography of the area, and to think about the life of a migrant worker.

List the crops that the students remember from the story. Ask students to surmise why those crops might grow so well in California. What clues did the illustrations give? What was life like for Amelia and other migrant workers? Amelia emphasized the disadvantages of her life. Do students see any advantages to such a lifestyle? If they were to pick a place to call home like Amelia did, would it be where they currently live or some other location? Explain why.

Activities

Agriculture and Its Role

After the discussion, have a group of students research the major crops grown in California, locating them on a large, student-drawn map to be shared with the rest of the class. A trip to the local grocery store to purchase California produce to sample later in class might be an enjoyable real-life learning experience.

Students should also research the geographic conditions that make California's valleys so bountiful. Zero in on what it would be like to live in a

California valley. Include information on landforms, bodies of water available for irrigation, climate, soil, and natural vegetation. Use the local newspaper and chart the temperatures in the area for two weeks. Examine the variation and discuss why there is or is not much variation in temperature. Study precipitation and weather charts that have been kept for an entire year and note the normal highs and lows for each season. Present findings in a handmade book form using one of the design suggestions in Appendix III.

Movement of People and Products in California

What brings people to this state? What kinds of products are manufactured here and transported out of state besides produce? How are goods transported? Where are major highways, railroads, and airports located? Amelia doesn't like roads but, obviously, they are important. Draw major modes of transportation on a map to be shared with the class and explain why these transportation arteries are situated where they are in the state. Finally, engage the class in a discussion about ways in which people may have changed the geography of California because of the demands agriculture places upon the land.

Cultural Diversity

Smoky Night examines different cultures and how important understanding between people can be. Remind students that geography is as much about people as it is about land formations. A group might read about the various cultures in this state, locate where they live, and discuss their roles influencing the makeup of the state. Focus should be on the geographic role of movement or migration and of humans interacting with each other for this group's work. To bring the various populations to life, the group could teach several songs to the class that originated with different cultures. Seek out samples of poetry to be read aloud and enjoyed, too.

Closure

Tell students to take out their sheet on images of the Pacific Coast states. Has their image of California changed after studying the state? Based on their work, students can surmise why one out of every nine Americans has chosen to live in California. Have the students briefly share their new ideas or defend their unchanged perceptions in talking triads.

Books Used in This Lesson

Altman, Linda J. *Amelia's Road.* Illus. by Enrique O. Sanchez. New York: Lee & Low Books, 1993.

Bunting, Eve. *Smoky Night.* Illus. by David Diaz. New York: Harcourt Brace, 1994.

Suggested Companion Titles

Boyle, Doe. *Otter on His Own: The Story of a Sea Otter.* Illus. by Lisa Bonforte. Norwalk, Conn.: Soundprints and the Smithsonian Institution, 1995.

Brown, Tricia. *The City by the Bay.* Illus. by Elisa Klevin. San Francisco: Chronicle Books, 1993.

Bunting, Eve. *A Day's Work.* Illus. by Ronald Himler. New York: Clarion Books, 1994.

Davis, James E., and Sharryl H. Davis. *Los Angeles.* New York: Raintree, 1990.

Fradin, Dennis B. *California: From Sea to Shining Sea.* Chicago: Children's Press, 1992.

Haddock, Patricia. *San Francisco.* New York: Macmillan, 1989.

Hamanaka, Sheila. *All the Colors of the Earth.* Illus. by author. New York: Morrow, 1994.

Harvey, Brett. *Cassie's Journey: Going West in the 1860's.* Illus. by Deborah Kogan Ray. New York: Holiday House, 1988.

Hinton, L. *Ishi's Tale of the Lizard.* Illus. by Susan L. Roth. New York: Farrar, Strauss & Giroux, 1992.

House, James. *The San Francisco Earthquake.* Illus. by Maurie Manning. San Diego, Calif.: Lucent Books, 1990.

Hoyt-Goldsmith, Diane. *Day of the Dead: A Mexican-American Celebration.* Photographs by Lawrence Migdale. New York: Holiday House, 1994.

———. *Hoang Anh: A Vietnamese-American Boy.* Photographs by Lawrence Migdale. New York: Holiday House, 1992.

Krull, Kathleen. *The Other Side: How Kids Live in a California Latino Neighborhood.* Photographs by David Hautzig. New York: Lodestar Books, 1994.

London, Jonathan. *Old Salt Young Salt.* Illus. by Todd L. W. Doney. New York: Lothrop, Lee & Shepard, 1996.

Polacco, Patricia. *Tikvah Means Hope.* Illus. by author. New York: Doubleday, 1994.

Say, Allen. *Grandfather's Journey.* Illus. by author. Boston: Houghton Mifflin, 1993.

Siebert, Diane. *Sierra.* Illus. by Wendell Minor. New York: HarperTrophy, 1991.

Thomas, Jane R. *Lights on the River.* Illus. by Michael Dooling. New York: Hyperion, 1994.

Vieira, Linda. *The Ever-Living Tree: The Life and Times of a Coast Redwood.* Illus. by Christopher Canyon. New York: Walker, 1994.

Williams, Shelly A. *Working Cotton.* Illus. by Carole Byard. New York: Harcourt Brace, 1992.

Wright, Courtni C. *Wagon Train: A Family Goes West in 1865.* Illus. by Gershom Griffith. New York: Holiday House, 1995.

Wood, Audrey. *Rainbow Bridge.* Illus. by Robert Florczak. New York: Harcourt Brace, 1995.

Lesson 4

Looking at the Pacific Ocean Through the Themes of Location and Place

Objectives

- to describe the relative location of the Pacific Ocean
- to map a portion of the ocean floor
- to observe humans' influence on the Pacific Ocean
- to understand how the ocean influences the coastal states
- to understand the moon's influence on tides

Materials

- paper and pencils
- *The Magic School Bus on the Ocean Floor* by Joanna Cole
- a globe, world map, student atlases
- butcher paper for mural and other art supplies
- maps of tide movement or navigational maps if available

Motivator

Have the students take out a piece of paper and a pencil and prepare an anticipation guide. Have them draw a straight line across the top of their paper with an arrow at each end. Write "Agree" on the right side of the continuum and "Disagree" on the left side. Invite students to suggest two other reactions for the middle of the line. Ask listeners to mark their responses on the continuum to the following questions:

1. The Pacific Ocean plays an important role in maintaining a healthy atmosphere. *(true)*
2. The earth's crust on the ocean floor is thinner than the crust under the continents. *(true)*

3. Mountains and valleys form the bulk of the ocean floor. *(false)*
4. If all of the land masses were put together, the Pacific Ocean would still be larger. *(true)*
5. The waters of the oceans could be called the sculptors of the coastline. *(true)*
6. The continental slope refers to a gentle slope just off the edge of the coastline. The richest variety of ocean life lives here. *(false)*

Discuss student responses to measure students' understanding. If possible, acquire enough paperback copies of *The Magic School Bus on the Ocean Floor* by Joanna Cole for students to read together in groups of three or four. Students can take turns reading these entertaining books. Once the book has been read, ask the students to review their original responses. Discuss the questions that weren't answered, suggesting resources where students can find the answers.

Activities

A Closer Look at the Pacific

Locate the Pacific Ocean on a globe, a world map, and a map of the United States. Discuss its size relative to other oceans in the world. Send a student or two on a quest to discover the size of the Pacific Ocean (64,000,000 square miles) as compared to the next largest ocean (the Atlantic; 31,815,000 square miles). Following the map presented in *The Magic School Bus,* make a large mural mapping the different levels of the ocean floor. In one corner of the map students might make a large insert illustrating the activity of an undersea volcano. Have a pair of students review vocabulary terms with the class from the topographical dictionary they may have created in chapter 1: ocean, gulf, bay, strait, channel.

Maps of the Ocean

If possible, get copies of maps of ocean tides or navigational maps for students to study. Have them read about ocean tides and the role the moon and gravity play in the movement of tides. Who needs this information and why would it be essential to understand? They might also ask and answer, Just how salty is salt water? How deep is the Pacific Ocean?

Closure

As students fill in key information on their United States maps, review what they have learned about these three states and the Pacific Ocean looking for commonalities between the states that would bind them together into a region. Record the conclusions drawn and store in manila folders or an ongoing notebook on the United States. Declare one day Pacific Ocean Day, dress in beach gear, plan a class picnic, and share all of the information gathered on the Pacific Ocean.

Book Used in This Lesson

Cole, Joanna. *The Magic School Bus on the Ocean Floor*. Illus. by Bruce Degen. New York: Scholastic, 1992.

Suggested Companion Titles

Helman, Andrea. *O Is for Orca*. Photographs by Art Wolfe. Seattle, Wash.: Sasquatch Books, 1995.

Hoff, Mary, and Mary M. Rodgers. *Oceans*. Minneapolis, Minn.: Lerner, 1992.

Johnston, Tony. *Whale Song*. Illus. by Ed Young. New York: Putnam, 1987.

McGovern, Ann. *The Desert Beneath the Sea*. Illus. by Craig Phillips. New York: Scholastic, 1991.

Parker, Steve. *Seashore: Eyewitness Books*. Photographs by David King. New York: Alfred A. Knopf, 1989.

Sheldon, Dyan. *The Whales' Song*. Illus. by Gary Blythe. New York: Dial, 1991.

Simon, Seymour. *Oceans*. New York: Morrow, 1990.

Sis, Peter. *An Ocean World*. Illus. by author. New York: Greenwillow, 1992.

Culminating Activity

After students have recorded pertinent information on their personal blank maps of the United States, invite them to booktalk a favorite book that they discovered during the study of the Pacific Coast states. Students should include title, author, illustrator, date of publication, and the dedication as they start their booktalk. A brief synopsis, a favorite illustration, or an overall reaction to the book could be parts of the talk. Time could be limited to five minutes to keep the pace lively.

3

The Mountain States:
Idaho, Colorado, Montana, Nevada, Utah, and Wyoming

Soaring high above the region called the mountain states, an eagle's panoramic view would reveal a long, high, wide area, with some parts quite rumpled in appearance. Tucking wings close to its body, diving, then gliding with ease on thermal currents, the eagle could travel from north to south down the chain of rugged Rocky Mountains, which resemble a curved backbone of this region. Able to see eight times better than humans, this bird would have quite a unique perspective as it drifts over magnificent ranges like the Tetons in Wyoming, the Bitterroot Range in Idaho, or the Wasatch Range in Utah, just a couple examples of the hundreds of individual ranges that comprise the Rockies. These relatively young (at least in terms of geologic time), rugged mountains have more than eighty peaks over 14,000 feet high. As further study will reveal, this impressive geologic creation figures heavily into life in the mountain states as it draws tourists, affects the climate, and often dictates where it is most advantageous for people to settle.

Sailing upward once again, the eagle travels onward. With its keen eyesight, it will easily discern several other key geologic areas that beg investigation. Basically an arid land rich in hidden minerals, an aerial view of this particular region would reveal the rolling short grass prairies of the fertile Great Plains, the Colorado Plateau's numerous canyons and mesas, and the windy, barren highlands of the Great Basin. It appears that this segment of the United States was created with infinite patience over millions of years. The topography is the result of cataclysmic actions like the incessant battering by glaciers, violent volcanic eruptions, and massive upheavals caused by the continental plates colliding beneath the earth's thin crust. The fact that much of this area is inaccessible and other parts are barely habitable directly relates to low state populations, particularly in Montana, Wyoming, and Utah. Yet people have settled in pockets along bands of productive land having been possibly drawn by the promise of wide, open spaces, a variety of jobs, and an abundance of rich natural resources.

It is no wonder that tourism ranks high in the economies of each of the mountain states. While parts of each state are dry and desolate, others are truly breathtaking as they are set against the backdrop of the magnificent ranges of the Rockies. Scattered throughout this region are marvels like Montana's awe-inspiring Glacier National Park, Colorado's Mesa Verde with its ghostly abandoned Anasazi ruins, and Utah's Dinosaur National Monument where the bones of some of the earliest inhabitants are naturally preserved in the earth itself. Miles of hiking trails in and around the Continental Divide and other areas draw thousands of tourists who appreciate the gifts and change of pace that nature has to offer. In brief, it is an area where, according to former President Theodore Roosevelt, "the scenery bankrupts the imagination."

Initiating Activity

Arrange to have students and their parents who might have vacationed in the mountain states share experiences and pictures with the class. As guest speakers, parents can bring in a selection of slides or short segments of vacation videos aimed at augmenting students' conceptions of the region. If parents are not available, the local library or a travel agency might be able to recommend someone who could bring the mountain states to life for these learners. It is important for students to be able to visualize the area, to get a sense of place before further study begins.

Lesson 1

The Mountain States from Origins to Present Day Through the Themes of Location, Place, and Region

Objectives

- to locate and identify Idaho, Montana, Wyoming, Nevada, Utah, and Colorado on individual outline maps of the United States
- to figure the absolute location of each state, recording latitude and longitude on the backs of student maps
- to locate and then draw the Rocky Mountains, the Colorado Plateau, the Great Basin, and key rivers on the outline maps
- to examine topographic maps and use the information to discover what the terrain is like in each state and why civilization is clustered as it is
- to read about and demonstrate the theory of plate tectonics as it moves continents and creates mountains

Materials

- student atlases
- individual outline map of the United States being filled in by each student
- colored pencils or markers

- *Rocky Mountain Seasons: From Valley to Mountaintop* by Diane L. Burns
- *The Eagle and the River* by Charles Craighead
- blank pie-slice diagram of the earth in Appendix III
- ingredients for Tectonic Sandwiches found in Appendix III

Motivator

Read *Rocky Mountain Seasons* by Diane L. Burns and invite students to pick up the book and study it later on their own. The use of language is wonderful, complemented by beautiful photographs of scenery and wildlife found throughout the mountain states. The book is a lovely introduction to the marvels of the Rockies, an integral part of these mountain states. Booktalk Craighead's *The Eagle and the River*, explaining that numerous eagles winter in Montana. The book also illustrates how the changing course of the Snake River alters life on its shores in the process. This is an informative book to read during independent reading time.

Activities

*A Look at the Earth
and Its Ever-Changing Structure*

Based upon further reading in suggested books at the end of this section and this brief overview, invite the students to take a closer look at the earth from the outside in and back again. Students can label the simple diagram of the earth's core as this information is discussed.

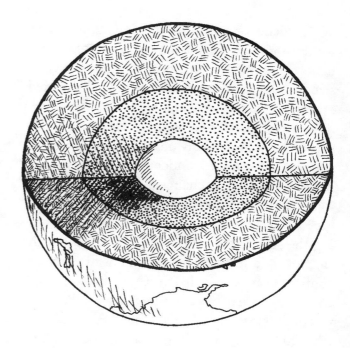

If a pie slice of earth could be removed for closer scrutiny, students would discover four basic layers: the thin outer crust, a thicker mantle, and the two layers of the earth's core. To begin with, an inspection of the outer crust shows that it is like a thin, brittle, rocky skin. The crust combines with the first layer of the mantle beneath it to form the rigid lithosphere. While numbers vary depending on the source consulted, this layer seems to vary in thickness from about 5 miles under the oceans to approximately 80 miles under some of the world's tallest mountain chains.

The next layer, the 1,800-mile-thick mantle, is made up of rock. Some of the rock is solid as one would expect, but the outer part is molten. The sluggish molten material might be likened in consistency to honey or molasses. This slow-moving, uppermost layer of the mantle is called the asthenosphere. Geologists believe that heat rising from the core of the earth makes this particular rock malleable. It stays in this state because of strong convection currents moving within the melted rock. Resting on this upper mobile mantle, the continents continually move and shift. Geographic sleuths will find that this unusual material is also responsible for earthquakes and volcanoes.

The final layer of the earth is the core, which is about 2,100 miles thick and may be as hot as 12,000 degrees Fahrenheit. Made up of both the inner core and outer core, it contains a mass of hot, heavy metals, primarily iron with some nickel. Convection currents are at work in the molten outer core, too, and the resulting movement of the liquefied outer core acts somewhat like a genera-

tor. It is here that the earth's magnetic field is created. That field, of course, is why compass needles point to the north. Lastly, there is the 800-mile-thick inner core. Despite the fact that it may be as hot or hotter than the sun, the inner core remains solid because of intense pressure at the center of the earth. These layers may look separate and distinct as they are diagramed, but geologists are finding that they can be broken down further into narrower bands so the inner view of the earth is much more complex than was once thought.

A Side Step to Discuss Convection Currents

To assure that students understand how convection currents work within the earth's layers, bring in a hot plate and a medium-sized pan filled with water. Set them in a safe place and heat the water. As it begins to heat, students can watch the motion of the water, which shows convection at work. The hot water rises to the surface, dropping back down to the bottom of the pan as it cools and is replaced with more heated water. If a student gently drops a cork into the water, observers will see how the currents move it around in the pan. The continents move a little like the cork, sliding around on the malleable layer of the mantle.

As little as a century ago many geologists would not have considered the idea that continents could move or that oceans might change in size. As new evidence continues to be discovered, however, many long-standing beliefs have been revised. While it isn't a noticeable movement, the earth's plates are actually traveling at an inch or so per year. At that rate residents of North America might unknowingly change locations by as much as 6 feet during the course of a lifetime. That progression seems barely measurable when considering the size of the continents that are doing the shifting, but in the scope of millions of years, the continents have traveled vast distances and will continue to do so. It is amazing to realize that what was once one large land mass called Pangea (more than 200 million years ago) has since broken up into seven recognizable continents, which continue to shift and move into their present locations.

As geologists work to better understand the earth, the discovery of one bit of information seems to open the door to other discoveries and questions. It appears that there are many intriguing mysteries ahead that geologists young and old will continue to try to solve.

Examining the Forces That Create Mountains

Geologists explain that plate tectonics is behind, or more accurately, beneath the movement of the continents. This relatively new theory suggests that the earth's crust, or lithosphere, is not a continuous layer of solid rock as was once thought. Instead, it is divided into seven enormous plates and about eighteen smaller ones that seem to float on the thick, slow-moving asthenosphere. Like huge turtles, the immense plates carry the continents and ocean basins on their backs. Most of North America and much of the Atlantic Ocean are on the North American Plate while Hawaii, part of California, Alaska, and most of the Pacific Ocean are part of the Pacific Plate. Since these plates move, there is always the possibility that they will bump into each other. In fact, that is just what

they do. The results of the crunching and grinding together over a time span of millions of years are mountain ranges like the Rockies, volcanoes that can create or destroy other mountains and landforms, and earthquakes that can reduce cities to rubble in a matter of minutes.

When plates just scrape by each other, fault lines like the San Andreas Fault in California are formed. This kind of slippage along fault surfaces is caused by stresses in the crust, which build up due to irregular plate movements. Think of one side of the fault getting stuck on a jagged piece of the opposite fault. As the first side tries to move on, stress is created. When it is eventually freed, the resulting motion is in the form of an earthquake. So common is this action that minor quakes occur with great regularity in various parts of the world.

Mountains are formed a little differently. Students are to work with their Tectonic Sandwiches as the formation of mountains is explained and demonstrated. Further instructions are located in Appendix III.

Fault-Block Mountains

These mountains are formed when the crustal plates move away from each other along a fault line or blocks of crust shift along fault lines within the plates. Large chunks of rock can slide down into the resulting opening or other chunks can be pushed up into the newly created space. Sometimes one block will rise while the other will fall or remain stationary. The landscape now has a new look. In addition, one block along a fault may tilt or rotate and, again, new mountains are formed. These mountains can often be identified by the steep face on one side and a gentle slope on the other. The Wasatch Range in Utah and the Tetons in Wyoming were created this way.

Colliding Continents and Folded Mountains

The collision of two crustal continental plates that were once separated produces folded mountain chains. As this action occurs, one plate slides beneath the other causing intense pressures and high temperatures, which eventually alter the composition of the rocks in the plates. The resulting upward movement produces mild, wavelike mountains or a range pleated like an accordion as are parts of the Rockies. The Appalachian Mountains in the South were also formed in such a manner. Another way students might visualize this is to bring in a cloth placemat. Hold one edge stationary while pushing the other edge gently toward it. The resulting folds illustrate how these mountains might also be built.

Subduction

This kind of activity has been happening on America's West Coast for the last 60 million years. When an oceanic plate like the Pacific Plate collides with a continental plate, the denser oceanic plate is forced beneath the continental plate by a process called subduction. The strong horizontal forces produced during this type of collision lift and fold the continental plate and the oceanic plate is forced deeper and deeper into the earth. The heat from the mantle eventually melts the bottom plate along its leading edge forming molten material. Because this material is less dense than the mantle rock, it may work its way up through the continent in the form of magma, fueling volcanoes in the mountains on the continent above. Part of the Rocky Mountains were created in this way. The Cascade Mountains are also an example of such a volcanic mountain range, while Mount St. Helens in Washington is a subduction-related volcano.

Dome Mountains

The Elk Mountains in Wyoming, the Black Hills of South Dakota, and the Adirondack Mountains in New York were formed when the earth's crust was forced upward as magma welled up underneath it. As it hardened, it formed a roughly circular bulge in the landscape. This is similar to a blister with liquid inside. A spectacular example that draws millions of tourists to California is Yosemite's Half Dome, a dome mountain that was cracked in half by glacial action. Similar structures that sink rather than being forced upward are called basins.

Closure

If students have been using pieces of their Tectonic Sandwiches to visualize the creation of mountains, it is now time to devour their handiwork. Hand out cartons of chilled milk and let the students consume their experiment as comprehension is checked during a wrap-up discussion of the earth and its interactions and reactions.

Applying What They Have Learned

Working in teams, select a mountain state and begin work on a topographic map. Instead of salt dough, make a three-dimensional map. Students can put their heads together to decide what kinds of materials they can use to represent different geographic regions. For example, stiff crumpled paper, wetted down and shaped carefully, might represent the Rocky Mountains. Shiny wide or narrow ribbon, gift wrap, or aluminum foil might be cut for rivers or lakes. What kinds of materials could represent the prairies? Creativity will be at its best as grass, pebbles, sticks, cardboard, string, and other materials are used to give an unusual but graphic view of Idaho, Colorado, Montana, Nevada, Utah, and Wyoming. Students are to include an elevation key in their final products. This would be one presentation to videotape as students share their work at the culmination of the activity.

Books Used in This Lesson

Burns, Diane L. *Rocky Mountain Seasons: From Valley to Mountaintop.* Photographs by Kent Dannon and Donna Dannon. New York: Macmillan, 1993.

Craighead, Charles. *The Eagle and the River.* Photographs by Tom Mangelsen. New York: Macmillan, 1994.

Suggested Companion Titles

Alessandrello, Anna. *The Earth: Origins and Evolution.* Austin, Tex.: Steck-Vaughn, 1995.

Fradin, Dennis.*Utah.* Chicago: Children's Press, 1993.

Heinrichs, Ann. *Wyoming.* Chicago: Children's Press, 1992.

LaDoux, Rita C. *Montana.* Minneapolis, Minn.: Lerner, 1992.

Lauber, Patricia. *Summer of Fire: Yellowstone, 1988.* New York: Orchard Books, 1991.

———. *Seeing Earth from Space.* New York: Orchard Books, 1990.

———. *Volcano: The Eruption and Healing of Mount St. Helens.* New York: Bradbury Press, 1986.

Patent, Dorothy Henshaw. *Eagles of America.* Photographs by William Munoz. New York: Holiday House, 1995.

Ride, Sally, and Tam O'Shaughnessy. *The Third Planet: Exploring the Earth from Space.* Photographs from the National Aeronautics & Space Administration. New York: Crown, 1995.

Rotter, Charles. *Mountains.* Mankato, Minn.: Creative Education, 1994.

Sattler, Helen Roney. *Our Patchwork Planet: The Story of Plate Tectonics.* Illus. by Giulio Maestro. New York: Lothrop, Lee & Shepard, 1995.

Time-Life Books for Children. *Geography: Understanding Science and Nature Series.* Alexandria, Va.: Time-Life, 1993.

Van Rose, Susanna. *Volcano & Earthquake: Eyewitness Books.* New York: Alfred A. Knopf, 1992.

Lesson 2

Looking at the Mountain States Through the Themes of Place and Human/Environmental Interactions

Objectives

- to understand the relationship between early settlers of this region and the land they called home
- to investigate the geographic question, What is it like there?
- to use history as a tool to understand the images or emotional responses that people might have to these states
- to chart the advantages and disadvantages of living in each of these states as a way of understanding why only four out of every one hundred Americans have decided to live here
- to map population density in each of the states while investigating what the relationship is between the people and the area in which they have chosen to live

Materials

- individual outline maps of the region including the mountain states
- a variety of picture books about early settlers like those listed below
- tapes of music representative of the groups to be studied like *Folk Songs of Idaho and Utah* by Rosalie Sorrels or *Songs of the Wild West* by Alan Axelrod

Motivator

Line up selected books on a table in front of the class. Include selections on the Anasazi like Betsy James's *The Mud Family*, A. S. Gintzler's *Rough and Ready Cowboys*, the pioneers in the amusing *Wagons West!* by Roy Gerrard, and women and miners in *Miners, Merchants, and Maids* by Suzanne Hilton. Looking at the area from the perspective of early explorers would be interesting, too. *Lewis and Clark: Explorers of the American West* by Steven Kroll is a wonderful start for interested students. While these men didn't stay, it will be informative to learn about what they found before others settled in the relatively unsettled regions. The workers on the transcontinental railroad make interesting study, too. *The Ten Mile Day and the Building of the Transcontinental Railroad* by Mary Ann Fraser tells about the battle between men, time, and the lay of the land as a team of men struggled to set a new record in laying the track.

Look for additional titles that might address the early lives of Basque sheepherders and Morman settlers as well. Hold each title up showing the cover and giving a brief synopsis. Ask students to think for a few minutes about what these books and their subjects might have in common. How can they be grouped together? Then ask for suggestions. Guide the discussion toward the idea that the books are all about people who once lived or explored in the mountain states, who chose to make the area their home for one reason or another.

The question to be investigated at this point and in upcoming research is, Why did these people pick this particular region? Delving a little deeper, students can answer questions like, What was it about the land, water, climate, soil, vegetation, or animal life that drew them? Did they stay? What did they contribute to the land or did they affect it in a negative way? What were the advantages or disadvantages of living in each state? List these questions on the board or type them on information-gathering sheets for the students to use. Students should pick a group of settlers that particularly interests them, get a list of the previous questions, and take the appropriate picture book along to share together.

Activities

Zeroing in on the Activity

To set the tone for the upcoming project, use a prop and a little time travel as students move imaginatively back in time. Each group might be given an item that symbolizes their group, something that is real, photocopied, or replicated out of tagboard. Suggestions might include a pick, ore, or tin pan for miners; a basket, dried corn, or pottery shard for the Anasazi; cornmeal, bag of beans, spoke from a broken wagon wheel for the pioneers, and so forth. Later, this prop can become the magical item that will take the class back in time as each group presents an informative skit about the lives of the settlers they studied at the culmination of this project.

A Framework for Research

Explain to the students that geographic thinkers look for answers to the questions, Where? and Why there? as they read books, maps, graphs, charts, and other pertinent materials in the quest to gather information. Once gathered, that information must be analyzed and organized into an appropriate format in order to be shared. As information is sifted through and scrutinized, some hypotheses or generalizations may occur that need to be substantiated or disproved. When satisfactory answers have been found to the initial questions, students can decide how to present their discoveries to others in an interesting and informative manner. Students are to keep these thoughts in mind as they learn about geography throughout the mountain states and across the continent in all of the projects they undertake.

Time Line

Using a long roll of shelf paper, create a time line across one wall in the classroom. As information is gathered, each group locates their settlers on the time line, adding enough information to make the entry interesting and then illustrating their work in an appealing way. The time line is a visual tool to enable all learners to get the whole picture of settlement across the mountain states as these projects progress. For example, the group studying the Anasazi might begin the time line at about A.D. 550, more than fourteen centuries ago. Around 1190, this culture built the wondrous city of alcove houses in what is now called Mesa Verde in southwest Colorado. This area was home to between 3,000 and 5,000 people until it was mysteriously abandoned in about 1300. For hundreds of years these buildings remained undisturbed. Then the Ute and Navajo tribes arrived in about 1390, and the Spaniards spent some time in the area as well. Later in the 1800s, new faces arrived: pioneers, miners, and ranchers. Students working with the latest group to settle in the mountain states can pick an ending date for this historical time line.

Closure

Present skits highlighting a few key points about each group of settlers. Use a tape such as *Folk Songs of Idaho and Utah* by Rosalie Sorrels as background music or a group could teach the class a catchy tune. Have the students summarize what they have learned about the influence people have had over the years on the geography of the mountain states. Explain where early settlers lived and where populations are concentrated today, having classmates record the information on their regional outline maps. Have students highlight how the geography helped or hindered the people. Ask each group of learners to make predictions for the future interactions between humans and geography in the region.

Books and Tapes Used in This Lesson

Axelrod, Alan. *Songs of the Wild West*. Arrangements by Dan Fox. New York: Simon & Schuster, 1991.

Fraser, Mary Ann. *The Ten Mile Day and the Building of the Transcontinental Railroad*. Illus. by author. New York: Henry Holt, 1993.

Gerrard, Roy. *Wagons West!* Illus. by author. New York: Farrar, Straus & Giroux, 1996.

Gintzler, A. S. *Rough and Ready Cowboys*. Illus. by Chris Brigman. Santa Fe, N.Mex.: John Muir Publications, 1994.

Hilton, Suzanne. *Miners, Merchants, and Maids*. New York: Twenty-First Century Books, 1995.

James, Betsy. *The Mud Family*. Illus. by Paul Morin. New York: Putnam, 1994.

Kroll, Steven. *Lewis and Clark: Explorers of the American West*. Illus. by Richard Williams. New York: Holiday House, 1994.

Sorrels, Rosalie. *Folk Songs of Idaho and Utah*. Washington, D.C.: Smithsonian/Folkways Recordings, 1992.

Suggested Companion Titles

Allen, Kate. *The Legend of the Whistle Pig Wrangler*. Illus. by Jim Harris. Del Mar, Calif.: Kumquat Press, 1995.

Arnold, Caroline. *The Ancient Cliff Dwellers of Mesa Verde*. Photographs by Richard Hewett. New York: Clarion Books, 1992.

Bodkin, Odds. *The Banshee Train*. Illus. by Ted Rose. New York: Clarion Books, 1994.

Dewey, Jennifer Owens. *Stories on Stone: Rock Art—Images from the Ancient Ones*. Boston: Little, Brown, 1996.

Fischer, Leonard Everett. *The Oregon Trail*. New York: Holiday House, 1990.

Geis, Jacqueline. *Where the Buffalo Roam*. Nashville, Tenn.: Ideals, 1992.

Gintzler, A. S. *Rough and Ready Homesteaders*. Santa Fe, N.Mex.: John Muir Publications, 1994.

Johnson, Neil. *Jack Creek Cowboy*. New York: Dial, 1993.

La Pierre, Yvette. *Native American Rock Art: Messages from the Past*. Illus. by Lois Sloan. Charlottesville, Va.: Thomasson-Grant, 1994.

Lyon, George Ella. *Dreamplace*. Illus. by Peter Catalanotto. New York: Orchard Books, 1993.

Martell, Hazel Mary. *Native Americans and Mesa Verde*. New York: Dillon Press, 1993.

Medearis, Angela Shelf. *The Zebra Riding Cowboy*. Illus. by Maria Cristina Brusca. New York: Henry Holt, 1992.

Metropolitan Museum of Art. *Songs of the Wild West*. New York: Simon & Schuster, 1991.

Morris, J. *The Harvey Girls: The Women Who Civilized the West*. New York: Walker, 1994.

Patent, Dorothy Henshaw. *West by Covered Wagon—Retracing the Pioneer Trail*. Photographs by William Munoz. New York: Walker, 1995.

Ratz de Tagyos, Paul. *Showdown at Lonesome Pellet*. New York: Clarion Books, 1994.

Rodanas, Kristina. *Dance of the Sacred Circle: A Native American Tale*. Boston: Little, Brown, 1995.

Roop, Peter, and Connie Roop. *Off the Map: The Journals of Lewis and Clark*. New York: Walker, 1993.

Sandler, Martin W. *Pioneers: A Library of Congress Book*. New York: HarperCollins, 1994.

Schlessel, Lillian. *Black Frontiers*. New York: Simon & Schuster, 1995.

Shirley, Gayle Corbett. *C Is for Colorado*. Illus. by Constance Rummel Bergum. Helena, Mont.: Falcon Press, 1993.

Stilz, Carol Curtis. *Grandma Buffalo, May, and Me*. Illus. by Constance R. Bergum. Seattle, Wash.: Sasquatch Books, 1995.

Trimble, Stephen. *The Village of Blue Stone*. Illus. by Jennifer Owings Dewey and Deborah Reade. New York: Macmillan, 1990.

Culminating Activity

Play the game Concentration with the class. Make "cards" out of tagboard, perhaps the size of a sheet of typing paper (8½ by 11). Using a dark-colored marker so that cards can be read from a short distance away, write a fact about a state. Make a matching card with the state's name on it. Obviously, facts should not be too obscure. It would be best during the initial games to include facts from materials that students had used in class.

Next, divide the class into two groups; each will play their own game. The number of cards to be used should be adjusted to the age or grade level of the players. The cards should be shuffled and then thumb-tacked, information side down, to a bulletin board or stuck to the wall with a re-usable adhesive product, like Fun Tak. There should be a monitor for each game.

Decide the order of play—alphabetical order by first or last names, perhaps, or the order children are sitting in. The first player turns over two cards, looks at them carefully while everyone else tries to remember what they say and where they are, and then the cards are turned over again. The next player takes a turn, and play continues until a student can match a fact with the correct state. That student keeps those two cards and gets a sec-

ond turn. If no match occurs, the next student takes a turn. The trick is to concentrate on the cards' locations. The player with the most matching cards at the end is the winner. At the conclusion of the game, teams can switch places, working with the other set of cards if time permits. As an extension of this activity, students will enjoy making their own version of the game using smaller cards (index cards would work) and playing with other classmates at the Geography Center during free time.

Some suggestions for cards follow:

Idaho

- a quarter of all of the French fries served in fast-food restaurants come from this state
- a state with such unusual shape and varied terrain that it could be three states in one
- Craters of the Moon National Monument so much resembles the landscape of the moon that astronauts trained here
- the Snake River is a primary water source
- Sun Valley Resort nestles in the Sawtooth Range of the Rockies
- there are more Basques living here than anywhere outside of northern Spain
- a solid copper, bronze-coated eagle perches atop the Boise capitol building

- Nez Perce and Shoshone were the largest early tribes here but the Coeur d'Alene left their mark as well
- fur trapping and trading were carried on for three decades beginning in the early 1800s

Colorado

- sometimes called "The Top of the Nation"
- claims fifty-five "fourteeners" or mountains that stand over 14,000 feet high
- straddles the Continental Divide
- Mother of Rivers is a nickname as more major rivers have their source here than in any other state
- Mesa Verde was home to the Basketmakers, some of the earliest inhabitants
- if they said, "Pikes Peak or Bust," they were headed for this state
- Katherine Lee Bates was inspired to write "America the Beautiful" here
- the mint here is the second largest depository of gold in the country
- capitol dome in the "Mile High City" is covered with 24-karat gold, testament to the city's origin as a gold-mining town

Montana

- home of Custer's Last Stand near the Little Bighorn River
- often referred to as "Big Sky Country"
- the fourth largest state
- so many bones have been found here that the town was named Skeleton Flats
- Lewis and Clark expedition traveled 1,600 miles up the Missouri River to end up in this state
- close ties to this land as hunters, trappers, farmers, ranchers, miners, and loggers made a living from the mountains and the prairies
- Great Depression in the 1930s plus severe drought and a plague of grasshoppers made life here nearly impossible

- home of Glacier National Park, Great Falls of the Missouri River, and Flathead Lake

Nevada

- the driest state in the country averaging between 7 and 9 inches of precipitation a year
- visit beautiful Lake Tahoe, the largest and second deepest alpine lake in the United States
- home of Hoover Dam, which holds back the Colorado River, and of the man-made Lake Mead
- important activities that help the economy are legalized gambling, tourism, and entertainment
- multimillion dollar Comstock Lode of silver and gold led to the settlement of Virginia City
- nuclear testing was done here from the 1950s to the 1970s
- it's possible to find a Roman palace, a medieval castle, a pirate ship battle, a circus, and magicians in two of the cities here (Las Vegas and Reno)
- is the turquoise capital of the world
- few of the rivers make it to the sea because they evaporate during the four-month dry season
- no other state except Alaska has such a large portion of unspoiled land

Utah

- named for the Ute Indians
- settled primarily by the Mormons
- named the Beehive State for the industrious people who settled there
- the western third of the state is a desert named after a lake
- second driest state in the United States
- Dinosaur National Monument is in the northeastern part of the state

- Golden Spike was driven into the ground here on May 10, 1869, connecting the East Coast and West Coast by rail
- one of the top salt-producing states

Wyoming

- first state to give women the right to vote
- state motto: Equal Rights
- unofficially the Cowboy State
- Continental Divide cuts diagonally across the state
- South Pass through the mountains made travel for pioneers easier
- home of Yellowstone, Grand Teton National Park, and Thunder Basin National Grasslands
- ranked fiftieth in state populations based on 1990 census
- Red Canyon or Hole-in-the-Wall sometimes sheltered the notorious gang lead by Butch Cassidy and the Sundance Kid

4

The Southwestern States:
Texas, Oklahoma, New Mexico, and Arizona

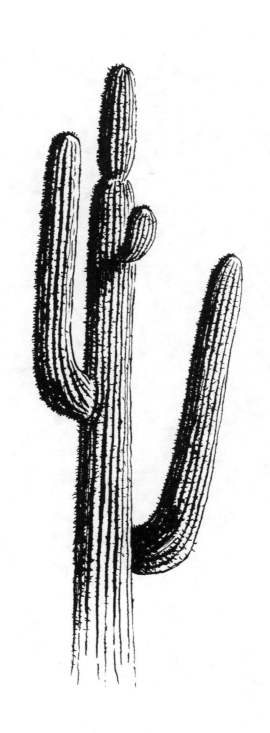

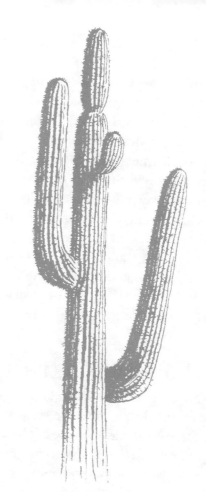

If asked for a one- or two-word reaction to the region of the Southwest, people might respond with constant sunshine, deserts, dry heat, chili peppers, wealth in oil, cowboys, saguaro cactus, rattlesnakes, and coyotes. Those images do fit, yet this is a surprisingly diverse land. There are barren areas of desert, but there are also the cool ponderosa pine forests surrounding the San Francisco Peaks in Arizona, the Ozark hardwood forests in eastern Oklahoma, and swamps and bayous along the Texas coast. From the tip of the 13,161-foot Wheeler Peak in New Mexico to the Texas Gulf Coast shore, this is a land of varied terrain.

The earliest inhabitants, however, would have chosen different words to describe the Southwest as it evolved from an area covered with shallow oceans 350 million years ago. It is challenging for people today to find words to describe those ancient people who left bits of their lives behind to tantalize current inhabitants and curious archeologists. Clovis points (projectile points found in New Mexico) are remnants of Ice Age hunters who roamed the area over 12,000 years ago. The Anasazi left carefully constructed cliff dwellings, pot shards, petroglyphs, and pictographs—puzzling pieces to their lives, which ended so mysteriously more than 2,000 years ago. Rich in Native American history, past and present, the movement of humans through the southwestern states makes a fascinating study. The Hopi, Navajo, Apache, Zuni, Hohokom, Pueblo, and Cherokee are just a few of the tribes who currently enrich the area with their customs, stories, and artwork. Here, too,

are memories of the arduous journey undertaken by the Cherokee during their relocation to Oklahoma. It became known as the Trail of Tears, another link between humans, history, and this land. And what a land it is.

If students wanted to learn geographic vocabulary terms in a real-life setting, the Southwest would make a fabulous textbook. Consider the Grand Canyon in Arizona for starters. What better way to define "canyon" while learning about geologic history back as far as 1.7 billion years than to a visit to this awesome creation. Both in the canyon and above it, words like gorge, mesa, butte, and arroyo could be defined by standing next to the feature itself. Volcano could be better understood by studying the Rocky Mountains in this area, which were formed by earth-shattering eruptions (process of subduction covered in chapter 3) over a period of many years. Not only are there mountains as a result of the volcanic action, but there remain fields of jagged black lava rock as barren and forbidding as a foreign planet.

Moving on to Oklahoma, and leafing back through history, students could experience the discovery of oil in the early 1900s and the prosperity that ensued. The next twenty-five to thirty years would bring learners into the dust bowl, which plummeted many farmers in the western part of the state into poverty. Not to be outdone, the Texas coast has something else to offer on-site learners as it is an excellent spot to experience fertile fields, huge cattle ranches, and wonderful beaches along with those swamps and bayous. The Southwest is a region with interesting lessons to teach and some surprises in store for geographic investigation.

Initiating Activity

To activate current knowledge and begin acquiring new knowledge, involve the students in a race for knowledge about the Southwest. This activity will also acquaint the students with some of the materials at hand for later research on these particular states.

Materials

- an ample supply of picture books on the Southwest, both fiction and nonfiction, selected from the Suggested Companion Titles listed at the end of each activity
- a textbook or two and atlases
- a variety of other materials on the states that may have been collected beforehand
- a small but audible bell
- a pack of index cards containing clues and answers for teacher use
- simple prizes for the winners

Rules for the Hunt

- In an accessible location, display the books that will be the resources for students to use as they look for clues.
- Divide the class into four or five teams, depending on the size of the class. Teams of four to five students would be ideal.

- When the hunt begins, the teacher will read a card. A designated member from each team goes to the materials table and may only take one reference or picture book to begin their search for the answer. He or she returns to the team and the hunt for the answer is on. This job of book picker rotates from team member to team member each time another card is read. Teams may only have one book in their possession at a time as they search for the state being described in the clue.
- When the team finds the correct state, they write the state name down on a numbered sheet of paper. The book picker quickly returns the book, rings the bell to signal to the other teams that an answer has been found, and sits down. If the answer is correct, the search for that answer is stopped. If the answer is incorrect, the other teams continue to search for the right answer. Teams draw a line by that answer slot. The teacher reads the next card, keeping the cards in order so that checking answers is possible later. A scout heads out for another book and the search continues.
- Courteous behavior and respect for the books must be observed at all times or a team may be warned and then disqualified if circumstances warrant it.
- When all of the clue cards have been read, the teacher will go back through them in order and ask teams for the answers. The team with the most correct answers is the winner. Appropriate prizes can be awarded at that time. It might also be fun to award a prize to any student who has a birthday on the date that one of the states received its statehood.

This is not meant to be a quiet activity as you can well imagine. It is an exciting race for knowledge designed to get everyone involved and keep them that way for the continued study of the southwestern states.

The following clues can be used or the teacher can develop a set of his/her own:

Arizona

1. Forty-eighth state: find the date it became a state (February 14, 1912)
2. Name comes from an Indian word meaning "small spring"
3. Mining products: copper, silver, lead, zinc
4. State bird: cactus wren
5. Geographical feature: one part of the only point in the United States where four states meet. List the states. (Four Corners—Arizona, Colorado, New Mexico, and Utah)
6. Economy: manufacturing, tourism, mining, arts and crafts, and agriculture

New Mexico

1. Forty-seventh state: find the date it became a state (January 6, 1912)
2. Nickname: Land of Enchantment
3. State bird: roadrunner
4. Agriculture: wheat, hay, grain, cotton, lumber, pecans, corn, livestock
5. Economy: a leading center of space and nuclear research
6. Geographical feature: Carlsbad Caverns

Oklahoma

1. Forty-sixth state: find the date it became a state (November 16, 1907)
2. Nickname: the Sooner State
3. Name comes from two Choctaw Indian words meaning "red people"
4. Agriculture: wheat, sorghum, hay, cotton, peanuts, mung beans, corn, alfalfa, cattle, dairy products, broiler chickens, sheep
5. Flower: mistletoe
6. Geographical feature: a prairie state with many mountains

Texas

1. Twenty-eighth state: find the date it became a state (December 29, 1845)
2. Flower: bluebonnet
3. Mining: cement, stone, sand, gravel
4. Name comes from the Indian word "tejas" meaning friends or allies
5. Geographical feature: Guadalupe Mountains National Park
6. Geographical feature: Colorado River is a major river

At the conclusion of the hunt, have students label the four states on their own copies of maps of the United States.

Lesson 1

Discovering Texas Through the Theme of Location

Objectives

- to plot the absolute location of the state of Texas using the reference system of latitude and longitude on student outline maps
- to describe the relative location of Texas using students' own descriptors
- to answer the geographic question, Why here? in regard to the placement of cities within Texas
- plot the cities and landforms described in *The Armadillo from Amarillo*
- to follow the pattern as it is used in the book to describe where children live to discover, Where in the world am I?

- to establish correspondence with children in Texas using postcards, building an informative postcard album
- to use the scale of miles on a map to calculate distances between cities mentioned in the book

Materials

- "They Don't Do Math in Texas" from *If You're Not Here, Please Raise Your Hand* by Kalli Dakos
- *The Armadillo from Amarillo* written and illustrated by Lynne Cherry
- a wall map of the United States
- individual student maps of the country

Motivator

Read the poem to introduce Texas. If there is a student in the class who has lived in Texas, have them talk about their real experiences in school. Display a stuffed toy armadillo or bring in large pictures of this unusual animal. Ask the students to share what they know about armadillos. Tell them they will be learning more about this ani-

mal as they listen to a beautifully illustrated book entitled *The Armadillo from Amarillo*. Be certain to read the endnote to the students after completing the book for additional information about the animal.

Next, ask for a volunteer to locate the state of Texas on a large wall map of the United States. Locate Amarillo as well. Finally, read the book aloud. Tell the students to just listen and enjoy the story the first time through. Then reread it so that they can take notes on what they have learned about Texas through this seemingly simple picture book. Before you start reading, have students label a piece of paper with the following columns:

| landforms | vegetation |
| wildlife | major cities |

They can quickly fill in the columns as they listen to the story a second time through. Discuss their information as a large group upon completion of the story.

Activities

Absolute Location

Using latitude and longitude, plot the location of Texas on individual student maps. Remind learners that latitude lines are also called parallels, and they are used to measure distances north and south of the equator. Longitude lines are called meridians, and they measure distances east and west.

Relative Location

When using relative location, students are to describe where Texas is in relationship to other places around it. They are to write down their descriptions and share them within small groups. They will quickly notice that no one's location will be exactly like anyone else's so relative location is less exact than absolute location. Discuss when each one might be the most appropriate to use.

Why There?

Using the large wall map or topographic maps in an atlas as references, locate and plot all of the cities that Sasparillo visits on student outline maps. Working in small groups, discuss why the cities might be located where they are. Look up the population of each city and discuss why one is larger than another in an effort to surmise why cities grew where they did and what attracts people to them.

Globe Work

Using a globe, locate Texas from an eagle's eye view. Pinpoint Cuba and Mexico as well.

Practicing with the Scale of Miles

Working in learning triads, use the scale of miles on a map of the students' choice to figure the distance Sasparillo traveled as he moved from one city to the next. Compare the results within a large group. Discuss why everyone might not come up with exactly the same numbers.

Where in the World Am I?

Follow the eagle's description of where Amarillo is in the scheme of things. Working from the inside out, students describe where they live from city to state, to United States, to continent, to planet earth, to solar system on the circle diagram. The center should be absolute location, the next ring should be relative location using north, south, east, and west of other points.

Geographic Postcard Exchange

Locate a Texas classroom where the students would be willing to be involved in a geographic postcard exchange. In this way both classrooms can learn more about another state.

Ask that the initial postcard be about a landform or common animal. Subsequent postcards can depict vegetation or tourist attractions.

One postcard should be completely designed by the students showing a specific aspect of their state that they have researched and illustrated themselves.

When postcards arrive, the children should share them with the class and then file them in a pocket-type photo album so that both sides can be enjoyed.

The goal of this activity is to learn as much as possible about Texas through postcards. In addition, students are learning and disseminating information about their own state. Time can be set aside to discuss the similarities and differences between the two states.

A Change of Pace

The students can create a lasting bouquet of bluebonnets and strengthen skills in following directions at the same time. See the Texas Bluebonnet Activity Sheet in Appendix III for directions.

Closure

Review the key points students have observed about the location of Texas and the large cities within the state. Ask students to share one particularly interesting thing they learned about this large state before moving on to another state in this region.

Books Used in This Lesson

Cherry, Lynne. *The Armadillo from Amarillo.* Illus. by author. San Diego, Calif.: Harcourt Brace, 1994.
Dakos, Kalli. *If You're Not Here, Please Raise Your Hand.* Illus. by G. Brian Karas. New York: Four Winds Press, 1990.

Suggested Companion Titles

Brett, Jan. *Armadillo Rodeo.* Illus. by author. New York: Scholastic, 1995.
dePaola, Tomie. *The Legend of the Indian Paintbrush.* Illus. by author. New York: Putnam, 1987.
———. *The Legend of the Bluebonnet.* Illus. by author. New York: Putnam, 1983.
Fraden, Dennis B. *From Sea to Shining Sea: Texas.* Chicago: Children's Press, 1992.
Harper, Jo. *Jalapeno Hal.* Illus. by Jennifer Beck Harris. New York: Four Winds Press, 1993.

Johnston, Tony. *The Cowboy and the Black-Eyed Pea.*
    Illus. by W. Ludwig. New York: Putnam, 1992.
Kellogg, Steven. *Pecos Bill*. New York: Morrow, 1986.

Rice, James. *Texas Alphabet*. Gretna, La.: Pelican,
    1988.
Sullivan, Charles. *Cowboys*. New York: Rizzoli, 1993.

Lesson 2

Discovering New Mexico Though the Themes of Place, Movement, and Human/Environmental Interactions

Objectives

- to examine the physical characteristics of New Mexico
- to investigate the human characteristics of the state noting how the population is distributed
- to compare and contrast lives of people and their jobs of New Mexico with the state in which the students live
- to understand how ethnic backgrounds influence popular foods from different regions
- to learn how crops grown in New Mexico are transported to other parts of the United States

Materials

- *Carlos and the Squash Plant* by Jan Romero Stevens
- student maps of New Mexico
- the spicy dish, calabacitas, for the students to sample
- small paper cups and spoons for tasting

Motivator

Discuss the fact that different parts of the United States are known for their special dishes, certain kinds of spices, or certain ethnic influences. Give students a small serving of calabacitas. Have them react in writing to the food and flavors. Ask them to list the ingredients to the best of their ability. Dur-ing a class sharing time decide where the ingredients might have come from. Explain to them that the foods are grown in New Mexico, and, in fact, the dish is a favorite of the main character in *Carlos and the Squash Plant*. Read the book. If at all possible, have someone read the Spanish version of the story at the same time.

Ask the students how life in Carlos's house is the same or different from life in their homes. How does the countryside differ? Since the family is farming, what kinds of conditions would it take to help the crops grow? Using the illustrations in the book, what can students learn about the crops grown, the kinds of animals in the area, and the nationality of the family? Why do students think there might be a strong Spanish influence in New Mexico?

Activities

Research the Climate and Farming Conditions in New Mexico

Give each student a deed for 50 acres of land of their choice to farm. Using topographical maps and a road map of New Mexico along with other resources they choose to consult, where would they locate their farm? What would they grow that would be profitable? How would they get their produce to market once it was harvested? After researching and locating their farm, invite students to share their decisions with the rest of the class. They must investigate climate, availability of water, soil and topography, and kinds of crops that fare well in New Mexico. In addition, ask the students how they would care for the soil so that it remained productive. Overall, what could the impact be of extensive farming on the land?

Physical and Human Characteristics

Divide the class into groups to research and create a topographic map of the state. Their task is to decide why the state is called, "The Land of Enchantment." Locate mountains, the Great Plains, canyons, deserts, and high mesas. Where are sources of water? Are there commonalities between areas in the state, like kinds of trees along rivers, types of vegetation in the mountains, and so forth? Learn how the size of New Mexico compares to other states. How do the students think the land has changed over time, since as long ago as the Anasazi Indians, for example? Students are to explain any geographical vocabulary they use such as the differences between the terms butte, mesa, and canyon, or river and tributary. When the topographic maps are completed, share the learning as a large group.

Closure

Ask the students to share what they have learned about New Mexico that they didn't know previously. Invite them to learn more about this state through other books in the classroom library. Students should fill in the state on their blank maps of the United States. They can put in cities and landforms as well.

In addition, it might be fun to have lunch together in the classroom and include as many authentic foods from this area as possible. Invite parents to contribute a dish or have owners of local restaurants bring in a dish to discuss and share.

Book Used in This Lesson

Stevens, Jan Romero. *Carlos and the Squash Plant.* Illus. by Jean Arnold. Flagstaff, Ariz.: Northland, 1993.

Suggested Companion Titles

Albert, Richard E. *Alejandro's Gift.* Illus. by Sylvia Long. San Francisco: Chronicle Books, 1994.

Anderson, Joan. *Roundup on an American Ranch.* Photographs by George Ancona. New York: Scholastic, 1996.

Ashabranner, Brent. *Born to the Land: An American Portrait.* Photographs by Paul Conklin. New York: Putman, 1989.

Fradin, Judith, and Dennis Fradin. *From Sea to Shining Sea: New Mexico.* Chicago: Children's Press, 1994.

Hausman, Gerald. *Coyote Walks on Two Legs: A Book of Navajo Myths and Legends.* Illus. by Floyd Cooper. New York: Philomel, 1995.

James, Betsy. *Blow Away Soon.* Illus. by Anna Vojtech. New York: Putnam, 1995.

Johnston, Tony. *Alice Nizzy Nazzy, the Witch of Santa Fe.* Illus. by Tomie dePaola. New York: Scholastic, 1995.

La Pierre, Yvette. *Native American Rock Art: Messages from the Past.* Illus. by Lois Sloan. Charlottesville, Va.: Thomasson-Grant, 1994.

Lowell, Susan. *The Tortoise and the Jackrabbit.* Illus. by Jim Harris. Flagstaff, Ariz.: Northland, 1994.

Paulsen, Gary. *The Tortilla Factory.* Illus. by Ruth Wright Paulsen. New York: Harcourt Brace, 1995.

Schoberle, Cecile. *Esmerelda and the Pet Parade.* New York: Simon & Schuster, 1990.

Sneve, Virginia Driving Hawk.. *The Navajos: A First Americans Book.* New York: Holiday House, 1993.

Stevens, Jan Romero. *Carlos and the Corn Field.* Illus. by Jeanne Arnold. Flagstaff, Ariz.: Northland, 1995.

Tinus, Arline Warner. *Young Goat's Discovery.* Santa Fe, N.Mex.: Red Crane Books, 1994.

Whitethorne, Baje. *Sunpainters: Eclipse of the Navajo Sun.* Flagstaff, Ariz.: Northland, 1994.

Lesson 3

Discovering Oklahoma Through the Themes of Movement, Place, and Human/Environmental Interactions

Objectives

- to trace on a map the route followed by Grandma Essie and her family
- to examine and explain the causes and effects of people migrating from one area to another
- to analyze the oil industry and the changes it has experienced in the last one hundred years
- to understand how the westward movement of people impacted certain states in the past and present

Materials

- *Grandma Essie's Covered Wagon* by David Williams
- paper and pencils
- classroom map

Motivator

Set the scene for the students by showing them the cover of the book. Tell them that their father has just come home brimming with excitement. He has heard about fertile land in Kansas and oil fields in Oklahoma. As soon as it can be arranged, you and your family will be leaving their home in Missouri and heading to one of those locations. Because you will be traveling in a covered wagon with your parents and five brothers and sisters, you can take very little with you. If you were limited to ten useful but small items, what might you take? Give students time to compile their lists and then share them.

Next, study the topography between Missouri and Kansas or Missouri and Oklahoma on a large classroom map. Speculate together about what a trip by covered wagon might have been like over that terrain. Read the book and discuss what life was like for Essie and her family. Compare the students' lives to the children's in the story. Figure out how long such a trip might have taken by covered wagon as compared to travel today.

Activity

Learning About Oklahoma from Different Perspectives

Divide students up into groups based on their interest in the following topics:

- One group could research the development of the oil industry in Oklahoma. Investigate the fossil fuels and discuss their limited life span. Students could present their information in the form of graphs, maps including working oil rigs in the 1800s and in the present, or a choice of their own.

- The state is divided into five geographic regions: the Ozark Plateau, the Arkansas Valley, the Ouachita Mountains, the Red River Region, and the Western Plains. Learn about each region: what it might be like to live there, if crops can be grown and transported from there, and what kinds of minerals might be mined there. In which regions did most of the people settle who moved to Oklahoma? Include information on advantages and disadvantages of different modes of transportation within the five regions (for example, cars for commuting, air travel for perishable goods, the availability of rail transportation).

- What is the weather like compared to Arizona, New Mexico, and Texas? Discuss the severe weather in the area like the tornadoes mentioned in the story. How could weather influence the movement of people within this region? Investigate the great drought of 1933 that turned the area into the dust bowl. What affect did this have on the movement of people? Chart or graph information and present it to the class.

- There are more Native Americans in Oklahoma than in any other state except California. Research several Indian tribes who once lived or now live in the area. What was life like for them when settlers first came to the area? How did the movement of people affect the Indians' lifestyle? Include information on the Trail of Tears. Students might present information in the form of a story written by a survivor of this ordeal or act out a play from the time the Indians learned they were to be moved until they reached reservations in Oklahoma. This information will present another perspective on the movement of people for the students to consider.

Closure

In a class discussion, compare and contrast what students have learned about the southwestern states thus far. Fill in the state and plot points of interest on the students' maps of the United States. In students' journals, write an entry explaining their reactions to the subject of geography in general. Then, ask for feedback on learning geography with a picture book as a starter. Ask students to evaluate the strengths and weaknesses as they see them for learning geography this way.

Book Used in This Lesson

Williams, David. *Grandma Essie's Covered Wagon.* Illus. by Wiktor Sadowski. New York: Alfred A. Knopf, 1993.

Suggested Companion Titles

Baker, Olaf. *Where the Buffaloes Begin.* Illus. by Stephen Gammell. New York: Puffin Books, 1985.

Birchman, David F. *The Raggly Scraggly No-Soap No-Scrub Girl.* Illus. by Guy Porfirio. New York: Lothrop, Lee & Shepard, 1995.

Fradin, Dennis. *Oklahoma in Words and Pictures.* Illus. by Richard Wahl. Chicago: Children's Press, 1981.

Greenlaw, M. Jean. *Ranch Dressing: The Story of Western Wear.* New York: Lodestar Books, 1993.

Krensky, Stephen. *Children of the Earth and Sky.* Illus. by James Watling. New York: Scholastic, 1991.

LaDoux, Rita C. *Oklahoma.* Minneapolis, Minn.: Lerner, 1992.

Mayo, Gretchen. *North American Indian Stories: Earthmaker's Tales.* Illus. by author. New York: Walker, 1990.

Medearis, Angela Shelf. *Dancing with the Indians.* Illus. by Samuel Byrd. New York: Holiday House, 1991.

Sandler, Martin W. *Cowboys: A Library of Congress Book.* Illus. by James Billington. New York: HarperCollins, 1994.

Lesson 4

Discovering Arizona Through the Theme of Region

Objectives

- to discover the distinct unifying characteristics that make up the physical region known as the Sonoran Desert
- to map the location of the desert in Arizona, California, and Mexico
- to examine the kinds of animal and plant life of the region to discover where life exists in the desert and how it does so
- to answer the questions, How and why is this desert similar to other deserts in the United States? How does it differ?
- to acquire knowledge so that students can later compare and contrast the Sonoran and Mojave Deserts as physical regions of the United States
- to map locations of deserts in each of the southwestern states

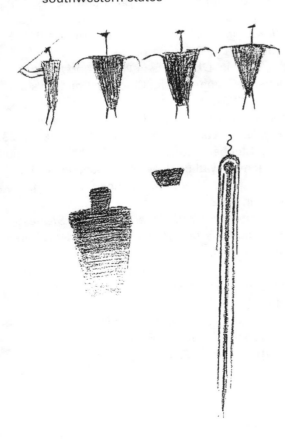

Materials

- *Cactus Hotel* by Brenda Z. Guiberson
- *Welcome to the Sea of Sand by* Jane Yolen
- an outline illustration of a saguaro cactus for each student

Motivator

Hand out shapes of a saguaro cactus made up ahead of time. Ask the students to label the first arm "What I Know," the second arm "What I Want to Learn," and the third arm "What I Have Learned." In the middle of the trunk, add "How Do I Find Out?" Model these directions on the chalkboard or on a large cactus at the front of the room. Give the students time to work on the first two arms and the trunk. After the allotted time is up, invite contributions from students, writing them on the large cactus. Discuss additional ways to find information on cacti, pointing out in-class resources, library materials, and places that students can write to for information.

Introduce *Cactus Hotel*. Show the title page and ask students to describe what they think the region might be like. Invite learners who have been to the desert to briefly share their experiences to activate background knowledge and provide information for students unfamiliar with the region.

Ask the students to use the backs of their cacti to jot down the kinds of animals that are mentioned in the story. Read the story.

When you have finished reading the book, ask for students' comments or reactions. Invite the students to come up to the giant cactus and write down an animal they met in the story. Animals include: pack rat, spotted ground squirrel, house finch, desert ants, jackrabbit, coyote, birds, bees, bats, Gila woodpecker, white-winged dove, elf owl, mice, lizards, snakes, foxes, millipede, scorpion, termites, collared lizard, and ground snake.

Go back to the third branch of the students' cacti and have them fill in what they have learned so far about the cactus. Discuss the importance of the saguaro cactus as a part of the desert. A key point to be learned is how interdependent animal and plant life are in this region, and any region for that matter. Ask students to describe the climate of the area, comparing it to the area in which they live. Finally, read Yolen's *Welcome to the Sea of Sand*. Have students listen to confirm what they have learned thus far and to add any new information that they learn.

Activities

Graphing Activity #1

Either on individual graphs or on a large graph on a bulletin board, graph the growth of a saguaro cactus in terms of inches and number of years it takes to grow. Students might plot a second graph using information they research on a tree that grows in their area. How long does it take a maple or pine tree to grow as compared to the saguaro?

10 years: 4 inches
25 years: 2 feet
50 years: 10 feet
60 years: 18 feet
150 years: 50 feet

Graphing Activity #2

Using the weather section of the newspaper, plot the daily temperatures in the Sonoran Desert over a period of two weeks. Add to that graph the daily temperatures in the area in which the students live. Discuss the differences and how they might affect animal, plant, and human life in both locations.

Directions for Further Research

Briefly introduce other titles of picture and non-fiction books in the classroom that students might want to use to learn more about this region and its importance as a geographic feature in the southwestern United States. Students should divide up into pairs to continue their work. They may choose to research such topics as:

- particular desert animals and how they survive
- people of the desert like the Papago Indians, past and present, and how their lives might differ from someone who lives in another area of the Southwest
- unique geographic features of the Sonoran Desert
- what the Mojave Desert is like and how it is similar to or different from the Sonoran Desert
- plant life and its importance to the region
- Arizona's other unique topographical features such as the Grand Canyon or the Santa Fe Peaks
- the state of Arizona itself
- other student suggestions with teacher approval

Closure

Ask listeners to recap the most interesting thing that they learned. Remind students to keep their cacti on hand to record any other information they discover about the saguaro in their future reading. Later, display the students' cacti on a wall or bulletin board to create a desert forest in the classroom.

The students will present the information they have compiled on their chosen topics to the class. They may write a report or a poem, use visual aids, sing a desert song, or utilize any other creative means in order to share their knowledge with the rest of the class. In the process they should answer the initial questions, How and why is this desert similar to other deserts in the United States? How does it differ?

Books Used in This Lesson

Guiberson, Brenda Z. *Cactus Hotel.* Illus. by Megan Lloyd. New York: Henry Holt, 1991.

Yolen, Jane. *Welcome to the Sea of Sand.* Illus. by Laura Regan. New York: Putnam, 1996.

Suggested Companion Titles

Bash, Barbara. *Desert Giant: The World of the Saguaro Cactus.* Illus. by author. New York: Little, Brown, 1989.

Baylor, Byrd. *Desert Voices.* Illus. by Peter Parnall. New York: Aladdin Books, 1993.

Buchanan, Ken. *This House Is Made of Mud.* Illus. by Libba Tracy. Flagstaff, Ariz.: Northland, 1991.

Buchanan, Ken, and Debra Buchanan. *It Rained in the Desert Today.* Illus. by Libba Tracy. Flagstaff, Ariz.: Northland, 1994.

Cobb, Vicki. *This Place Is Dry: The Sonoran Desert.* Illus. by Barbara Lavallee. New York: Walker, 1989.

Filbin, Dan. *Arizona.* Minneapolis, Minn.: Learner, 1993.

Fradin, Dennis B. *Arizona.* Chicago: Children's Press, 1993.

Fraser, Mary Ann. *In Search of the Grand Canyon: Down the Colorado with John Wesley Powell.* Illus. by author. New York: Henry Holt, 1995.

Geis, Jacqueline. *Where the Buffalo Roams.* Illus. by author. Nashville, Tenn.: Ideals, 1992.

Johnson, Paul B., and Celeste Lewis. *Lost.* Illus. by Paul Johnson. New York: Orchard, 1996.

Lee, Sandra. *Rattlesnakes.* New York: The Child's World, 1992.

Lerner, Carol. *Cactus.* Illus. by author. New York: Morrow, 1992.

———. *A Desert Year.* Illus. by author. New York: Morrow, 1991.

Lowell, Susan. *The Three Little Javelinas.* Illus. by Jim Harris. Flagstaff, Ariz.: Northland, 1992.

Marsh, Carole. *Don't Be Square: Let's Quilt Arizona.* Historic Bath, N.C.: Gollpade Publishing Group, 1990.

Pallotta, Jerry. *The Desert Alphabet Book.* Illus. by Mark Astrella. Watertown, Mass.: Charlesbridge, 1994.

Siebert, Diane. *Mojave.* Illus. by Wendell Minor. New York: HarperTrophy, 1988.

Simon, Seymour. *Deserts.* New York: Morrow, 1990.

Wallace, Marianne D. *America's Deserts: Guide to Plants and Animals.* Golden, Colo.: Fulcrum Publishing, 1996.

Weaver, Dorothy H. *Arizona A to Z.* Illus. by Kay Wacker. Flagstaff, Ariz.: Northland, 1992.

Wright-Frierson, Virginia. *A Desert Scrapbook: Dawn to Dusk in the Sonoran Desert.* Illus. by author. New York: Simon & Schuster, 1996.

Culminating Activity

Divide students into four groups based on their interests in a particular southwestern state. Bring drama into the classroom by having each group act out a book of their choice from the list of Suggested Companion Titles at the end of the lesson pertaining to their chosen state. After the group reads the book together, they can decide how to present the story. As a means of introduction before the actual performance, a member of the group might briefly highlight some factual information about their state.

Perhaps one person could be the narrator reading the story, pausing at specific parts for the rest of the group to act out in a scene. Another option might be to have a narrator read the book while the other students present a tableau of a favorite scene in the book. Of course the complete story could be acted out based on a simple script written by the group as a whole. Invite another class or two to watch the four performances so that they can also learn about the Southwest.

5

The Heartland: North Dakota, South Dakota, Nebraska, Kansas, Minnesota, Iowa, and Missouri

It is astounding to contemplate what the natural forces of the earth can do. Almost like sculptors, some of these forces shape and mold, carve and reshape, sometimes gently, at other times with ferocity. Consider the power that melting glaciers had upon the states known as the Heartland. North Dakota, South Dakota, Nebraska, Kansas, Minnesota, Iowa, and Missouri make up some of the most fertile lands in the world and they acquired that distinction because of the work of glaciers that deposited rich soils, gouged out pockets in the earth that became tiny lakes, and left gently rolling hills in their wakes. It is interesting to note that these particular states include less than 15 percent of the land in the United States, but because of such rich soil and the bounty produced as a result, they have been nicknamed the Breadbasket of the United States.

As with other regions of the United States, the Heartland has special characteristics that make it distinctive. An artist could depict its endless open skies, plenty of sunshine, incessant winds, and rolling, grass-covered lands sparsely dotted with trees. A close inspection of this area will reveal interesting differences like 10-feet-tall prairie grasses in the eastern area and a variety of shorter grasses in drier areas to the west. Moisture ranges from almost humid conditions in the east to arid conditions on the Great Plains, the latter of which brought drought and dust bowls in the past. One of North America's major river systems flows through the area, evolving in time into a key transportation system. When moun-

tains can be seen on the horizon, they resemble low, age-worn hills. Finally, the eastern borders of these states are artistically curved by rivers like the indomitable Mississippi while the western borders are straight and angular.

In the past this land was a daunting challenge to the pioneers who dreamed of making it their home. However, once John Deere perfected a plow that could withstand the tough, root-filled soil, farmers' lives changed from the nightmares of horse-drawn plowing to manageable, amazingly productive farming. So important is agriculture to the Heartland, in fact, that the businesses that have grown up as a result are termed "agribusinesses." Today, this type of manufacturing is second to agriculture in states that are well known for corn, wheat, and beef cattle production. Minneapolis, St. Paul, Wichita, and St. Louis have become major manufacturing meccas. Further investigation of the bountiful Heartland and its geographic roots makes compelling study for geographers of all ages.

Initiating Activity

The goal of this initiating activity is to establish an ongoing pen-pal activity that will have students personally involved in geography. Begin a discussion about the fact that the food and products from the Heartland region are moved in a number of ways across the United States, and the ways that they are transported bear geographic investigation. In fact, Missouri is a leading trucking and shipping center. Ask the students to brainstorm about what kinds of products they have in their homes or the classroom that might have been transported by trucks. List answers on the chalkboard or overhead. Beside the items, invite students to speculate where those items might have come from. This could generate a lively discussion as students share their opinions and try to justify them. Now, explain to the students that they are going to learn about the geographic theme of movement as related to goods transported to and from the Heartland states and other states in the United States. This will be accom-

plished in a rather unique way, by becoming a pen pal with a trucker.

Introduce the students to the Trucker Buddy Program. Distribute the information previously acquired about the Trucker Buddy Program begun by twenty-six-year-old driver Gary D. King. This innovative program was started in 1992 and now involves 10,000 truck drivers who reach students across the United States as traveling pen pals. Information can be acquired by contacting them at:

> Trucker Buddy
> P.O. Box 7788
> Madison, WI 53707-7788
> (800) MY-BUDDY

Further information on this program is available in Appendix I. Ask if any of the learners have a parent or relative who is a trucker. That person would make a timely resource person to come in to talk to the class.

Once a pen pal has been established, students can track his or her progress across the classroom's map of the United States using yarn and thumbtacks to denote cities where the trucker has stopped. In the process, students are seeing the movement of goods from origin to destination in a memorable way. They might want to devise a chart to keep track of the movement of products as a visual representation of the theme of movement. Ask students how they can learn more about the cargo carried by these truckers and where it goes once it is delivered. The learning center director, trucking firm, or local librarian might be an asset in this research. Since the Heartland states might be the origin of many of these products, this is an excellent time to become involved in the pen-pal program. A highlight of this activity would be to meet the trucker, of course.

Lesson 1

Studying the Heartland Through the Themes of Location, Place, Human/ Environmental Interactions, and Region

Objectives

- to locate the Heartland states on individual copies of outline maps of the United States
- to recognize that these states are grouped into a region based upon their proximity, climates, common geographic features, and history
- to generate the characteristics that make up the prairie region based upon the study of topographic maps, fiction and nonfiction picture books, and other pertinent materials
- to compare life on the prairie, past and present
- to identify and locate the major industries that grew up because of available natural resources and man's adaptation to the land

Materials

- *Heartland* by Diane Siebert
- *If You're Not from the Prairie …* by David Bouchard
- student atlases like *Nystrom's Atlas of Our Country*
- copies of "Looking at Regions" chart
- pens or pencils

Motivator

Read *Heartland* by Diane Siebert. Students should just sit back and listen to the book, enjoying the rhythm of the words and illustrations the first time through. Then read the book again, this time asking students to write down what they have learned about this region from the book. For example,

What products come from the Heartland? What does it look like? What might you do if you lived there? How does the weather differ from where the students live? What might they surmise about the geography of the land? After the second reading and subsequent recording of observations, share thoughts together as a class. What else might students add if they have lived in one of the Heartland states or visited there on vacations? This discussion will lay the groundwork for further study of this area.

Activities

Defining a Region

Introduce the concept of the prairie as a region of the United States by reading aloud *If You're Not from the Prairie …* by David Bouchard. Remind listeners that a region is an area with unifying characteristics. Tell the students that they will be approaching this part of the country in the role of geographic investigators. During this activity readers will be doing some inductive thinking as they move from a variety of facts or pieces of information to forming a generalization. Thus, they will be accumulating clues to discover what the unifying characteristics are that make this region a prairie.

It would be wonderful if teachers could have several copies of this book available for students to study because the illustrations are superb, packed with information about life on the prairie. Students should use both text and pictures to ferret out the clues to what makes this region unique.

Gathering the Facts

Using the chart "Looking at Regions" in Appendix III, have students fill in pertinent facts as the book is read through a second time or as they scour shared copies of the book. Readers should add any different information that they gleaned from Siebert's *Heartland* to try to form a more complete picture of the prairie. Using student atlases like *Nystrom's Atlas of Our Country*, have the learners study topographic, climate, growing seasons, land use, and annual rainfall maps as additional sources of information. Tell them that they are on a quest to prove or disprove their initial observations and to add additional details to the chart by using a number of maps, other picture books, and nonfiction resources. Work in triads, collecting and comparing observations.

Then, on a large master chart, record the class's observations. Based upon recorded observations and class discussions, have each group write a definition of the prairie. Groups will then share their definitions with the entire class, building and refining a single definition as a sound generalization of the prairie emerges. As a result of their quest, it is likely that students will discover that prairie lands exist in several other states and into Canada as well as being a major part of the Heartland.

A Picture of Life Past and Present

Students can delve into additional picture books, novels, and factual materials to learn more about early life on the prairies. They could use a copy of the Venn diagram in Appendix III to compare life in the past and changes that have evolved to create the present day. Images of sod houses, hoards of crop-destroying insects, drought, and neighbors miles away contrast with quite a different picture today. What has happened to the tall grass prairie that once covered over 400,000 square miles? One way to report findings might be via informational newspaper articles set up like a newspaper from the 1800s along with a contemporary version. Just the front pages might be done. Another approach might be to record journal entries from one fictitious family across several generations illustrating the changes students find pertinent. Papers could be stained with a wash of tea or coffee or the edges burnt slightly to make them look like aged pages of old journals or diaries. One strand of thinking might be to consider what kinds of improvements humans have generated to make life more pleasant and more productive in this region.

Closure

An appealing bulletin board could be completed including the polished definition describing the prairie, maps of the enlarged states colored with topographic information, products grown or manufactured, and stories, news articles, journal excerpts, or poetry about life past and present on the prairie.

Books Used in This Lesson

Bouchard, David. *If You're Not from the Prairie ...* Illus. by Henry Ripplinger. New York: Atheneum, 1995.

Nystrom's Atlas of Our Country. Chicago: Nystrom Division of Herff Jones, 1996.

Siebert, Diane. *Heartland.* Illus. by Wendell Minor. New York: HarperTrophy, 1989.

Suggested Companion Titles

Brandenburg, Jim. *An American Safari: Adventures on the North American Prairie.* New York: Walker, 1995.

Bunting, Eve. *Dandelions.* Illus. by Greg Shed. New York: Harcourt Brace, 1995.

Cobb, Mary. *The Quilt-Block History of Pioneer Days with Projects Kids Can Make.* Illus. by Jan Davey Ellis. Brookfield, Conn.: Millbrook Press, 1995.

Dvorak, David, Jr. *A Sea of Grass: The Tallgrass Prairie.* Illus. by author. New York: Macmillan, 1994.

Ernst, Lisa C. *Little Red Riding Hood: A Newfangled Prairie Tale.* Illus. by author. New York: Macmillan, 1995.

Harvey, Brett. *My Prairie Christmas.* Illus. by Deborah Kogan Ray. New York: Holiday House, 1990.

———. *My Prairie Year.* Illus. by Deborah Kogan Ray. New York: Holiday House, 1986.

Hirschi, Ron. *Save Our Prairies and Grasslands.* Photographs by Erwin Bauer and Peggy Bauer. New York: Delacort Press, 1994.

Kirkpatrick, Patricia. *Plowie: A Story From the Prairie.* Illus. by Joey Kirkpatrick. New York: Harcourt Brace, 1994.

Lottridge, Celia Barker. *The Wind Wagon.* Illus. by Daniel Clifford. Parsippany, N.J.: Silver Burdett Press, 1995.

McGugan, Jim. *Josepha: A Prairie Boy's Story.* Illus. by Murray Kimber. New York: Chronicle Books, 1994.

MacLachlan, Patricia. *What You Know First.* Illus. by Barry Moser. New York: HarperCollins, 1995.

———. *Three Names.* Illus. by Alexander Pertzoff. New York: HarperCollins, 1991.

Moroney, Lynn. *The Boy Who Loved Bears: A Pawnee Tale.* Illus. by Charles W. Chapman. Chicago: Children's Press, 1994.

Rotter, Charles. *The Prairie.* Mankato, Minn.: Creative Education, 1994.

Saunders, Susan. *The Jackrabbit and the Prairie Fire.* Norwalk, Conn.: Trudy Management Corporation, 1991.

Siy, Alexandra. *Native Grasslands.* New York: Dillon Press, 1991.

Sorensen, Henri. *New Hope.* Illus. by author. New York: Lothrop, Lee & Shepard, 1995.

Turner, Ann. *Dakota Dugout.* Illus. by Ronald Himler. New York: Macmillan, 1985.

Williams, David. *Grandma Essie's Covered Wagon.* Illus. by Victor Sadowski. New York: Alfred A. Knopf, 1993.

Lesson 2

Studying the Heartland Through the Themes of Location, Human/Environmental Interactions, and Movement

Objectives

- to develop an understanding of movement of goods being transported from one place to another through continued participation in the Trucker Buddy Program
- to use the scale of miles on state maps or the classroom wall map to figure distances between the place of origin of goods and their destination
- to examine the Mississippi River, its tributaries, and other key waterways to learn what geographic implications they have for people who live in the Heartland

Materials

- props like a live turtle in an aquarium, plush turtle or puppet
- *Minn of the Mississippi* by Clancy Holling
- a large map of the United States and students' maps of the United States
- reference materials about the Mississippi River and other key waterways in the Heartland available from the United States Geologic Survey Information Service (see Appendix I)

Motivator

If possible, bring in a live turtle and its aquarium to class, or use a plush turtle or turtle puppet. To tweak student interest, discuss probable habits of turtles. What might be the pros and cons of a river as a possible home? Discuss student responses before introducing the book, *Minn of the Mississippi.* Locate the river on the classroom map along with some of the main tributaries. Then, read aloud chapters 1 and 2 in this classic book, stopping to discuss key points. Older students can complete the book independently or in small groups, reading the story and tracing Minn's journey on the real map. Work can be done outside of class for several days and progress discussed in class daily. For younger students, the book can be used as a teacher resource pulling pertinent facts from it as students trace Minn's journey down this impressive river in class. They may enjoy illustrating a favorite part of Minn's journey and creating a bulletin board featuring the river and their work.

Activities

The Many Roles of the Mississippi

Folklore suggests that Paul Bunyan and Babe the blue ox were responsible for digging a 1,000-mile ditch from Minneapolis to the Ohio River, which became the mighty Mississippi River. Set the students to work to discover the real truth behind this river. For instance, discuss how the river, its tributaries, and other connected waterways became major transportation routes for people and goods just as highways have for truck transportation. Examine the communities that have grown up along the shores of the river on the classroom map. Students might estimate the length of the river as it forms the eastern border of the Heartland states. Using Minn's story and nonfiction references like Porter's *Minnesota*, locate the origin of the river. Learn the history of some of the key cities along this river's shores, especially those in the Heartland. Look into how people have affected the area and the waterways with growth and change. One direction that study might take is a closer investigation into pollution as the relationship between humans and river has strengthened over the years. Excellent materials to guide the study of pollution can be found in *Ranger Rick's NatureScope* issue entitled, *Pollution: Problems and Solutions*.

A Collection of Thoughts

Students can create a scrapbook about the Mississippi River or one of the other key rivers in the Heartland. They might compare the lengths of the rivers in this region. Artifacts might include hand-drawn "snapshots" of scenes that relate an important fact about the river, postcards they may have collected from vacations or contacts with schoolmates in the Heartland states, pictures cut from travel brochures received from the state's tourism department, paragraphs expressing their concerns and suggestions to deal with pollution, or whatever categories of information the class decides upon. Work can be displayed in the learning center or in the classroom.

Closure

Map the Mississippi, the Missouri, the Des Moines, the Platte, and the Kansas Rivers and other tributaries on students' personal copies of the United States maps along with any other pertinent information students want to include. Continue to plot locations based upon pen-pal letters, figuring mileage between stops on a large classroom map. Be certain students are corresponding with their pen pal regularly.

Books Used in This Lesson

Holling, Clancy. *Minn of the Mississippi*. New York: Houghton Mifflin, 1989.

Porter, A. P. *Minnesota*. Minneapolis, Minn.: Lerner, 1992.

Ranger Rick's NatureScope: Pollution: Problems and Solutions. Washington, D.C.: National Wildlife Federation, 1990.

Suggested Companion Titles

Badt, Karin L. *The Mississippi Flood of 1993*. Chicago: Children's Press, 1994.

Crisman, Ruth. *The Mississippi*. New York: Franklin Watts, 1984.

Locker, Thomas. *The Land of Gray Wolf*. Illus. by author. New York: Penguin, 1991.

Marston, Hope Irwin. *Big Rigs*. Dutton, N.Y.: Cobblehill Books, 1993.

Schmid, Eleonore. *The Water's Journey*. Illus. by author. New York: North-South Books, 1989.

Wurmfeld, Hope Herman. *Trucker*. New York: Macmillan, 1990.

Lesson 3

Looking at Each Heartland State
Through the Five Geographic Themes

Objectives

- to survey the other Heartland states, selecting one for more in-depth study
- to improve reading, writing, thinking, speaking, and listening skills through the process of creating a group presentation, teaching the rest of the class more about a Heartland state
- to pick one or more of the geographic themes and explain how they apply to the state under study
- to summarize information about the state into four key facts illustrated by a completed quadrarama

Materials

- *Antler, Bear, Canoe: A Northwoods Alphabet Year* by Betsy Bowen
- *Gathering: A Northwoods Counting Book* by Betsy Bowen
- paper and art supplies to make quadraramas
- a variety of materials that might include: travel videos, materials from tourist offices in each state, fiction and nonfiction book titles, atlases, and state maps

Motivator

Read *Antler, Bear, Canoe: A Northwoods Alphabet Year* to the class as an introduction to life in one part of Minnesota. Perhaps several students would like to follow up this book by reading the companion volume, *Gathering: A Northwoods Counting Book,* to the class as well. Talk about the kinds of insights students gained about life in rural Minnesota from these two books. They might describe any physical and human characteristics that they picked up from the text and illustrations. How did people depend on the natural environment? How did they adapt? Did they alter the environment in any way? Explain that each one of the Heartland states has its own story to tell and that it is now time to look at them closely.

Activity

Individual State Group Work

Place the names of the seven Heartland states up on the chalkboard. Pick a democratic way for students to sign up for the state that they are interested in so that groups are fairly even in size. Perhaps students could choose a number from a box as it is passed around. Going to the board in numerical order, they can put their name under the state of their choice. Another enjoyable way to divide into groups is to pass around a container of flavored lollipops, counted out ahead of time by flavor to match group sizes. Everyone who has grape, for instance, gets to choose a state first. Those who chose lemon go next, and so forth. Before each group begins work, they will be given a worksheet to follow to help them organize their discoveries of the state and to provide continuity during the group presentations.

A worksheet like the sample in Appendix III might include absolute location, relative location, key geographic features, agriculture, climate, and manufacturing and recreational opportunities. Individuals within the group can pick an area to research, organize the information, and practice presenting it to the small group initially. Then, the group as a whole will teach the remainder of the class what they have learned in a fifteen-minute presentation. A colorful prop for the presentation would be quadraramas made following the directions in Appendix III. Students will have to evaluate the information they collect and put it in concise form to display in the four-sided quadrarama.

Closure

Groups will present the information they have gathered to the class in a fifteen-minute presentation. They can use the quadraramas to highlight specific aspects of the state on which they became an expert. Later, the quadraramas can be grouped together to make attractive mobiles or they can be displayed singly on a bookshelf or table for others to enjoy. Group presentations can be videotaped for assessment purposes. It would be fun to invite parents in for an informative session from the experts on the Heartland states.

Books Used in This Lesson

Bowen, Betsy. *Gathering: A Northwoods Counting Book*. Boston: Little, Brown, 1995.

———. *Antler, Bear, Canoe: A Northwoods Alphabet Year*. Illus. by author. Boston: Little, Brown, 1991.

Suggested Companion Titles

Anderson, Joan. *The American Family Farm: A Photo Essay*. Photographs by George Ancona. San Diego, Calif.: Harcourt Brace Jovanovich, 1989.

Andryszewski, Tricia. *The Dust Bowl: Disaster on the Plains*. Brookfield, Conn.: Millbrook Press, 1993.

Bruchac, Joseph. *A Boy Called Slow: The True Story of Sitting Bull*. Illus. by Rocco Baviera. New York: Philomel, 1995.

Carson, Jo. *The Great Shaking: An Account of the Earthquakes of 1811 and 1812 by a Bear Who Was a Witness in New Madrid, Missouri*. Illus. by Robert Andrew Parker. New York: Orchard Books, 1994.

Chall, Marsh W. *Up North at the Cabin*. Illus. by Steve Johnson. New York: Lothrop, Lee & Shepard, 1992.

Conrad, Pam. *Prairie Visions: The Life and Times of Solomon Butcher*. New York: HarperCollins, 1991.

Esbensen, Barbara Juster. *Great Northern Diver*. Illus. by Mary Barrett Brown. Boston: Little, Brown, 1990.

Fradin, Dennis B., and Judith B. Fradin. *South Dakota*. Chicago: Children's Press, 1995.

Goble, Paul. *Adopted by the Eagles*. Illus. by author. New York: Bradbury Press, 1994.

———. *Dream Wolf*. Illus. by author. New York: Bradbury Press, 1990.

———. *Iktomi and the Berries: A Plains Indian Story*. Illus. by author. New York: Franklin Watts, 1989.

Hargrove, Jim. *Nebraska*. Chicago: Children's Press, 1992.

Kellogg, Steven. *Paul Bunyan*. Illus. by author. New York: Morrow, 1988.

LaDoux, Rita C. *Missouri*. Minneapolis, Minn.: Lerner, 1991.

Matthaei, Gay, and Jewel Grutman. *The Ledgerbook of Thomas Blue Eagle*. Illus. by Adam Cvijanovic. Charlottesville, Va.: Thomasson-Grant, 1994.

Regguinti, Gordon. *The Sacred Harvest: Ojibway Wild Rice Gathering*. Photographs by Dale Kakkak. Minneapolis, Minn.: Lerner, 1992.

Sans Souci, Robert D. *Kate Shelly—Bound for Legend*. Illus. by Max Ginsburg. New York: Dial, 1995.

———. *North Country Nights*. Illus. by author. New York: Bantam, 1990.

Schroeder, Alan. *Ragtime Tumpie*. Illus. by Bernie Fuchs. Boston: Little, Brown, 1989.

Shannon, George. *Climbing Kansas Mountains*. Illus. by Thomas B. Allen. New York: Bradbury Press, 1993.

Stroud, Virginia A. *The Path of the Quiet Elk*. New York: Dial, 1996.

Taylor, C. J. *Bones in the Basket*. Montreal, Que.: Tundra Books, 1994.

Tunnell, Michael O. *Mailing May*. Illus. by Ted Rand. New York: Greenwillow, 1997.

Weitzman, David. *Thrashin' Time: Harvest Days in the Dakotas*. New York: Godine, 1991.

Culminating Activity

Give the students copies of the official transportation map for Kansas and the quiz sheet entitled "There's More to a Name than You Think: Riddles and Absolute Location" from Appendix III. Tell them they will have a specified amount of time to work in pairs to solve the riddles. They are to first predict or make an educated guess as to what the answer might be, recording that answer in one color pen or pencil in the margin. Then, they are to use the coordinates listed to find the correct answer and write it in the blanks provided. They can compare answers and quickly move on to the next riddle. Do not make the time period so short that stress develops, but keep the students moving right along. To de-emphasize the competition and to celebrate everyone's learning, give a small prize to each learner at the end of the activity. On their own students might want to develop their own page of riddles using maps of the other Heartland states. The completed sheets could be duplicated and kept in a classroom geography center to be filled out during students' free time.

6

The Great Lakes States:
Illinois, Indiana, Michigan,
Wisconsin, and Ohio

What do Abraham Lincoln, Henry Ford, Sojourner Truth, John Glenn, Chris Van Allsburg, and Raggedy Ann have in common? The ties may seem elusive but they do exist. These personalities all originated in or emigrated to the Great Lakes states where they put down roots and prospered. Raggedy Ann can be considered a member of this elite group as she was the creation of John Gruelle, an Indiana cartoonist. He repaired an old doll at his daughter's request, and a much-loved personality came to life for children for generations to come. As for the people, they are but a few industrious individuals who chose to call this fertile part of the United States home. Some of them joined easterners who moved west in the 1800s in search of opportunity and better land to farm. Numbers swelled as the Amish settled in the Ohio and Indiana areas. Immigrants from countries like Germany, Ireland, Poland, Italy, and Russia arrived with few belongings but well supplied with dreams. Together people from a variety of backgrounds and places inhabited this area, providing the roots for what it is today.

The Great Lakes states cover a region that is as rich in fertile farmlands as it is in cultural diversity. Farms stretch across land once covered with prairie grasses that grew higher than a man could reach. Rolling hills have become pastureland for vast herds of dairy cattle. As the years passed, the people and the land built and refined a partnership, one that hasn't always benefited both parties equally. Elements of nature like tornadoes, fire, and drought have destroyed crops and communities. Great cities like Chicago fell victim to sparks

and consuming fire. Repeated planting of the same crops depleted the once fertile soil until wisdom prevailed. Crop rotation and dairy farming were instigated to rejuvenate and save that soil. Hardwood and white pine forests that blanketed the land were logged almost into oblivion as the demands for wood for settlers' homes grew. Today, only patches of the abundant forests remain. Then, in the 1960s, Lake Erie was declared dead because of its high level of pollutants. Reality dictated a change in the notion that America's vast resources were unlimited. With Wisconsin leading the way, conservation efforts have been prioritized in order to preserve the remaining natural resources and to protect the environment for future generations.

Topographically, this is a region with a flavor all its own. From flat, fertile prairie lands to rolling hills to surprisingly rugged terrain ending abruptly with limestone cliffs, it has a restful beauty to share. A drive through rolling farm country at dusk on a balmy summer evening is an experience one doesn't quickly forget. Rows of stately, towering cornstalks bedecked with silken-tasseled corn form green walls on each side of the road. Flitting and twinkling above them are hundreds of fireflies creating a piece of midwestern summer night magic. Chances are the mosquitoes are there, too, for they thrive in a land doused with frequent violent thunderstorms. Some say the southern part of the Great Lakes states is much like the South. Others believe that pieces of New England were transplanted to this part of the country. It appears that both views are right but there is a piece to be discovered that is uniquely the Midwest as well.

Here farm towns sit shoulder to shoulder with sprawling cities like Chicago, Cincinnati, Milwaukee, Detroit, and Indianapolis. High-rises with the clamor and high energy generated by the cities are in contrast to the towns' broad-porched bungalows and Victorian homes with cobblestoned city squares, band shells with summer appeal, and wide streets shaded by mature maples and oaks. There are steel mills belching sun-dimming smoke, Chicago's John Hancock Building, and the roar of motors at the Indianapolis 500. Add to that acres of undulating, grain-filled fields, miles of sandy beaches along Lake Michigan's shoreline, and a pristine lighthouse on Door County's Cana Island and you have just a few of the pieces that make up the mosaic that is the Great Lakes states.

Initiating Activity

Collect a variety of items that represent the Great Lakes states such as a Raggedy Ann doll; a toy racing car; a toy Model T or other Ford car; a bar of soap; a chunk of cheese; several fresh apples; a container of salt; two boxes of cereal (one Post®, the other Kellogg's®); a bag of dried soybeans; a can of corn or an ear of dried corn; a hand-drawn map of a route used on the Underground Railroad; an empty, clean milk carton; and so forth. Each item will fit into a lunch-size brown bag. Tie with thick, bright yarn and place on a table or desks across the front of the room.

Invite one volunteer at a time to pick a bag, then go back to his or her desk and open it. After sharing what is in the bag, encourage the student to tell anything he or she might know about the object. Go on to the next volunteer until all of the bags have been opened. Ask the students to line up in front of the room with their items. Have the rest of the class decide what these products could possibly have in common. If a connection hasn't been made after some time is spent brainstorming, explain that they are all tied in some way to the Great Lakes states, the next region to be studied. Now it's up to the students to speculate and try to match product to state:

- Raggedy Ann: invented by cartoonist John Gruelle in Indianapolis, Indiana
- Racing car: Indianapolis 500
- Model T: Henry Ford and the auto industry in Dearborn, Michigan
- Corn and soybeans: Illinois in particular, but also the other states
- Milk carton and cheese: Wisconsin is a key dairy farming state but the others are, too
- Cereals: Battle Creek, Michigan, nicknamed the "Cereal Bowl of the World"
- Soap: Cincinnati, Ohio
- Underground Railroad: routes were throughout the area but abolitionists helped escaping slaves board boats in Ohio and sailed them across Lake Erie to freedom in Canada
- Salt: Ohio
- Apples: either an example of the fruits grown in Michigan or to illustrate that Johnny Appleseed (John Chapman) is buried in Fort Wayne, Indiana

Once the activity is completed, display the nonperishable items on a classroom table, which can be covered first with a state map or two. Products could be labeled with the state where they are produced. Students can add other items or information to this display area as they are discovered. Following that, slice up the apples and cheese and serve them with a selection of Keebler® crackers, a company based in Illinois. As the students munch, tell them that they will be discovering these states more closely in the following weeks.

Getting the Broad Picture of the Great Lakes States Through the Themes of Location and Place

Objectives

- to locate the Great Lakes states on individual outline maps and regional maps
- to discover and record topographic features including landforms, vegetation, and elevation changes plus key lakes and rivers on the regional maps
- to investigate why people might have settled where they did
- to look at how the natural environment inhibits or encourages the growth of cities or towns
- to discuss the advantages and disadvantages of living in a city; in a town; on a farm
- to understand population distribution by graphing the population of a selection of large and small cities across the states

Materials

- classroom map, student atlases, state maps, *Rand McNally Road Atlas*
- students' outline maps of the United States plus regional maps of the Great Lakes states
- pens, pencils, colored pencils, markers
- graph paper
- *Heartland* by Diane Siebert
- *Town Mouse, Country Mouse* by Jan Brett

Motivator

Begin the discovery of the Great Lakes states by sharing *Heartland* by Diane Siebert, which is a poetic tribute to the Midwest. If students are not familiar with the book, take some time to discuss the area that the book describes.

Activities

Getting the Broad Picture Through Map Work
Direct students to the landform map using their atlases or the topographical classroom map if one is available. They are to look for different kinds of landforms in the Great Lakes states and color them in according to the legend. They will find smaller areas of hills, basins, and plains. Then, using a different marking system, denote the types of vegetation throughout the area. Research will reveal grass, broadleaf trees, and evergreens or needleleaf trees. To better understand the importance of the waterways, label the Great Lakes, key rivers, and several of the smaller lakes. Conclude this activity by writing a statement about the elevation using the elevation key in the atlases. Briefly discuss the terrain and natural resources of these states before moving on to the next activity.

People and Places
Read Jan Brett's colorful *Town Mouse, Country Mouse* to lead into the discussion of population distribution throughout the Great Lakes states. Start a class discussion by querying, "Why do people live where they do?" List suggestions on the board. Next, students are to choose two large cities and two small cities or towns in each state, locate them on their individual outline maps, and graph the population of each city on a sheet of

graph paper. Copies of state maps or the *Rand McNally Road Atlas* would be useful resources. Direct students to set up the graph by cities and states across the horizontal bar, and population numbers up the vertical bar.

Completed graphs can be illustrated simply, collected, and displayed in an album with clear plastic envelopelike pages or in a student-created book. This work provides a visual picture of large and small communities as they address cities in the Great Lakes states. The completed book would be a perfect addition to the display area where state products are set up.

Looking at Differences

Finally, have students do some reading about life in cities, towns, and farms. In their journals or on notebook paper, they should jot down notes on the advantages and disadvantages to living in each place. In a general class discussion, have students explain why the larger cities are located where they are. Speculate on why the smaller towns have stayed that way. Look at farming communities as well. According to their reading, are farms growing or declining in size? If the students discover a change, ask them to figure out why. Students share their personal preferences verbally or in a journal entry, justifying them based upon the reading they have done.

The Weather and What It Means to Place

The Midwest is noted for its violent summer thunderstorms and destructive tornado season. Signs of trouble are heavy, moist air, ominous yellow-green color of the sky, absolutely still air, and towering black clouds. Some students may wish to research the weather in this region and report to the class why tornadoes are so prevalent here, how they are caused, and what kinds of precautions can be taken to ensure people's safety.

Closure

A number of topics have been investigated so far. Invite students to join in a general discussion of the Great Lakes states, what they have found most interesting, which activities were the most challenging, and what they are still curious about. If students are involved in the Trucker Buddy Program, have an update on recent mail and continue the correspondence. Then, move on to the next geographic challenge.

Books Used in This Lesson

Brett, Jan. *Town Mouse, Country Mouse.* New York: G. P. Putnam's Sons, 1994.

Siebert, Diane. *Heartland.* Illus. by Wendall Minor. New York: HarperTrophy, 1989.

Suggested Companion Titles

Alexander, Sue. *Sara's City.* Illus. by Ronald Himler. New York: Clarion Books, 1995.

Andrews, Jan. *The Auction.* New York: Macmillan, 1990.

Aylesworth, Thomas, and Virginia Aylesworth. *Chicago.* New York: Rosen, 1990.

Balterman, Lee. *Girders and Cranes: A Skyscraper Is Built.* Morton Grove, Ill.: Albert Whitman, 1991.

Bial, Raymond. *Portrait of a Family Farm.* Boston: Houghton Mifflin, 1995.

———. *Amish Home.* Boston: Houghton Mifflin, 1993.

Bushnell, Jack. *Sky Dancer.* Illus. by Jan Ormerod. New York: Lothrop, Lee & Shepard, 1996.

Davis, James E., and Sharryl Davis Hawke. *Chicago.* Milwaukee, Wisc.: Raintree/Steck-Vaughn, 1990.

Geisert, Bonnie. *Haystack.* Illus. by Arthur Geisert. Boston: Houghton Mifflin, 1995.

Harshman, Marc. *The Storm.* Illus. by Mark Mohr. New York: Cobblehill Books, 1995.

Hiscock, Bruce. *The Big Storm.* Illus. by author. New York: Atheneum, 1993.

Johnson, Stephen T. *Alphabet City.* Illus. by author. New York: Viking, 1995.

Kent, Deborah. *Jane Addams and Hull House.* Chicago: Children's Press, 1992.

Mitchell, Barbara. *Down Butternut Lane.* Illus. by John Sanford. New York: Lothrop, Lee & Shepard, 1993.

Myers, Christopher A., and Lynne B. Myers. *McCrephy's Field.* Illus. by Normand Chartier. Boston: Houghton Mifflin, 1991.

Osofsky, Audrey. *Dreamcatcher.* Illus. by Ed Young. New York: Orchard Books, 1992.

Platt, Richard. *The Apartment Book: A Day in Five Stories.* Illus. by Leo Hartas. Orlando, Fla.: Dorling Kindersley, 1995.

Polacco, Patricia. *Just Plain Fancy.* Illus. by author. New York: Bantam, 1990.

———.*Thunder Cake.* Illus. by author. New York: Philomel, 1990.

Provensen, Alice, and Martin Provensen. *Town & Country.* San Diego, Calif.: Harcourt Brace, 1994.

Simon, Seymour. *Weather.* New York: Morrow Junior Books, 1993.

———. *Storms.* New York: Morrow Junior Books, 1989.

Stone, Lynn M. *Prairies.* Illus. by author. Vero Beach, Fla.: Rourke, 1989.

Sturges, Philemon. *Ten Flashing Fireflies.* Illus. by Anna Vojtech. New York: North-South Books, 1995.

Tripp, Nathaniel. *Thunderstorm!* Illus. by Juan Wijngarrd. New York: Dial, 1994.

Winter, Jeanette. *The Christmas Tree Ship.* Illus. by author. New York: Philomel, 1994.

Lesson 2

Looking at the Great Lakes States Through the Themes of Place, Movement, and Human/Environmental Interactions

Objectives

- to get a sense of place by investigating how that place was created
- to understand how people and place interact and what the results of that interaction are
- to consider the movement of people over time and how that creates place as it is today
- to investigate the ethnic diversity of a region

Materials

- a long roll of paper per group
- atlases, books for researching each state
- pens, markers, and materials to decorate time line
- multiple copies of the following books: *Who Came Down That Road?* by George Ella Lyon; *The Backyard* by John Collier; *In My Own Backyard* by Judi Kurjian; and *Under the Moon* by Dyan Sheldon

Motivator

Divide the class into five groups, one per state. Locate enough copies of the picture books so that each group can have one of each book. They are to read the book together and discuss what the state they are working on might have been like if they went back in time. Invite the readers to share their books with the other groups who may want to read them during free time.

Activity

Past, Present, and Future

Instruct the class to think about the area in general and their state in particular along with its inhabitants as far back as they can find information. Using a variety of resources including books on each state, the group is to research a state, making a vertical, illustrated time line with what the state looked like when earth was created. Follow the pattern of the books that were shared.

Prepare a worksheet for each group with guiding questions like, How was the land formed?

Were glaciers at work there? Who were the earliest known inhabitants? Which American Indian tribes made this area their home and for how long? When did settlers first arrive? Who were they and why did they come? How did things change as a result? What was the consequence of increasing population and larger cities? What role does water play in the state as far as industry, tourism, and daily life? Why do people stay here? Keep the facts following a similar line as those in the books as a way of organizing and presenting the compiled information. Students can roll up and secure their completed project with ribbon or yarn until it is time to unveil it for the class.

Closure

In a class presentation, each group can display their time line, highlighting the most interesting points. It would be fun to play a tape of folk songs or have each group teach the class a tune popular in the early years in their state. Children love toe-tapping music. For some learners, in fact, music opens the door to better comprehending the material at hand. Make it a goal to incorporate music into classroom activities frequently. Tapes that might be handy:

- Donohoe, Kitty. *Bunyan and Banjoes: Michigan Songs and Stories.* (audiocassette). Hillsdale, Mich.: Hillsdale Educational Publishers, 1987.
- Michigan Traditional Arts Program and the Michigan State University Museum. *Michigan in Song.* Spring Lake, Mich.: River Road Press, 1990.

Books Used in This Lesson

Collier, John. *The Backyard.* Illus. by author. New York: Viking, 1993.

Kurjian, Judi. *In My Own Backyard.* Illus. by David R. Wagner. Watertown, Mass.: Charlesbridge, 1993.

Lyon, George Ella. *Who Came Down That Road?* Illus. by Peter Catalanotto. New York: Orchard Books, 1992.

Sheldon, Dyan. *Under the Moon.* Illus. by Gary Blythe. New York: Dial, 1993.

Suggested Companion Titles

Ackerman, Karen. *The Tin Heart.* Illus. by Michael Hays. New York: Atheneum, 1990.

Altman, Susan, and Susan Lechner. *Followers of the North Star.* Illus. by Byron Wooden. Chicago: Children's Press, 1993.

Aylesworth, Thomas, and Virginia Aylesworth. *Eastern Great Lakes: Ohio, Indiana, Michigan.* New York: Chelsea House, 1991.

Bial, Raymond. *The Underground Railroad.* Photographs by author. Boston: Houghton Mifflin, 1995.

Bonvillain, Nancy. *The Huron.* New York: Chelsea House, 1989.

Bratvold, Gretchen. *Wisconsin.* Minneapolis, Minn.: Lerner, 1991.

Faber, Doris. *The Amish.* New York: Doubleday, 1991.

Fiday, Beverly, and David Fiday. *Time to Go.* Illus. by Thomas B. Allen. San Diego, Calif.: Harcourt Brace Jovanovich 1990.

Glass, Andrew. *Folks Call Me Appleseed John.* New York: Doubleday, 1995.

Halsey, John R. *Beneath the Inland Seas.* Lansing: Michigan Department of State Bureau of History, 1990.

Harshman, Marc. *Uncle James.* New York: Penguin/Cobblehill, 1993.

Kellogg, Steven. *Johnny Appleseed.* New York: Morrow, 1988.

———. *Paul Bunyan.* New York: Scholastic, 1984.

Kent, Zachary. *Tecumseh.* Chicago: Children's Press, 1992.

Lawlor, Laurie. *The Real Johnny Appleseed.* Illus. by Mary Thompson. Morton Grove, Ill.: Albert Whitman, 1995.

Lindberg, Reeve. *The Legend of Johnny Appleseed.* Illus. by Kathy Jakobsen. Boston: Little, Brown, 1990.

Peters, Lisa Westberg. *Treasure in the Air.* Illus. by Deborah Durland DeSaix. New York: Henry Holt, 1995.

Ogden, Dale R. *Indiana.* Chicago: Children's Press, 1990.

Sanders, Scott Russell. *Warm as Wool.* Illus. by Helen Cogancherry. New York: Bradbury Press, 1992.

————. *Aurora Means Dawn.* Illus. by Jill Kastner. New York: Bradbury Press, 1990.
Scholastic Voyages of Discovery. *Wind and Weather.* New York: Scholastic, 1995.
Shelby, Anne. *Homeplace.* Illus. by Wendy Anderson. New York: Hyperion, 1995.

Shemie, Bonnie. *Houses of Bark: Tipi, Wigwam and Longhouse: Native Dwellings of Woodland Indians.* New York: Tundra Books, 1990.
Van Leuuwen, Jean. *Going West.* Illus. by Thomas B. Allen. New York: Dial, 1992.
Winter, Jeanette. *Follow the Drinking Gourd.* New York: Alfred A. Knopf, 1988.

Lesson 3

Looking at the Great Lakes States Through the Themes of Location and Movement

Objectives

- to continue correspondence with Trucker Buddies, noting their travels on a classroom map
- to discover and discuss the connections between industry and agriculture in this region, the rest of North America, and the world
- to create a regional product map illustrating an understanding of what products originate in the Great Lakes states
- to investigate the role of lakes and rivers in the development and growth of industries in the region
- to continue to learn about the partnership between humans and geography and what it takes to make it "equal"

Materials

- a large regional map of the Great Lakes states
- student atlases
- labels, pictures, advertisements for products created in the area
- *In Coal Country* by Judith Hendershot
- *Up the Road to Grandma's* by Judith Hendershot

Motivator

Read *In Coal Country* and *Up the Road to Grandma's* to the students. Since these are true stories of life in a 1940s coal-mining region, locate the Ohio community on the map. Use student atlases to find coal deposits in this region. Discuss the value of this natural resource before explaining the task ahead.

Activity

Products and Destinations

Students will learn about and locate industrial and agricultural products in the Great Lakes states and trace their paths to their possible destinations. Students may already have some of this information at their fingertips from the Trucker Buddy with whom they are corresponding.

First, groups of learners are to create a large regional map of the Great Lakes states. They can sketch it freehand, making it about 2 feet by 3 feet, or larger if they so choose. After researching the kinds of products made in the states, have them begin collecting labels from those products as they are used up at home. Students should not have to go to the grocery store and spend their allowances on a variety of foods, of course. It might be fun to have several maps designating specific themes including foods;

home, office, and personal care products; or building materials and ores. While a group of students could have primary responsibility for a specific map, everyone in class could be on the lookout for appropriate products to match each theme. As labels or pictures are brought in, they can be glued to the outer edges of the map. Brightly colored yarn tacked with pushpins will connect product with location of its manufacture.

Closure

At a designated time, share the completed maps in class. Discuss what the students learned about the products of the region and where they go from this point. They might ponder just how important the geographic theme of movement is to daily life. It would be wonderful to display the maps in the hallway outside of class or in the learning center where other students could appreciate them and learn from them as well.

Books Used in This Lesson

Hendershot, Judith. *Up the Road to Grandma's.* Illus. by Thomas B. Allen. New York: Alfred A. Knopf, 1993.

———. *In Coal Country.* Illus. by Thomas B. Allen. New York: Alfred A. Knopf, 1987.

Suggested Companion Titles

Bial, Raymond. *Corn Belt Harvest.* Photographs by author. Boston: Houghton Mifflin, 1991.

Burns, Diane L. *Cranberries: Fruit of the Bogs.* Photographs by Cheryl Walsh Bellville. Minneapolis, Minn.: Carolrhoda Books, 1994.

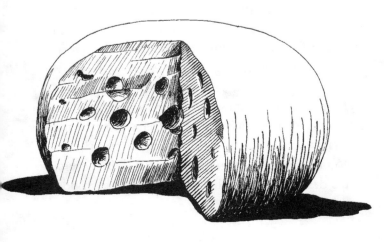

Collins, David R. *Pioneer Plowmaker: A Story About John Deere.* Minneapolis, Minn.: Carolrhoda Books, 1990.

Diller, Harriett. *Grandaddy's Highway.* Illus. by Henri Sorensen. Honesdale, Pa.: Boyds Mill Press, 1993.

Jaspersohn, William. *Cranberries.* Boston: Houghton Mifflin, 1991.

Kent, Zachary. *The Story of Henry Ford and the Automobile.* Chicago: Children's Press, 1990.

McFarland, Cynthia. *Cows in the Parlor: A Visit to a Dairy Farm.* New York: Atheneum, 1990.

Micucci, Charles. *The Life and Times of the Apple.* Illus. by author. New York: Orchard Books, 1992.

Mitchell, John, and Tom Woodruff. *Great Lakes and Great Ships: An Illustrated History for Children.* Illus. by authors. Suttons Bay, Mich.: Suttons Bay Publications, 1991.

Ross, Catherine, and Susan Wallace. *The Amazing Milk Book.* Illus. by Linda Hendry. Reading, Mass.: Addison-Wesley, 1991.

Culminating Activity

If your class is participating in an ongoing project like Quilts of the United States, spend time adding the Great Lakes to the project. A just-for-fun writing activity would be to break the class up into four or five groups and do some round-robin writing. The teacher can give the groups a prompt to get them started or students can come up with their own. An example of a starter might be, "I was driving through the Great Lakes states one hot summer day, when I looked in my rearview window and saw … " Each student writes for a specified period of time then the teacher tells writers to pass the papers to the right. The second writer reads what the first writer has written and carries on the thread of the story. After a designated time, the papers are passed to the right again and so forth until each member of the group has added something to the original story. Writers should try to tuck in tidbits that they have learned throughout the study of this region. Then, have a read-aloud session, with each student sharing his/her very unique creation. This is one upbeat way to conclude the study of the Great Lakes states.

7

The New England States: Vermont, Massachusetts, New Hampshire, Connecticut, Maine, and Rhode Island

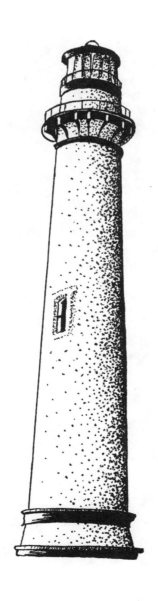

Tucked up into the northeastern corner of the United States is a collection of mountainous, heavily forested states including Vermont, Massachusetts, New Hampshire, Connecticut, Maine, and Rhode Island. Enduring long winters and often battered by the elements like the infamous Nor'easters, these New England states also are bathed in sparkling summer sunlight and in stunning fall colors. No matter what the season, tourists are drawn to the area to ski on snow-covered slopes, tour historic sites, wander ocean beaches, or take on the wilderness as they camp, hike, and canoe. Patiently grinding their way across the land, glaciers left behind a rugged, rock-strewn countryside for these New England states. Early immigrants imbued the area with a rich history. By combining topography and people, past and present, you gain an inviting viewpoint for looking into an engrossing region awaiting geographic discovery.

One approach to the study of New England is through its geographic features including mountains, rivers, valleys, and the coast. Formed over 440 million years ago when plate tectonics were in high gear, the mountains are a dominant feature throughout the region. Part of the Appalachian Mountains, head high over the others, is Mount Washington rising to a height of 6,288 feet. A popular destination for summer visitors, it is abandoned to the fierce winds and bitter weather in the winter. Close behind in size is Mount Katahdin in northern Maine, nearly a mile high. It is an interesting weathered rock called a monadnock, which has endured many a storm showing little telltale damage. The lovely Berkshire Hills in Massachusetts draw tourists, artists, writers, and musicians including the popular Boston Symphony. Topographic maps show ranges like the Longfellow Range, the Taconic Range, and the White Mountains and the Green Mountains in the Northeast. These heavily forested hills in varying heights and sizes are a dominant feature of all the New England states except tiny Rhode Island.

As in other regions of North America, the role that rivers play in the past and present is an important one. Beginning in a boggy area a few hundred miles south of Canada, the Connecticut River touches four of the six New England states before emptying into Long Island Sound. An eastern boundary of Vermont, it splits the Appalachian Mountains into two ranges and provides a fertile river valley where farms have taken root. It is New England's longest river, a watery road for transporting goods to and fro. Along with other major rivers, it has long been a source of inexpensive power from the earliest textile, grist, and sawmills to hydroelectric power for current industries. Other key rivers like the Merrimack, Penobscot, Thames, Providence, and Kennebec appealed to early settlers as towns sprang up on the shores, many of which grew, prospered, and flourish today. Often abused and taken for granted over the years, rivers in this part of the country are a primary concern of environmentalists today. Thus, rivers have played a critical role in development within the New England states and continue to be an important resource.

This region has been shaped, chiseled, and ground out by glacial action that left behind a countryside that beguiles tourists and challenges farmers with its thin, rocky soil. So rocky is the ground, in fact, that in Connecticut alone resigned farmers have built 25,000 miles of rocky fences around pastures, fields, and homes over the years.

The rock-strewn ocean shoreline dominates the coastal region where names like Bar Harbor, Portsmouth, Cape Cod, Nantucket, Mystic, and Martha's Vineyard represent a once thriving fishing and whaling industry. They still support a declining fishing industry, but whaling has been replaced with droves of tourists each season. It is interesting to note that Vermont has no coastline at all, while New Hampshire has only 18 miles, the shortest in the nation. Maine boasts the longest of these states, an amazing 3,478 miles of curving, cove-filled shoreline including nearby islands. Stretched out in a straight line these miles would carry one from New York to San Francisco! New England's shoreline is a boon to the shipping industry, excellent for commercial and recreational fishing, and appeals to throngs of tourists. A remnant of glacial action, it certainly is an asset to the region.

The New England states evoke visions and impressions all their own. Part of the original thirteen colonies, the states have accumulated a unique and memorable history filled with people like the Pilgrims, the Lowell millworkers, and Eli Whitney along with events like the Boston Tea Party, Salem Witch Trials, and Paul Revere's Ride. Here, too, is the land of Norman Rockwell, pristine white-steepled churches set on the town square, and a tapestry of green rolling hills surrounding quaint small towns. A riot of color in the fall, this area kindles images of lighthouses, seagulls atop the pilings, the smell of sharp salt air, and the tantalizing thought of fresh lobster. Miles of untamed waterways are inviting to white-water rafters and beg to be explored. Able-bodied hikers might tackle the Long Trail, which runs through the peaks of the Green Mountains from Massachusetts through Vermont and up into Canada. This land that welcomed the Pilgrims, provided jobs for immigrants from a number of countries, and served as the roots of contemporary America still draws people today and bears closer investigation.

Initiating Activity

Bring in a variety of music that students can stand up and sing along with or just listen to quietly as you paint a musical picture of the New England states. Amy L. Cohn's collection of American folklore and folk songs, *From Sea to Shining Sea*, has a useful chapter entitled "The Shot Heard 'Round the World" including several appropriate songs. Try tapes of the ocean water slapping the shore and gulls crying in the background, the song of the loon from a secluded forest lake, the historical sounds of a whaling song, or the famous "Yankee Doodle Dandy" from Revolutionary War days. The last song can be followed up with Steven Kellogg's book version—a rollicking, action-filled book that ends with the history of the tune. In addition, talk to the librarian, scout music stores or local bookstores to find appropriate music to share. It is so important to have music permeate the study of geography across North America as it is another avenue of learning for many a child.

Lesson 1

Looking at the New England States Through the Themes of Location, Place, and Human/Environmental Interactions

Objectives

- to locate the New England states on personal outline maps
- to describe a New England state of choice in terms of relative location
- to develop a profile of a state examining both tangible and intangible characteristics that set it apart from other states
- to zero in on one state and answer the geographic questions, Where?, Why there?, and What is it like there?
- to investigate human/environmental interactions by looking at the advantages and disadvantages of living in a particular state
- to present the state profile to the class in the form of an accordion book

Materials

- paper, ribbon or yarn, glue, scissors for accordion book
- *A River Ran Wild* by Lynne Cherry

Motivator

Read *A River Ran Wild* to the class, showing the maps on the endpapers before reading. Locate the Nashua River on a wall map. Because so much background of the story is told through pictures around the page borders, which share additional information, encourage students to pick this book up later and reread it on their own, paying special attention to the details. Tell the class that the illustrations will give them a sense of what the environment of New England looks like plus a sense of history of the area at the same time. As they

listen, students should be thinking about the interactions between the people and the land plus the role of the river in the development of communities. Discuss these points after reading the book.

Activity

Creating the Profile of a State

Tell the class that they will be choosing a state that they are particularly interested in after spending some time scouting and reading about this area in general. They are going to make a profile of that state, presenting the information in an accordion book. They will include basic information like:

- relative location and state size in terms of population and miles
- overview of the topography of the state including key features: rivers, lakes, mountains, river valleys, and shoreline
- industry and why it has developed in these particular states

- industries that have died and been replaced by something new
- the advantages and disadvantages of living in the state
- several places of historical significance
- several particularly appealing tourist attractions
- several unique and fun tidbits of information about the state

For example, students might enjoy knowing that there are more toothpicks made in Maine than anywhere else and that the tall white pines in Maine had originally been earmarked for the masts of ships long ago. Each year 100,000 Christmas trees are harvested in New Hampshire. Half a million gallons of maple syrup are shipped annually from Vermont, and more than half of the nation's cranberries are grown in Massachusetts. Interesting tidbits, indeed!

Since each student-made accordion book will have sixteen folds or "pages," it will be up to the student to decide how to lay out the information. Each page could be filled with information and only have a small key illustration. Maybe the writer will have so much information, he or she will use two pages or accordion folds for each topic. Another option is to skip every other page as text is recorded, then go back to the blank pages to add illustrations. After data are collected, the rough draft should be proofread by a classmate and fine-tuned. That version should be given to the teacher for additional scrutiny. Once that copy has been polished, the text can be transferred to the book. Put on a quiet tape of ocean sounds or sounds of nature in the background as students work to create their state profile. Specific directions for making the book are included in Appendix III.

Closure

Set aside a morning or afternoon to "publish" the books. At that time each student is to booktalk their book in a three- to five-minute presentation. Afterward, display the books so that they are available for others to read following the booktalks or during free time. Later, an eye-catching exhibit in the learning center might tempt others to learn more about the New England states from the class authors.

Books Used in This Lesson

Cherry, Lynne. *A River Ran Wild.* Illus. by author. San Diego, Calif.: Harcourt Brace, 1992.

Cohn, Amy L. *From Sea to Shining Sea: A Treasury of American Folklore and Folk Songs.* New York: Scholastic, 1993.

Kellogg, Steven. *Yankee Doodle Dandy.* Illus. by author. New York: Aladdin, 1996.

Suggested Companion Titles

Bedard, Michael. *Emily.* Illus. by Barbara Cooney. New York: Doubleday, 1992.

Blackstone, Margaret. *This Is Maine.* Illus. by John Segal. New York: Henry Holt, 1995.

Fradin, Dennis Brindell, and Judith Blook Fradin. *Connecticut.* Chicago: Children's Press, 1994.

Hall, Donald. *The Farm Summer 1942.* Illus. by Barry Moser. New York: Dial, 1994.

Holmes, Efner Tudor. *Deer in the Hollow.* Illus. by Marlowe DeChristopher. New York: Philomel, 1993.

Kinsey-Warnock, Natalie. *The Bear That Heard Crying.* Illus. by Ted Rand. New York: Cobblehill Books, 1993.

Lindbergh, Reeve. *View from the Air.* Photographs by Richard Brown. New York: Viking, 1992.

McCloskey, Robert. *Blueberries for Sal.* Illus. by author. New York: Puffin, 1948.

McCully, Emily Arnold. *The Bobbin Girl.* Illus. by author. New York: Dial, 1996.

MacLachlan, Patricia. *All the Places to Love.* Illus. by Mike Wimmer. New York: HarperCollins, 1994.

McNair, Sylvia. *New Hampshire.* Chicago: Children's Press, 1991.

McPhail, David. *Farmboy's Year.* Illus. by author. New York: Atheneum, 1992.

Maass, Robert. *When Autumn Comes.* New York: Henry Holt, 1990.

Mason, Cherie. *Wild Fox: A True Story.* Illus. by JoEllen McAllister Stammen. Camden, Maine: Down East Books, 1993.

Pelta, Kathy. *Vermont.* Minneapolis, Minn.: Lerner, 1994.

Rylant, Cynthia. *The Whales.* Illus. by author. New York: Blue Sky Press/Scholastic, 1996.

Savageau, Cheryl. *Muskrat Will Be Swimming.* Illus. by Robert Hynes. Flagstaff, Ariz.: Northland, 1996.

Slawson, Michele Benoit. *Apple Picking Time.* Illus. by Deborah Kogan Ray. New York: Crown, 1994.

Turkle, Brinton. *Thy Friend, Obadiah.* Illus. by author. New York: Puffin, 1969.

Wells, Rosemary. *Waiting for the Evening Star.* Illus. by Susan Jeffers. New York: Dial, 1993.

Yolen, Jane. *Letting Swift River Go.* Illus. by Barbara Cooney. Boston: Little, Brown, 1992.

Lesson 2

Looking at the New England States Through the Themes of Location and Place

Objectives

- to look at a region in one of the New England states from the perspective of a vacationer in order to map an appealing three-day road trip
- to polish map skills as students draw a map of the region to be traveled
- to investigate both historical and cultural features in order to learn more about a place
- to organize and present the information in an appealing pamphlet or poster

Materials

- maps, videos, and guidebooks for each of the New England states
- brochures and information from Departments of Tourism in each state
- paper, pencils
- a supply of books on the New England states that highlight history, vacations, or other useful information
- *Time of Wonder* by Robert McClosky

Motivator

Show a video of the New England states as an overview of the area. Invite a travel agent to class who is familiar with the New England states and can talk about places of interest in order to provide background information for the students and spark their enthusiasm for this project. Then read the Caldecott-winner *Time of Wonder* by Robert McCloskey. With its rhythmic language, the story pulls the reader right into island life off the coast of Maine. After hearing this story, an island just might be included in the students' extended road trip.

Activity

Planning a New England Road Trip

Using maps, travel guides, and other materials in the classroom, students are to plan a road trip that will take a minimum of three days. After preliminary research the students are to:

- Divide their plans into a one-day trip and the longer trip, showing both on their maps in different colors and providing a color key to identify them.
- Write a brief, two- or three-sentence, enticing explanation of the sites found during the trip in a separate column of the pamphlet.
- Sketch a map of the section of the state they are visiting including state routes, U.S. routes, and interstate highways, using the appropriate symbols for each one.
- Calculate the mileage from point to point and indicate that with mile markers or a scale of miles on their maps.

- Number and describe attractions to be seen in a corresponding key.
- Include something for every member of the "family" so nature stops, museums, historic sites, shopping, recreation, zoos, and amusement parks might be included. One side trip should be included in case travelers have some extra time. Each trip should be coded by color or symbol as to its category: historical site, nature activity, and so forth.

Using a 12-by-18-inch sheet of paper, students can fold it in half, putting the map on one side of the inside and the other information in columns or paragraphs on the other side. They can decorate the cover and present it as a pamphlet or brochure. They may choose to leave the sheet flat, putting the map at the top and the information across the bottom.

Closure

Display the road trip maps on a bulletin board decorated with scenes from each of the states. Old calendars might have excellent scenic pictures that can be used as accents on the bulletin board. If there is time in the already packed curriculum, students might be encouraged to give a three-minute sales pitch for their trip.

Book Used in This Lesson

McClosky, Robert. *Time of Wonder.* New York: Viking, 1957.

Suggested Companion Titles

Aylesworth, Thomas G., and Virginia L. Aylesworth. *Northern New England: Maine, New Hampshire, Vermont.* New York: Chelsea House, 1990.

Carrick, Carol. *Whaling Days.* Illus. by David Frampton. New York: Clarion Books, 1993.

Cohlene, Terri. *Little Firefly: An Algonquin Legend.* Illus. by Charles Reasoner. Vero Beach, Fla.: Watermill Press, 1990.

Dean, Julia. *A Year on Monhegan Island.* New York: Ticknor & Fields, 1995.

Fradin, Dennis Brindell. *Maine.* Chicago: Children's Press, 1994.

Lasky, Katherine. *She's Wearing a Dead Bird on Her Head!* Illus. by David Catrow. New York: Hyperion, 1995.

———. *Fourth of July Bear.* Illus. by Helen Cogancherry. New York: Morrow Junior Books, 1991.

McMillan, Bruce. *Grandfather's Trolley.* New York: Candlewick Press, 1995.

Sewell, Marcia. *People of the Breaking Day.* New York: Atheneum, 1990.

Taylor, C. J. *How Two-Feather Was Saved from Loneliness.* Northampton, Maine: Tundra Books, 1990.

Van Rynback, Iris. *Everything from a Nail to a Coffin.* New York: Orchard Books, 1991.

Weller, Frances Ward. *I Wonder If I'll See a Whale.* Illus. by Ted Lewin. New York: Putnam, 1991.

Zolotow, Charlotte. *The Seashore Book.* Illus. by Wendell Minor. New York: HarperCollins, 1992.

Lesson 3

Looking at the New England Coast Through the Theme of Place

Objectives

- to identify unique characteristics of the New England coast as they pertain to the theme of place
- to portray a sense of the coast through poetry, art, or creative writing
- to create a bulletin board that teaches the different categories of place as it relates to the coastal region

Materials

- *Until I Saw the Sea: A Collection of Seashore Poems* by Alison Shaw
- *Sea Watch: A Book of Poetry* by Jane Yolen
- *Spray* by Robert J. Blake

Motivator

Fill the students' heads with sights and sounds of the ocean. Read several of the poems about the sea from both of the suggested poetry books while a tape of sea sounds plays softly in the background. Then pick up the pace with the imaginative tale of Justin who sets sail off the coast of Martha's Vineyard and nearly loses his life when his boat capsizes. Saved by the famous, mysterious Captain Slocum, he must test his courage and determination before arriving safely back home. What a great introduction to one aspect of ocean life!

Activities

Examining the Theme of Place

On the board or the overhead, list the following three categories: physical characteristics, feelings about a place, and human characteristics. Refresh students' minds by telling them that physical characteristics deal with landforms, bodies of water, native plants, animal life, and climate. Human characteristics deal with what humans do to the environment like building roads and towns or creating pollution. Feelings are probably self-explanatory. How do they feel when they think of this particular place? Remind them that these are the elements that make up place in terms of geography.

Next, ask the students to listen to *Spray*. Based on what they hear and what they already know and feel, have them write reactions to the story and the place, perhaps for three to five minutes. Tell them to just let their thoughts flow. When the time is up, ask for volunteers to share key words, ideas, or phrases about the ocean and coasts. Put them on the chalkboard or overhead into the categories where they are the most appropriate. These will eventually be transferred to a bulletin board created by the students. They could arrange the display as a Place Web with the three categories in separate boxes or balloons, and their words and impressions surrounding the appropriate balloon with yarn. The display could be completed with student work including poetry, stories, and pictures.

Student-Centered Specific Projects

Giving students a choice in the direction of their learning is always a sensible idea. They can demonstrate what they have learned about the New England coast in a number of ways. They might write poetry about it, write a short story set in the area, make a mosaic or other art project that evokes a sense of what the place is like, or work with several others to create an ocean alphabet book that addresses the three components of "place." Student suggestions are always welcome, of course.

Closure

It is time to talk and share everyone's creative endeavors. In addition, students might be asked to compare this region with another previously studied discussing the differences and similarities and which region has the most appeal to them and why. Work on any ongoing projects and continue the correspondence with the Trucker Buddy if students are involved in that program.

Books Used in This Lesson

Blake, Robert J. *Spray.* Illus. by author. New York: Philomel, 1996.
Shaw, Alison. *Until I Saw the Sea: A Collection of Seashore Poems.* New York: Henry Holt, 1995.
Yolen, Jane. *Sea Watch: A Book of Poetry.* Illus. by Ted Lewin. New York: Philomel, 1996.

Suggested Companion Titles

Arnosky, Jim. *Near the Sea.* Illus. by author. New York: Lothrop, Lee & Shepard, 1990.

Cole, Joanna. *The Magic School Bus Inside a Hurricane.* Illus. by Bruce Degen. New York: Scholastic, 1995.

———. *The Magic School Bus on the Ocean Floor.* Illus. by Bruce Degen. New York: Scholastic, 1992.

Ganeri, Anita. *The Oceans Atlas.* Illus. by Luciano Corbella. Orlando, Fla.: Dorling-Kindersley, 1994.

Gemmell, Kathy. *Storms and Hurricanes.* Illus. by Gary Bines and Ian Jackson. New York: Scholastic, 1995.

Gibbons, Gail. *Surrounded by the Sea: Life on a New England Fishing Island.* Illus. by author. Boston: Little, Brown, 1991.

Graff, Nancy P. *The Call of the Running Tide: A Portrait of an Island Family.* Illus. by Richard Howard. Boston: Little, Brown, 1992.

Hirshi, Ron. *Where Are My Puffins, Whales, and Seals?* New York: Bantam, 1992.

Hoff, Mary, and Mary M. Rodgers. *Oceans.* Illus. series: Our Endangered Planet. Minneapolis, Minn.: Lerner, 1992.

Hoff, Syd. *The Lighthouse Children.* Illus. by author. New York: HarperCollins, 1994.

Jenkins-Pearce, Susie, and Claire Fletcher. *The Seashell Song.* Illus. by Susie Jenkins-Pearce. New York: Lothrop, Lee & Shepard, 1992.

Kesselman, Wendy. *Sand in My Shoes.* Illus. by Ronald Himler. New York: Hyperion, 1995.

Livingston, Myra Cohn. *If You Ever Meet a Whale.* Illus. by Leonard Everett Fisher. New York: Holiday House, 1992.

Ryder, Joanne. *Winter Whale.* Illus. by Michael Rothman. New York: Morrow, 1991.

Simon, Seymour. *Oceans.* New York: Morrow, 1990.

Sis, Peter. *An Ocean World.* Illus. by author. New York: Greenwillow, 1992.

Smith, Maggie. *Counting Our Way to Maine.* Illus. by author. New York: Orchard Books, 1995.

Weller, Frances Ward. *Riptide.* Illus. by Robert J. Blake. New York: Philomel, 1990.

Culminating Activity

Invite parents and family to participate in a "Taste of New England and Knowledge" exhibition. Volunteer parents can be invited to contribute snacks or regional dishes; students can prepare songs and explain projects completed during the study of the region. Sharp Vermont cheddar cheese and crackers, sliced apples, clam chowder, deviled eggs to represent the dairy industry, maple sugar candy, and other products and tasty recipes can be researched and presented that afternoon or evening. A valuable resource would be *Cooking Up U.S. History* by Suzanne I. Barchers and Patricia C. Marden as noted in Appendix I. Colorful student-generated invitations might include a map to the school to polish those skills, a poem written by someone in class, and the request to come dressed for an activity they would do if they vacationed in the New England states. Beach gear, hiking attire, casual wear with a fishing pole might be fun. Then settle in for the fun generated by these memorable northeastern states.

8

The Mid-Atlantic States:
New York, New Jersey, Pennsylvania,
Delaware, and Maryland

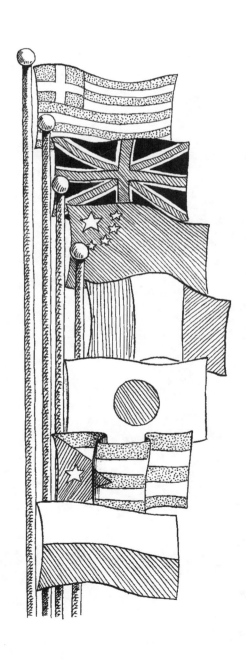

The Mid-Atlantic states are an impressive collection of opposites: past and present, topographic highs and lows, mountains and farmlands, the call of the loon and bustling crowds, and states, large and small. To illustrate, consider the stately, sprawling old plantations scattered throughout the area. They are rooted in colonial history, wrapped in issues of slavery, monuments to a gentile life and tobacco profits. Compare these pillared homes with the geometrically clean lines of glass and steel skyscrapers that stretch vertically toward the sky. Offices and corporate headquarters, these buildings are testaments to the success of big business.

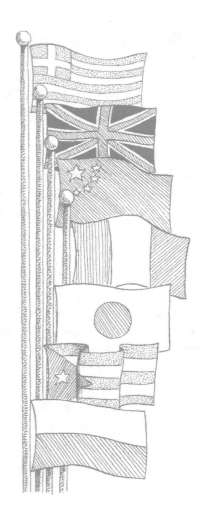

Now think topographically. Consider how mountainous the lands of Pennsylvania and New York are with peaks between 3,000 and 5,000 feet high. In contrast, visualize Delaware where the land rarely raises 80 feet above sea level. In different terms, there are the age-old Allegheny Mountains offering beauty and solitude to those who seek it set against the often frenetic hustle and motion of a metropolis like New York City, Philadelphia, or Baltimore.

There, too, is a difference between the central Pennsylvania mountains riffled with roads steep and winding as they work their way down the slopes and the state's fertile, pastoral lands in Lancaster County. Here many farms are run quietly and efficiently without the help of modern machinery. Horse-drawn teams, ingenuity, and muscle of the hard-working Amish, Mennonites, and Moravians get the job done. In terms of actual size of these states there are obvious differences to note as well. New York and Pennsylvania simply dwarf their neighbors New Jersey, Maryland, and Delaware, which is not to say the smaller are any less important, of course. These are but a few of the interesting opposites to be found in the Mid-Atlantic states.

While these states have some distinct differences, there are common denominators that run across the region. The first is scenery: Each state is rich in this commodity. The trails, lakes, waterfalls, and vistas of the Catskills, Poconos, Adirondacks, and Kittatinny Mountains are havens for many fisherpeople, hikers, and nature lovers. Look to the east and find some of the most scenic shoreline in the United States along the coasts of New Jersey, Delaware, and Maryland. Many New Yorkers throng to the sanctuary of Long Island for seaside summer vacations. Throughout the region ocean beaches and the tangy salt air draw thousands of harried city dwellers who are seeking a respite from the city's oppressive, humid summer heat.

Fertile farmlands are yet another commonality. With the Garden State, New Jersey, leading the way, a bounty of fresh fruits, crisp vegetables, and multicolored flowers are raised and shipped to nearby markets. Industry and commerce are strong throughout the region as workers of great diversity head to jobs in flour mills, steel mills, coalfields, assembly plants, and other manufacturing options. Because almost half of the goods shipped into this country come through these states, the ports are alive with jobs and activity as well.

Finally, ethnic diversity ties this region together to a degree not experienced in any other area. Immigrants from a wide variety of countries who arrived through Ellis Island often opted to stay in the area. Early years of overwork and abuse were dismal for all too many newcomers to the country, but they were tenacious. Good fortune, strong dreams, and diligent labor combined so that life for their descendants generally improved over the years. In brief, history, people, and bounty of the region have combined to make the Mid-Atlantic states absorbing subjects for further investigation.

Initiating Activity

To set the mood, a teacher-made tape with versions of the states' theme songs or tunes like "New York, New York" could be played. As students enter the room on the day study of this region begins, hand them a business-sized, sealed envelope. On the outside of each envelope will be a student's name and a number or other designation that indicates a team. Working in threes or fours, students will be members of units involved in the exciting Mid-Atlantic States Scavenger Hunt (M.A.S.S.H.). Set up classroom rules for the hunt and list them on a colorful poster displayed at the front of the room. Discuss them before the learning begins.

Each group will have the same clues but it might be fun to change the order so that units are not trying for the same bit of information at the same time. Materials for finding the answers should be in the classroom unless the teacher has made special arrangements with the librarian or another adult to have part of the investigation to be done in other areas of the school. If that is the case, the items to be found outside of the classroom should be starred and limited in number to maintain control of the learning situation. A list of possible clues is included in Appendix III but they are just starters. Teachers can add their own imaginative ideas to the list. Items connected to locations like pieces of saltwater taffy originating in Atlantic City or Hershey's Kisses® representing Hershey, Pennsylvania, might be in containers for teams to discover. Maps, travel guides, state tourist information, student atlases, books on the states, and colorful posters from an area are all

options of sources for finding answers to the clues. Teachers should be available to monitor progress, to check the winning team's clue sheet, and to give units something appropriate to do while others complete the activity. Certainly this would be an opportunity to delve into some of the fabulous books on this area.

When the hunt is completed, gather as a group to discuss each clue and answer. After a general discussion, suggest that students can develop a miniversion of the scavenger hunt for their parents or guardians to complete during the celebration of learning at the conclusion of this unit of study.

Lesson 1

Looking at the Mid-Atlantic States Through the Themes of Location, Place, and Human/Environmental Interactions

Objectives

- to locate New York, New Jersey, Pennsylvania, Delaware, and Maryland on students' individual outline maps
- to locate one major city in each state using absolute location and write the absolute location only on a 3-by-5-inch index card for future use
- to locate on regional maps: the Allegheny, Pocono, Catskill, and Adirondack Mountains; key rivers including the Hudson, St. Lawrence, Delaware, Potomac, and Susquehanna; bodies of water including the Finger Lakes, Niagara Falls, Lake Ontario, Lake Erie, Delaware Bay, and Chesapeake Bay
- to get an overview of the topography by coloring in the elevations according to an elevation map on regional maps
- to study the cultural diversity of the area and its importance in relation to what the area is like today

Materials

- individual and regional outline maps
- pens, pencils, markers
- butcher paper to make a large regional map
- materials to make a piece of the quilt of diversity
- a variety of fiction and nonfiction books for reference and reading
- *Cinder-Elly* by Frances Minters
- *Snow White in New York* by Fiona French
- *Immigrants* by Martin W. Sandler

Motivator

Read *Cinder-Elly* by Frances Minters as an upbeat introduction to life in the Big Apple. Briefly booktalk *Snow White in New York*, another fairy tale adapted to the city, as a title for free reading. Have students get a general understanding of where these states are and what they look like by completing the map work: locating states, completing the absolute location note cards, looking at topography, and thinking about what influences the bodies of water in the area have on the way the states develop.

Activity

Creating a Quilt of Diversity
Once map work has been completed, move to the interaction of people and place. Explain that one

of the fascinating facets of life in the Mid-Atlantic states is human diversity. Share several excerpts from *Immigrants* by Martin Sandler. It reveals graphically, through superb pictures and brief snippets of informative text, just what life as an immigrant was like. Every student should read and think about this book as this lesson is being completed. Locate Ellis Island on individual regional maps. It was a gateway to reaching the American dream, but in reality, life in this country was a nightmare for the majority of newcomers. Who came? Why did they do so? This lesson will acquaint students with the courageous people who left so much behind to start in a land they knew little about. While some of the immigrants continued their journeys beyond the area, many stayed. Their descendants still make the region their home. There is no more diverse region in the United States.

The project to lead students to understand people and places better is to create a large wall map of diversity. Give the students the param-

eters of the project. Then they are to decide how the map quilt should be titled, bordered, and divided up to eventually make an attractive pattern. Learners should make two identical large-size maps of the region. One will be the background upon which pattern pieces will be glued and it will hang on the classroom wall. The other map will be cut into pieces, each one representing a specific culture. Students could work individually or in pairs on a selected nationality decorating a representative quilt piece. Some of the suggested companion titles at the end of this segment will be helpful. In addition, students can seek help from the school or city librarian or interview people of their selected nationality.

Some nationalities to be discovered:

African American
British
Chinese
Cuban
Eastern European
German
Greek
Haitian
Hispanic
Irish
Italian
Japanese
Jewish
Korean
Native American
Pennsylvania Dutch
Polish
Puerto Rican
Scandinavian
Vietnamese

On the day the quilt is completed each pair of students will present their culture as they glue their piece on the map. Each presentation should be a celebration of culture as the quilt pieces are fitted together. Presentations will include a brief background including why these people came to America, where they settled, and what kinds of jobs they did. As an extra, poetry, music, holiday celebration, illuminating picture book, or powerful excerpt from a pertinent novel could be shared with the class to further illustrate the culture. In this visual way, the class will get the picture of the wonderful diversity that makes up this part of the United States and perhaps see how it has enriched other parts of the country as well.

Closure

After assembling the quilt, ask students to share what they have learned in general about diversity and its role in creating a sense of place here in America. Have them apply this knowledge to the community in which they live. What richness is there to appreciate because of different nationalities? Then have them exchange the 3-by-5-inch index cards they made while completing the initial map work. Students who wrote the cards should have secreted the names of the cities at the absolute locations so that there is nothing on the cards to give them away. Using their atlases, classmates are to try to find the city according to its absolute location. Later, the cards might be kept in a file box in the geography center to be added to and used during free time.

Books Used in This Lesson

French, Fiona. *Snow White in New York.* Illus. by author. New York: Oxford University Press, 1992.

Minters, Frances. *Cinder-Elly.* Illus. by G. Brian Karas. New York: Viking, 1994.

Sandler, Martin W. *Immigrants: A Library of Congress Book.* New York: HarperCollins, 1995.

Suggested Companion Titles

Aylesworth, Jim. *The Folks in the Valley: A Pennsylvania Dutch ABC.* Illus. by Stefano Vitale. New York: HarperCollins, 1992.

Bartone, Elisa. *American Too.* Illus. by Ted Lewin. New York: Lothrop, Lee & Shepard, 1996.

Bunting, Eve. *Cheyenne Again.* Illus. by Irving Toddy. New York: Clarion Books, 1995.

Chinn, Karen. *Sam and the Lucky Money.* Illus. by Cornelius Van Wright and Ying-Hwa Hu. New York: Lee & Low, 1995.

Choi, Sook Nyal. *Halmoni and the Picnic.* Illus. by Karen M. Dugan. San Diego, Calif.: Houghton Mifflin, 1993.

Cooney, Barbara. *Hattie and the Wild Waves.* Illus. by author. New York: Viking, 1990.

Dorros, Arthur. *Abuela.* Illus. by Elisa Kleven. New York: Dutton, 1991.

Fisher, Leonard Everett. *Ellis Island: Gateway to the New World.* Illus. by author. New York: Holiday House, 1986.

Good, Merle. *Reuben and the Blizzard.* Illus. by P. Buckley Moss. Intercourse, Pa.: Good Books, 1995.

———. *Reuben and the Fire.* Illus. by P. Buckley Moss. Intercourse, Pa.: Good Books, 1993.

Goss, Linda, and Clay Goss. *It's Kwanzaa Time!* Illus. by award-winning artists. New York: Putnam, 1995.

Greenberg, Melanie Hope. *Aunt Lilly's Laundromat.* Illus. by author. New York: Dutton, 1994.

Hamanaka, Sheila. *Bebop-a-Do-Walk!* Illus. by author. New York: Simon & Schuster, 1995.

Heo, Yumi. *Father's Rubber Shoes.* Illus. by author. New York: Orchard Books, 1995.

Jacobs, William Jay. *Ellis Island: New Hope in a New Land.* New York: Charles Scribner's Sons, 1990.

Kalman, Esther. *Tchaikovsky Discovers America.* Illus. by Laura Fernandez and Rick Jacobson. New York: Orchard Books, 1995.

Knight, Margy Burns. *Who Belongs Here? An American Story.* Illus. by Anne Sibley O'Brien. Gardiner, Maine: Tilbury House, 1993.

Krull, Kathleen. *City Within a City: How Kids Live in New York's Chinatown.* Photographs by David Hautzig. Lodestar Books, 1994.

Levinson, Riki. *Soon, Annala.* Illus. by Julie Downing. New York: Orchard Books, 1993.

Mitchell, Margaree King. *Uncle Jed's Barbershop.* Illus. by James Ransome. New York: Scholastic, 1993.

Moss, Marissa. *In America.* Illus. by author. New York: Dutton, 1994.

Orie, Sandra De Coteau. *Did You Hear Wind Sing Your Name?* Illus. by Christopher Canyon. New York: Walker, 1995.

Polacco, Patricia. *The Keeping Quilt.* Illus. by author. New York: Simon & Schuster, 1988.

Ringgold, Faith. *Tar Beach.* Illus. by author. New York: Crown, 1991.

Soto, Gary. *Chato's Kitchen.* Illus. by Susan Guevara. New York: Putnam, 1995.

Torres, Leyla. *Subway Sparrow.* Illus. by author. New York: Farrar, Straus & Giroux, 1993.

Waters, Kate, and Madeline Slovenz-Low. *Lion Dancer: Ernie Wan's Chinese New Year.* Photographs by Martha Cooper. New York: Scholastic, 1990.

Watson, Mary. *The Butterfly Seeds.* Illus. by author. New York: Tambourine, 1995.

Lesson 2

Looking at the Mid-Atlantic States Through Student-Selected Themes and Individual Investigations

Objectives

- to give students the option of choice in their learning
- to investigate a state or a geographic area in depth
- to refine reading, writing, speaking, listening, and thinking skills through geographic research
- to use personal judgment to select the most appropriate geographic theme or themes for the area being researched

Materials

- books, articles, tourist information, atlases, and other materials that will help students learn more about the selected area
- *Jamaica Louise James* by Amy Hest
- *Catskill Eagle* by Herman Melville
- *The Legend of Sleepy Hollow* retold by Will Moses
- *Hand in Hand: An American History Through Poetry* collected by Lee Bennett Hopkins
- *Celebrate America in Poetry and Art* edited by Nora Panzer

Motivator

Read several books about different areas of one state or of the region to pique students' interest. One group of titles might include *Jamaica Louise James* by Amy Hest to show one aspect of life in New York City related to the subways. *Catskill Eagle* by Herman Melville shows the area's marvelous mountain scenery. Finally, the classic *The Legend of Sleepy Hollow*, retold and illustrated by Will Moses, the great-grandson of Grandma Moses, could be enjoyed. Discuss the impressions of place that these books give listeners as they think about the state of New York.

For a change of pace, the teacher might read selections from the wonderful poetry book, *Hand in Hand.* Poems like "The Erie Canal," "Subways Are People," "Skyscraper," and "Song of Myself" might be thought-provoking choices. Another poetry option is the richly illustrated *Celebrate America.* Selections like Sandburg's "Niagara," Carol Snow's "Drumbeats," Lazarus's "The New Colossus," or Lehman's "Song of the Builders" would fit perfectly with images of these states.

Activity

Geographic Investigation Sheets

Place a number of Geographic Investigation Sheets (instructions to follow) out for students to browse through. Tell budding investigators that they can choose an area of particular interest for the next learning activity and become the resident expert in that area. They are to use the laminated investigation sheets as an aid for organizing their work but are free to discuss other options with the teacher. Include a request that students read a book connected with the area. They are to jot down anything they learned about the area from the book. In the process of doing further research, they are to check their first impressions to see if they were correct. A presentation of information will culminate their work. Students may negotiate how that will be done with the teacher, too. While this activity will be student generated, the teacher's careful planning will undergird the learning process.

To create the Geographic Investigation Sheets, type a guideline for each activity including a reminder to read a book, pertinent questions to think about, a suggested project to get students thinking about how they would like to present their knowledge to the class, and several helpful resources. Decorate the page in an appealing manner and glue to a piece of tagboard or to the inside of a file folder. Sheets might be laminated so that they will survive until another group uses them in the future. (See Appendix III for an example.) Here are some suggested ways to use the Geographic Investigation Sheets.

Pick a State

Students can select one of the five Mid-Atlantic states and research it geographically. How was it formed? What are its important natural resources? What role do those resources play in the day-to-day lives of the people who live in the state? How do people interact with the land in a positive or negative way? Could the state be considered a re-

gion? If so, how would the area be defined? (Teacher-generated guidelines like these would be listed on the Geographic Investigation Sheet for students to use.)

The Chesapeake Bay

Used for commerce, shipping, fishing, and vacationing by people and as full-time or temporary homes for a wide variety of wildlife, this is a fascinating area to research. How was the bay formed? Why is it an asset to people who live nearby? Could you give its absolute location? What is it like there? Have people changed it in any way? These are but a few questions that could be answered by the sleuths.

The Erie Canal

Here is a human-made canal that was quite a feat to build. Why was it built? What was the lay of the land that people had to deal with as they built the canal? What changed as a result of the canal? What are the advantages or disadvantages of its creation? How is it used today? After some reading, the investigator may have different directions of interest to pursue. Those should be checked out with the teacher to be certain the time being spent is being used wisely.

The Hudson and Potomac Rivers

What roles do either of these rivers play in the lives of people in the area? Who lives near them? Who settled there initially? How have people affected the rivers? What is it like along the shores of the rivers? What can you learn about the geographic life of a river?

Cities Through the Eyes of a Geographer

Cities like New York City and Buffalo, New York; Wilmington, Delaware; Bethlehem, Pittsburgh, and Philadelphia in Pennsylvania; or Annapolis, Maryland, are a few of the options open for investigation. Students might look at what it is like to live there, who lives there and why, how humans and location work together, where exactly is the city under investigation, and what keeps it alive.

Delmarva Peninsula

This unusual area is shared by Delaware, Virginia, and Maryland. It might be an interesting spot to learn more about. How large is the area? What does it look like? Who lives there? Why would a piece of land like this be important to three different states?

The Pine Barrens

The Barrens is an area in New Jersey that includes 1 million acres of forests, swamps, bogs, and some of the cleanest water on earth in the Cohansey Aquifer. It is a fabulous wetlands area that certainly has possibilities for geographic investigation.

The Coastline of the Mid-Atlantic States

Students might study the ocean floor in the area. In addition, they could investigate the way humans and animals interact with the land and ways to preserve it. What might be advantages and disadvantages of living in a shoreline community? Could it be defined as a distinct region? How would it feel to live there? If learners have had personal experiences with the shore, those insights could enrich the presentation.

Weather and Its Affect on People and the Land

Students might investigate weather throughout the area, comparing weather in several spots at several different times throughout the year and charting it for presentation. Hurricanes wreak havoc on communities in the region periodically. What causes them? Is geography affected by them? How far inland do they reach? Weather surely has an influence on what it is like to live in a place and bears investigation for this particular region.

These are but a few topics that students might explore. As the teacher talks through some of these options, students may come up with others. Have

them design the Geographic Investigation Sheet following those already completed so that it will help organize their research. Once it is approved, the sheet can be typed up by the teacher or student and tucked in a folder or laminated.

Books Used in This Lesson

Hest, Amy. *Jamaica Louise James.* Illus. by Sheila White Samton. Cambridge, Mass.: Candlewick Press, 1996.

Hopkins, Lee Bennett, coll. *Hand in Hand: An American History Through Poetry.* Illus. by Peter M. Fiore. New York: Simon & Schuster, 1994.

Melville, Herman. *Catskill Eagle.* Illus. by Thomas Locker. New York: Putnam, 1991.

Moses, Will, reteller. *The Legend of Sleepy Hollow.* Illus. by author. New York: Philomel, 1995.

Panzer, Nora, ed. *Celebrate America in Poetry and Art.* New York: Hyperion, 1994.

Suggested Companion Titles

Aliki. *Those Summers.* Illus. by author. New York: HarperCollins, 1996.

Ancona, George. *Riverkeeper.* Photographs by author. New York: Macmillan, 1990.

Aylesworth, Thomas G., and Virginia L. Aylesworth. *Mid-Atlantic: Delaware, Maryland, Pennsylvania.* New York: Chelsea House, 1991.

Bendick, Jeanne. *Exploring an Ocean Tidal Pool.* Illus. by Todd Telander. New York: Henry Holt, 1992.

Blos, Joan W. *The Days Before Now: An Autobiographical Note by Margaret Wise Brown.* Illus. by Thomas B. Allen. New York: Simon & Schuster, 1994.

Fredeen, Charles. *New Jersey.* Minneapolis, Minn.: Lerner, 1993.

Garland, Sherry. *The Summer Sands.* Illus. by Robert J. Lee. New York: Gulliver Green, 1995.

George, Jean Craighead. *To Climb a Waterfall.* Illus. by Thomas Locker. New York: Philomel, 1995.

Gillerman, Gayle. *The Reverend Thomas's False Teeth.* Illus. by Dena Schutzer. New York: BridgeWater Books, 1995.

Greene, Ellin. *The Legend of the Cranberry: A Paleo-Indian Tale.* Illus. by Brad Sneed. New York: Simon & Schuster, 1993.

Grimes, Nikki. *C Is for City.* Illus. by Pat Cummings. New York: Lothrop, Lee & Shepard, 1995.

Harding, Emma. *The Headless Horseman: A Retelling of Washington Irving's "The Legend of Sleepy Hollow."* Illus. by author. New York: Henry Holt, 1995.

Harness, Cheryl. *The Amazing Impossible Erie Canal.* Illus. by author. New York: Macmillan, 1995.

Harrison, Troon. *The Long Weekend.* Illus. by Michael Foreman. San Diego, Calif.: Harcourt Brace, 1994.

Hathorn, Libby. *Way Home.* Illus. by Gregory Rogers. New York: Crown, 1994.

Henderson, Kathy. *A Year in the City.* Illus. by Paul Howard. Cambridge, Mass.: Candlewick Press, 1996.

Hest, Amy. *How to Get Famous in Brooklyn.* Illus. by Linda Dalal Sawaya. New York: Simon & Schuster, 1995.

Hirschi, Ron. *Save Our Wetlands.* Photographs by Erwin Bauer and Peggy Bauer. New York: Delacorte, 1994.

Jakobsen, Kathy. *My New York.* Boston: Little, Brown, 1993.

Jauck, Andrea, and Larry Points. *Assateague: Island of the Wild Ponies.* New York: Macmillan, 1993.

Jenkins, Priscilla Belz. *Falcons Nest on Skyscrapers.* Illus. by Megan Lloyd. New York: HarperCollins, 1996.

Lee, Huy Voun. *At the Beach.* Illus. by author. San Diego, Calif.: Harcourt Brace, 1994.

Levine, Laura. *Ollie Knows Everything.* Illus. by Lynn Munsinger. Morton Grove, Ill.: Albert Whitman, 1994.

Macquitty, Miranda. *Ocean.* Photographs by Frank Greenaway. New York: Alfred A. Knopf, 1995.

Mitchell, Barbara. *Waterman's Child.* Illus. by Daniel San Sousi. New York: Lothrop, Lee & Shepard, 1997.

Rotner, Shelley, and Ken Kerisler. *Citybook.* Photographs by Shelley Rotner. New York: Orchard Books, 1994.

Rotter, Charles. *Hurricanes.* Mankato, Minn.: Creative Education, 1994.

Stein, R. Conrad. *New York.* Chicago: Children's Press, 1989.

Twist, Clint. *Repairing the Damage: Hurricanes and Storms.* New York: Dillon Press, 1992.

Closure and Culminating Activity

Parents can be invited to an evening celebration of learning in the classroom. They might be sent on a short, simple scavenger hunt to learn a little about the Mid-Atlantic states just like their children did. Students could put the absolute location note cards to use again, challenging or teaching parents to find the cities. Then they can sit back and listen to the geographic experts present the information they have gleaned on a particular area through song, poetry, charts, mural, short skit, or simple lecture. Students will already have had their final presentations approved by the teacher and have polished them for a smooth display of their knowledge. Serve a variety of simple Mid-Atlantic snacks and enjoy a lively, informative evening.

9

The Appalachian Highlands: North Carolina, Virginia, West Virginia, Kentucky, and Tennessee

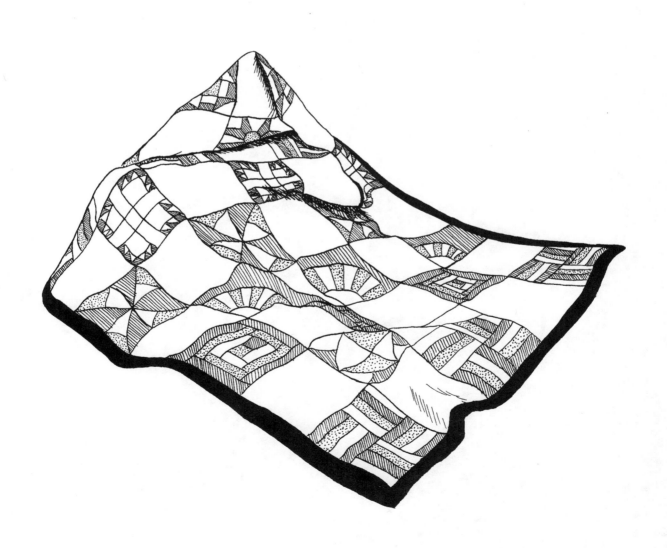

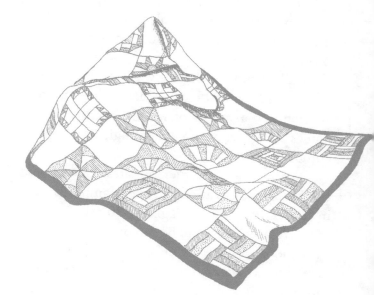

The closer one studies it, the more obvious it becomes that no matter which set of states or what area in North America is studied, something absorbing, beautiful, or of wonder is there. A riveting feature of this particular region, the 300-million-year-old Appalachian Mountains, demand respect and command attention as the Upper South is studied. Once thought to be as high as the Himalayas, these eroded elder statesmen of the mountains sweep through North Carolina, Virginia, West Virginia, Kentucky, and Tennessee, creating a stunning countryside filled with forested peaks, jagged ridges, and isolated deep, narrow valleys. People who choose to live in this mountainous country are hearty, self-reliant, independent individuals who seem to prefer a quieter pace of life.

To the east and west of the rugged Appalachian chain lies land more fertile and more hospitable than that of the mountains. Beyond the often mist-veiled Blue Ridge and Smokey Mountains to the east is the Piedmont Plateau including rolling, forested hills and fertile, farm-filled valleys. To the west of the mountains is the Bluegrass region of Kentucky and Tennessee. Here one finds some of the world's finest horse farms, crisply outlined with white fences. Tennessee walking horses thrive on the abundant bluegrass, which is filled with vital nutrients from the limestone bedrock from which it grows.

In addition, deep, vital coalfields dot the Upper South, bringing a livelihood to some, death to others, and scaring the landscape in the process.

Here the controversial practice of strip-mining is under fire because use of large machinery has replaced many a worker. It also razes the land, pollutes streams, and destroys farmland, forests, and numerous wildlife habitats. Geologists report that there is such an abundance of coal to be retrieved in both Tennessee and Kentucky that it could be mined by a more sensible means for hundreds of years to come.

To the east of the mountains in the Piedmont Plateau region of North Carolina and Virginia, white-pillared plantations sit in quiet elegance. These opulent homes are a testament to the successful tobacco and cotton farming of the past and present. Then, moving onward down onto the Atlantic Coastal Plain there are extensive swamps and lowlands like North Carolina's 750-acre Great Dismal Swamp. Overgrown with creeping vines and populated with knobby cypress trees, part of this amazing area is a refuge for hundreds of birds and other wildlife.

Finally, one reaches the coast, and it is an impressive one indeed. On the rugged Atlantic Coast the traveler faces the intimidating Outer Banks, the longest chain of barrier islands in the United States. Around these islands the treacherous shoals became the final resting place for many an ancient ship and sailor. The inlets and coves of these islands were once a hideout for the infamous Blackbeard and his band of pirates until the English killed him in the early 1700s. Islands like Assauteague and Chincoteague dotting the coast are home to a variety of wildlife including wild ponies. The area is popular to anglers and sports enthusiasts today.

Not to be outdone, there are sites below ground that demand one's attention like Mammoth Cave in Kentucky, a mind-boggling 330 miles of cavern systems, some yet to be explored. In Virginia's Shenandoah Valley, Skyline Caverns offers a spectacular sight. The ceilings are decorated with delicate anthodites: mineral "flowers" of snow-white calcite that grow minutely over thousands of years. Imagine this scene in the Grand Caverns of Virginia—considered so appealing they were used for candlelight dances during the Civil War. Humans could never create a ballroom equal to these extraordinary limestone creations, remnants of the work of an ancient sea. There seems to be no end to the marvels of the Upper South.

Nature takes center stage throughout the Upper South as truly spectacular scenery awaits the traveler or resident of this region. Rimmed with water, there is beauty to be found in the area rivers, lakes, and rocky Atlantic shoreline. Earthquake-created Reel Lake in northwest Tennessee is the winter home to approximately 200 bald eagles. Throughout the mountains, cascading waterfalls of varying sizes abound, like Blackwater Falls in West Virginia. No matter the size, they are demanding of a hiker's reflection. Another not-to-be-missed site is Cumberland Falls in Kentucky where a rainbow, or moonbow, can be seen through its mists during the full moon.

Armed with paintbrush, camera, or just an appreciation for the geography of the region, a traveler can revel in the colors and beauty no matter what the season. Flowers abound in the spring with the pinks of the rhododendrons and the lovely mountain laurel. The meadows in summer are filled with a variety of blooms including black-eyed Susans, goldenrod, and daisies. Fall has to be seen to be believed as the vibrant colors of the various hardwoods are contrasted with the greens of the pines, fir, and spruce. Mountains, valleys, lowlands, and swamps beckon the interested visitor. It is a truly spectacular part of the United States, attested to by the increasing number of tourists who visit this region each year.

Initiating Activity

The majority of time on this section of the United States will be spent in creating a book based on the Appalachian region. The cover of the book will be a quilt pattern like those done by hand over the years by Appalachian women. There are several ways the cover can be done. Using one of the patterns in Appendix III, enlarge the pattern on a photocopy machine to the appropriate size. Students can color it in attractively, cover each segment with pieces of colorful paper, or actually make a hand-stitched quilt square using the pattern as a guide.

If the latter option is chosen, write a letter to parents or guardians explaining the following project. Ask parents if they would contribute some fabric remnants purchased from the local sewing store or brought from home. They may also send in pieces of fabric from clothing no longer needed. Those pieces should be washed, pressed, and cut so that they lie flat. Since those used scraps are what most quilters took advantage of throughout the years, it would be fun to incorporate some into the quilt designs. Colorful paper and patterned gift wrap can also be contributed to make the designs. In addition, ask for parent volunteers to come to class to help assemble the covers at a later date.

Ask students to return the letters promptly. An organizational suggestion would be to collect materials as they arrive and store them in plastic tubs that students can browse through as they are thinking of colors and designs to be used in their quilt square.

To begin the study of these beauty-filled, historical states, hand each child a 36-inch length of string and a large button. The students are to thread the string through two of the holes in the button (if there are four holes, thread diagonally). Knot the ends of the string to form a loop. Holding the string between their thumbs and forefingers, students should whirl it around until it is tightly wound. Then, begin to pull the fingers toward each other and away, easing and increasing the tension on the string in the process. The button will start whirring and spinning. Explain that this simple toy was popular with some of the children in the Appalachian region in the past and may still be today. Tell the students they will be learning more about this region in particular, and the Upper South in general, during the upcoming unit. If students want to know more about other handmade toys, refer them to *Foxfire 6*, edited by Elliot Wigginton and Margie Bennett. It covers one hundred toys and games, including gourd banjos, song bows, and other absorbing topics.

Have the students tuck their new toys away and direct their attention to the bulletin board that is filled with travel brochures, maps, and captivating scenes from magazines like *National Geographic*. Point out the states to be studied on the classroom map, showing generally where Appalachia is. Then highlight some of the information on the bulletin board to give the learners an intriguing overview of the states in the Upper South.

To get the students thinking about quilting and to provide a glimpse of life in the hills of Appalachia, read *The Rag Coat* by Lauren Mills and discuss students' reactions. Invite quilters from the area in to talk to the students, display several quilts as they explain their craft, and give a brief history of some of the quilt patterns if possible. If the students are going to quilt the cover of their books, ask these talented stitchers if they would conduct a short workshop on how to quilt so that students can practice a bit before attempting their own quilt squares. The following patterns have been used over the years in Appalachia according to *Foxfire 9*, edited by Eliot Wigginton and Margie Bennett: Joseph's Coat of Many Colors, Monkey Wrench, Fishtail, Irish Chain, Grandmother's Fan, Log Cabin, Bear Paw, Churn Dash, Dresden Plate, and Spiderweb. Examples of several of these regional choices are located in Appendix III.

Lesson 1

Understanding the Appalachian Highlands Through the Themes of Location, Place, Human/Environmental Interactions, and Region

Objectives

- to locate the five states on personal outline maps of the United States

- to locate key geographic features in each state including rivers, lakes, mountains, and areas of mining/minerals as a means of learning what makes this group of states different from other groups of states

- to study this area in relation to key features that make Appalachia a unique region by looking at similarities and differences within the states
- to list characteristics of the land and characteristics of the people who live in the Appalachian region, noting how they both work together to help the people to survive
- to answer the question, What are the advantages and disadvantages to living here?

Materials

- individual student maps, pens or pencils
- students atlases or individual road maps of the states
- *Appalachia: The Voices of Sleeping Birds* by Cynthia Rylant
- *When I Was Young in the Mountains* by Cynthia Rylant
- *Pioneer Children of Appalachia* by Joan Anderson

Motivator

Read both of Cynthia Rylant's books aloud. As the teacher reads, students should jot down what life was like in the books. Listen for clues to questions like, How were family relationships portrayed? What kinds of things seem to be important to the people who live in this region? How would the students feel living in the hills and hollows as compared to where they live presently? Discuss reactions. Students will extend their learning about these people and the places in which they live as study continues.

Activities

Understanding the Lay of the Land

While students fill in their outline maps with key geographic features of the five states, play a tape of music featuring the dulcimer, banjo, mouth harp, or fiddle—instruments common to the Appalachian region. Listening to John Denver's "Country Roads," a song about West Virginia might be fun, too, or selections by Dolly Parton, a native of the region.

Getting a Sense of the Place and the People

Bring in a selection of fiction and nonfiction titles about Appalachia along with several Foxfire titles. As students read, have them fill in a two-columned sheet of notebook paper. One column lists characteristics of the region, the other, characteristics of the people. Sample observations about the geography might include: The area is relatively inaccessible; the valleys or "hollows" are narrow; the terrain is mountainous, which isolates people; and the availability of coal is the reason why some communities exist. As to the people who live there, they are independent and perhaps reserved with strangers, know about living off the land, choose a different lifestyle than people who live in bustling cities, enjoy nature and every season for what it offers, work with their hands, and are self-reliant. The picture books used illustrate closely knit families, love of the land, and strong religious ties, too.

After working for a designated period of time, ask students to share their observations. Two students, one per column, could record key points on a chart made of a large sheet of butcher paper hung in the front of the room. Discuss what students have discovered. Have each student write a reflective essay about what they have learned about this region called Appalachia and how they see the people and land interacting to support their lifestyle. Display the edited copies on a bulletin board created to introduce the area.

A Book of One's Own

Introduce the culminating project at this point so that students can begin thinking, planning, and gathering information as the whole region is being studied. Students will be writing a book, fiction or nonfiction, based upon some aspect of the highlands. The cover will be a quilt square stitched of fabric or made of colorful paper prints. Specific directions for completing the book can be found in Appendix III.

Explain that people of Appalachia are renowned for their craftwork when making toys, furniture, baskets, pottery, dulcimers, and quilts. Because quilts are a thread to understanding the people as they interacted with one another and with the geography over the years, students will be working with quilting in this section, too. In the process, students will be relating to their ancestors and emulating quilters of years gone by as they choose a quilt pattern and make a cover for their own books.

An Overview of the Project

Students are to select a quilt pattern and learn its name and a little history about it so that they can include a brief description on the inside of the front cover once it is done.

Decide on the kind of book to be done from the four options below:

1. Write a fictional story about a character who lives in Appalachia. The character needs to have a problem to solve or an interesting conflict to resolve to move the story along.
2. Address the rich history of this area by retelling several important events from the life of a well-known person from this region like Abraham Lincoln, George Washington, Thomas Jefferson, Davy Crockett, Booker T. Washington, Daniel Boone, or the Wright brothers. The setting of the story should reflect this region as do the illustrations.
3. Retell a well-known fairy tale or folktale but set it in the Appalachian highlands. Use examples like *Ashpet* by Joanne Compton or *Moss Gown* by William Hooks. Be certain to make appropriate changes in the tale like setting, dress, dialect, and historical period.

4. Write a book about "childhoods" using three generations of your family including yourself, one of your parents, and a grandparent, preferably of the same sex. Examine how life has changed for girls or boys over the years.

This is similar to the work done in the Foxfire books where students learn by doing and from people in the community by interviewing them about their lives. The Foxfire series or selected titles from it would be excellent to have on hand in the classroom as resources for both the students and the teacher.

1. Use the graphic organizer in Appendix III to structure the story.
2. Choose one of the five geographic themes to emphasize and weave into the story.
3. Make a "dummy" or practice copy of the book before the final copy is started. Use large sheets of newsprint divided into pages that are exactly the same size as the finished pages. Artists use these books to play around with text and illustrations, position and content until they get them just right. Then they proceed with the book. Directions for constructing the book are in Appendix III.
4. Time will be spent both in class and out working on the students' books. The stories will begin with the sequencing worksheet and be proofread as they develop. Students will lay out their final copies in a dummy made of newsprint, moving text and quickly sketching illustrations before deciding how the final book will be designed. Books will be made in class with the help of parent volunteers if possible.
5. Establish a schedule for when parts of the project are due: the cover and method of quilting, the story graphic organizer, the rough draft, the completed dummy, the final draft of the story, the session to work on final covers, and so forth.

6. Decide how to celebrate authorship. Final copies of students' books can be read to other classes or shared with parents at a Celebration of the Appalachian Highlands Gathering at the close of this segment.

Books Used in This Lesson

Anderson, Joan. *Pioneer Children of Appalachia.* Photographs by George Ancona. New York: Clarion Books, 1986.

Rylant, Cynthia. *Appalachia: The Voices of Sleeping Birds.* Illus. by Barry Moser. San Diego, Calif.: Harcourt Brace, 1991.

———. *When I Was Young in the Mountains.* Illus. by Diane Goode. New York: Dutton, 1982.

Suggested Companion Titles

Bates, Artie Ann. *Ragsale.* Illus. by Jeff Chapman-Crane. Boston: Houghton Mifflin, 1995.

Birdseye, Tom. *Soap! Soap! Don't Forget the Soap!* Illus. by Andrew Glass. New York: Holiday House, 1993.

Bradby, Marie. *More than Anything Else.* Illus. by Chris K. Soentpiet. New York: Orchard Books, 1995.

Bruchac, Joseph, and Gayle Ross. *The Story of the Milky Way: A Cherokee Tale.* Illus. by Virginia A. Stroud. New York: Dial, 1995.

Compton, Joanne. *Ashpet.* Illus. by Kenn Compton. New York: Holiday House, 1994.

Giblin, James Cross. *Thomas Jefferson: A Picture Book Biography.* Illus. by Michael Dooling. New York: Scholastic, 1994.

Gray, Libba Moore. *My Mama Had a Dancing Heart.* Illus. by Raul Colon. New York: Orchard Books, 1995.

Hooks, William H. *The Ballad of Belle Dorcas.* Illus. by Brian Pinkney. New York: Alfred A. Knopf, 1990.

———. *The Three Little Pigs and the Fox.* Illus. by S. D. Schindler. New York: Macmillan, 1990.

———. *Moss Gown.* Illus. by Donald Carrick. New York: Clarion Books, 1987.

Hopkinson, Deborah. *Sweet Clara and the Freedom Quilt.* Illus. by James Ransome. New York: Alfred A. Knopf, 1993.

Houston, Gloria. *My Great Aunt Arizona.* Illus. by Susan Conie Lamb. New York: Scholastic, 1992.

Isaacs, Anne. *Swamp Angel.* Illus. by Paul O. Zelinsky. New York: Dutton, 1994.

Johnston, Tony. *Amber on the Mountain.* Paintings by Robert Duncan. New York: Dial, 1994.

Kellogg, Steven. *Sally Ann Thunder Ann Whirlwind Crockett.* New York: Morrow Junior Books, 1995.

Lester, Julius. *John Henry.* Illus. by Jerry Pinkney. New York: Dial, 1995.

Lyon, George Ella. *Come a Tide.* Illus. by Stephen Gammell. New York: Orchard Books, 1990.

Ransom, Candance F. *When the Whipporwill Calls.* Illus. by Kimberly Bulcken Root. New York: Tambourine, 1995.

Schulz, Walter A. *Will and Orv.* Minneapolis, Minn.: Carolrhoda Books, 1991.

Van Laan, Nancy. *Possum Come a-Knockin'.* Illus. by George Booth. New York: Trumpet, 1990.

Wigginton, Eliot, and Margie Bennett, eds. *Foxfire 9.* New York: Doubleday, 1986.

———. *Foxfire 6.* New York: Doubleday, 1980.

Lesson 2

Looking at Coal and Strip-Mining in the Appalachian Highlands Through the Themes of Location and Human/Environmental Interactions

Objectives

- to plot geographic location of the minerals in each state on individual outline maps

- to write out the relative location of coal deposits in each state

- to investigate the origins of coal and explain the geology of one state in particular

- to research and report on better ways of mining coal in order to avoid pollution and the ravaging of the land
- to report findings on a chart with the theme of environmental impact of the mining process upon humans

Materials

- individual outline maps of the states grouped as a region
- student atlases, reference materials on coal and mining
- tagboard, markers, pictures and/or materials to create chart
- *Mama Is a Miner* by George Ella Lyon

Motivator

Read *Mama Is a Miner* to the students. Ask them to share three interesting things they learned about mining from this picture book. Invite students to share what they know about coal as a resource, how it is used, and if there are any drawbacks to using it.

Activity

A Closer Look at Mining

Explain how strip-mining is used as an alternative to underground mining. Tell the students that their task is to learn as much as they can about coal mining in general and this process in particular as they work in learning triads. After gleaning an understanding of strip-mining, each group is to note the advantages and disadvantages of this process. Point to address: Where are coal deposits located in the Upper South? Note them on regional outlines of the states. Be prepared to give their relative locations later when information is shared. Investigate how coal is formed, learning about the geology of this region in the process. In addition, check on present ways that the geography of the land can be mined with the least impact. Can learners find alternatives to mining coal that won't destroy and pollute?

Several groups might focus on one aspect of the research while other groups highlight different parts so that the same information is not repeated during class presentations. Using a chart as a concise visual aid, each group can share what was learned, followed by a general discussion to end this activity. Address key points including deaths, explosions, black-lung disease, destruction of the land, and effect on agriculture. In addition to resources in the school and local library, students can write to the following address requesting information about coal and coal-related activities:

Energy Information Administration
U.S. Department of Energy
Forrestal Building, EI-231
Washington, DC 20585
(202) 586-8800

An excellent catalog is available free from this group. It is entitled *Energy Education Resources, Kindergarten Through 12th Grade*. It was updated in February 1996 and contains a list of organizations that offer generally free or low-cost energy-related educational materials.

Book Used in This Lesson

Lyon, George Ella. *Mama Is a Miner*. Illus. by Peter Catalanotto. New York: Orchard Books, 1994.

Suggested Companion Titles

Brooks, Felicity. *Protecting Trees and Forests*. New York: Scholastic, 1991.

Fradin, Dennis B. *Kentucky*. Chicago: Children's Press, 1993.

Hansen, Michael C. *Coal: How It Is Found and How It Is Used*. Hillside, N.J.: Enslow Publishers, 1990.

Pack, Janet. *Fueling the Future*. Chicago: Children's Press, 1992.

Sirvaitis, Karen. *Tennessee*. Minneapolis, Minn.: Lerner, 1991.

Smucker, Anna Egan. *No Star Nights*. Illus. by Steve Johnson. New York: Alfred A. Knopf, 1989.

Stewart, Gail B. *Acid Rain*. San Diego, Calif.: Lucent Books, 1990.

Lesson 3

Looking at a Specific Region in the Upper South Through the Themes of Location, Human/Environmental Interaction, and Region

Objectives

- to locate on maps of the states grouped by region: the Cumberland Plateau, the Allegheny Mountains, the Piedmont Plateau, the Shenandoah Valley, the Atlantic Coastal Plain, and the Tidewater or Outer Banks
- to examine other regions of the Appalachian highlands in more detail
- to use travel brochures and maps to plan a vacation to one of the regions above
- to present the vacation package to the class in such an appealing way that others will want to go there

Materials

- outline map of the states in the Appalachian highlands
- travel materials from each state's Department of Tourism
- individual state maps
- *Stringbean's Trip to the Shining Sea* by Vera Williams and J. Williams
- paper, pencils, materials needed to plan a vacation for a family of four
- enough play money or a check written out to each child to equal $2,000

Motivator

Read *Stringbean's Trip to the Shining Sea* by Vera Williams and J. Williams. Stringbean went from Kansas to the Pacific Ocean. Tell the students that they are going to plan a vacation that may or may not include the sea, but that they will be heading east rather than west from wherever they live. Using play money or a "check," hand each student $2,000. This money is to be spent on a vacation for a family of four that will last a week or a little longer, depending on travel time to their destination. The destination will be one of the geographic areas in the Upper South like the Piedmont Plateau, the Shenandoah Valley, or the Atlantic Coastal Plain.

Activity

The Trip

1. Plan a car trip so that students practice using maps to figure mileage and route. They must decide how many hours they will drive per day and how long the trip will take just to reach their destination. Figure in gas, motel, and meals both coming and going and compare it to current airfares for a family of four. Which way would be the most economical?
2. Once they arrive, the family has five days to spend in the geographic region.
3. Figure money for meals, motel, gas, souvenirs, and entrance fees to various sites per day.
4. Tell the class why the area they chose appealed to them.
5. Present information in an appealing booklet, pamphlet, or poster decorated with pictures from travel brochures, sketches, and drawings.

Closure

Set aside a "Hear All About It: Vacation Travel Day." Students have an opportunity to "sell" the particular region and vacation they zeroed in on to the class as a package deal. They should use the large classroom map to trace their journey briefly from origin to destination. Then they can highlight their vacation activities.

Book Used in This Lesson

Williams, Vera, and J. Williams. *Stringbean's Trip to the Shining Sea.* Illus. by authors. New York: Scholastic, 1988.

Suggested Companion Titles

Aylesworth, Thomas G., and Virginia L. Aylesworth. *Atlantic: District of Columbia, Virginia, West Virginia.* New York: Chelsea House, 1991.

Kramer, Stephen. *Caves.* Photographs by Kenrick L. Day. Minneapolis, Minn.: Carolrhoda Books, 1995.

Mead, Robin, Polly Mead, and Andrew Gutelle. *Our National Parks.* New York: Smithmark, 1992.

Miller, Christina, and Louise A. Berry. *Coastal Rescue: Preserving Our Seashores.* New York: Atheneum, 1989.

Peterson, David. *Great Smoky Mountains National Park.* Chicago: Children's Press, 1993.

Pinkney, Gloria Jean. *Back Home.* Illus. by Jerry Pinkney. New York: Dial, 1992.

Reef, Catherine. *Monticello.* New York: Macmillan, 1991.

Robbins, Ken. *Make Me a Peanut Butter Sandwich and a Glass of Milk.* Illus. by author. New York: Scholastic, 1992.

Weber, Michael. *Our National Parks.* New York: Millbrook Press, 1994.

Wood, Jenny. *Caves: Facts, Stories, and Activities.* New York: Scholastic, 1990.

Culminating Activity

Upon completion of the books centering on Appalachia, it is time to celebrate being authors and learning about a fascinating region of the United States. Perhaps students will read their books to each other, to other classes, and to parents who come in to celebrate the learning with their children. Regional foods might be enjoyed along with quiet background music. Students might also like to highlight their vacation plans and other knowledge gleaned from studying the states in the Upper South.

10

The Southeastern States: Arkansas, Mississippi, Alabama, Georgia, South Carolina, Louisiana, and Florida

If students were to assemble a puzzle of the United States, it wouldn't be difficult to fit the southeastern states together. Their boundaries are distinctive, making the matching process relatively easy. No one could miss the boot shape of Louisiana, the nearly triangular South Carolina, or the peninsula of Florida jutting 400 miles out into a saltwater world. Rippled and ruffled, the Atlantic coastline is intriguing in itself. Havens for wildlife and pirates in the past, the bays and beaches beckon tourists today as do other areas of the Southeast. Much more than pieces in a national puzzle, however, these states are distinctive in themselves and interesting in combination.

Looking specifically at geographic features of the area, moving from mountains to sandy beaches, the first area to note is the mountainous region of Alabama, Georgia, and South Carolina. Here the southernmost ridges of the Appalachians stretch as far south as they are going to go. Arkansas can boast of mountains, too. There the Ozarks are appreciated for their beauty and for the practical hydroelectric power created along the fall line where the Ozark Plateau drops down to the coastal plain. Lower, and one step closer to the Atlantic Ocean, are the Piedmont foothills in South Carolina and Georgia. They lie between the mountains and the Atlantic or Gulf Coastal Plains. At this point the land throughout the region is basically flat. In fact, two-thirds of South Carolina is made up of the Atlantic Coastal Plain while the Gulf Coastal Plain borders the Gulf of Mexico in Louisiana, Mississippi, Alabama, and Florida. While the upper areas of the plains are fertile farmlands, the spots closer to the ocean where land is so low are filled with bogs, marshes, and swamps—home to a melange of plant and animal life. In fact, New Orleans is actually 5 feet below sea level protected by a series of levees that hold back the water. Speaking of low, Florida has the distinction of being the nation's lowest, flattest state. Once part of the sea bottom, it is a land of porous limestone whose pitted surface is filled with freshwater streams, rivers, ponds, and lakes tipped by the marvelous Everglades.

In the lowlands of the region there are four important wetland areas: Atchafalaya in Louisiana, Georgia's Okefenokee Swamp, Four Holes Swamp in South Carolina, and the famous Everglades in Florida. Islands string along the coastline, offering some protection from severe storms to coastline communities. Rich with timber and wildlife, the islands along the coast of South Carolina are also home to many of the Gullah people, descendants of those who were once slaves on plantations in the South. From top to bottom, mountain to island, the Southeast is a beautiful and productive region.

A key player in this part of the country is the Mississippi River. Over the years its flooding has left rich alluvial soils, which promote farming. One particularly rich area is called the Black Prairie, located in Mississippi and Alabama. In the Delta area of the South, the topsoil is an unbelievable 25 feet thick! Unfortunately, in the past, continuous planting of cotton crops throughout the area depleted the soil, forcing farmers to seek a living from other crops. The appearance of the destructive boll weevil in the 1900s sealed the decision to diversify. Today, crops like sugarcane, soybeans, rice, peanuts, peaches, and catfish come from this area. It is interesting to note that once a crop has been harvested, some enterprising Delta area farmers flood their fields and concentrate on a finned crop, raising catfish for a growing market.

It appears that not all of the change in diversity has been for the good. For instance, the poultry industry has become a major source of income in recent years. With this successful enterprise comes a problem as humans inadvertently change the environment. There is so much fertilizer from the chickens subsequently spread on farmers' fields that its chemicals are filtering into the lakes and rivers. As a result, more and more algae are growing in the water, clogging waterways and eventually suffocating fish. Solutions are being sought, and proper composting may be a means to reestablish a balance between humans and nature.

The feel of this place called the Southeast is different from that of other regions in the United States. Its warm, humid summers dictate a slower pace of life. History quietly asserts itself. One could easily imagine ghosts from the past gracing the dance floors of the lovely plantation homes or hear the bark of the auctioneer as slaves are heartlessly auctioned off. Antebellum plantations and lovely gardens depict a unique style of living and a sense of that era before the Civil War that still lingers.

It would be interesting to ask people what comes to mind when they think of the South. Reactions will be varied, no doubt, but images of Florida's Disney World, Spanish moss draping from live oaks, alligators, delectable seafood, miles of beaches, azaleas and fragrant camellias, and foot-stomping Cajun music might be suggested. Some might add that poverty and wealth live side by side while others remark about the lazy Mississippi, jazz, the French Quarter, Mardi Gras, pralines, and beignets and coffee at Cafe Du Monde in New Orleans. There's no place with the color and feelings evoked by the South.

Initiating Activity

Explain to the learners that during the Ice Age this whole area was dry land. The water level was lower then because water was frozen as part of the glaciers. As time passed and the glaciers melted, the water rose. Florida was long underwater as its limestone base formed from millions and millions of skeletons of sea creatures. Today, parts of that once dry land are still submerged, a continental shelf running along the coast. At one time woolly mammoths and saber-toothed tigers roamed the Florida coast, and bones discovered offshore attest to their lives. It might be fun to show Rafe Martin's captivating and imaginative *Will's Mammoth* to the class as an option for free time reading. This wordless book just might spark imaginations for work on the upcoming project.

Pass out a sheet of white paper to each student. It should be larger than 8½ by 11 so that students have plenty of room to work. They will need a pencil or pen, something with which to do some quick sketching. Ask students to close their eyes and visualize each of the states in the Southeast one at a time: Alabama, Arkansas, Louisiana, Georgia, Florida, and South Carolina. Tell listeners you are going to call out one of the states and they are to quickly sketch whatever comes to mind. Reassure the class that this is not a test but an opportunity to experience a sense of place, if they have one, for a state.

If students are stumped because of lack of background experiences, tell them to jot down thoughts that run through their minds and then wait for the next state to be called. At the conclusion of the activity, invite volunteers to share one sketch or thought as each state is discussed. Tally responses or reactions to each state to see with which one the students are most familiar. (Chances are it will be Florida if family vacations have taken them to Disney World.) Briefly describe the upcoming lessons that center on the southeastern states.

Lesson 1

Understanding the Southeastern States Through the Themes of Location, Physical and Human Characteristics, and Human/Environmental Interactions

Objectives

- to locate the southeastern states on individual outline maps
- to locate geographic areas on individual regional outline maps including the Appalachian, Blue Ridge, and Ozark Mountains; the Savannah, Tennessee, Arkansas, and Mississippi Rivers; the Mississippi Delta; the Piedmont Plateau; the Atlantic Coastal Plain; the Gulf Coastal Plain; the Everglades; the Gulf of Mexico; and the Atlantic Ocean
- to learn the key crops and industries that provide area jobs
- to investigate vacation opportunities that bring tourist dollars to each state, later concentrating on one state in particular
- to delve into one particular state and cull out a baker's dozen Fascinating Facts to teach the rest of the class
- to create a Topography, Tourists and Products Poster for a state of one's choice
- to participate in a Geographic Review and Art Show

Materials

- scratch paper to use for planning the layout of the exhibition map
- a variety of reference books and materials including student atlases
- paints, markers, colored paper, and other items to make the map
- *Celebrate America in Poetry and Art* by Nora Panzer
- *The Talking Eggs* by Robert D. San Souci

Motivator

Fill the student's minds with a variety of impressions of the southeastern states. Teachers might read a selection of poetry to give a sampling of this area. *Celebrate America in Poetry and Art* is inspiring because of the artwork as well as the poetry. A sampling might include "In Hardwood Groves" by Robert Frost, "At Sea" by Jean Toomer, "Front Porch" by Leslie Neson Jennings, "A Poem for Myself" by Etheridge Knight, and "A Lazy Day" by Paul Laurence Dunbar. Then switch gears and read the upbeat Cajun folktale, *The Talking Eggs* by Robert D. San Souci.

Discuss the poetry. What did students visualize as they heard the poetry? Then, after reading the Caldecott Honor Book, *The Talking Eggs,* ask for comments about a sense of place evoked by the tale and detailed illustrations. What do students think it would feel like to live in the South based upon the illustrations and story? Have students lived there and what can they share? Just what lessons can be learned from the folktale? Have any impressions of this area changed or been confirmed based upon vacation experiences? Advise the students to keep imaginations sharp and minds in high gear through the following lessons.

Activity

Topography, Tourists, and Products Poster

Each student is to pick a state and begin to research it using materials that have been collected in the classroom. They are looking at products produced in the state, the growth of industry and how it has affected people and the place they live, and vacation opportunities that would bring tourist dollars into the state. As they collect information and are ready to place it on their state map, they should set it up on a planning copy. Once the layout and ideas have been discussed with the teacher, the art can be started. Artwork might be done with collage, paints, or markers—whatever will best foster individual student creativity.

As students collect information, they will find some amazing tidbits that will go into their lists of Fascinating Facts. For example, in the late eighteenth century, the notorious Revolutionary War leader called the Swamp Fox hid in the swamps around South Carolina frustrating the British who were trying to capture him. In Arkansas there is a park called Crater of Diamonds State Park, which is the only place in North America where visitors can dig for diamonds and keep what they find. The longest overwater bridge in the world is the bridge or causeway across Lake Pontchartrain in Louisiana. It should be an absorbing search to unearth points of interest unique to the Southeast.

Basic Steps for This Activity

1. Conduct research.
2. Plan a copy of the state map. The background of the state is to reflect the topography of the land with mountains, major rivers, lakes, plains, large ports, and so forth. An elevation key should be included in the finished product.
3. Students are to keep notes on what they learn as they study their state, looking for a baker's dozen of Fascinating Facts that they think others would like to know.
4. For the final product, using a large sheet of study paper or tagboard, the students are to draw the shape of the state, filling it in to be as colorful and appealing as possible. It is going to become a part of a walk-through educational exhibit on the southeastern states.
5. The Fascinating Facts sheet is to be attached to the lower right-hand corner of the map so that students attending the exhibit can read it as they enjoy the informative map.
6. On the designated day, hang the maps around the room, place them on tables, or on as many easels as can be collected. Invite another class in to examine the artwork and ask questions of each student as they stand by their masterpiece. Play a variety of music from the South quietly in the background. It might include gospel, spirituals, jazz, West African rhythms, or the beat of brass bands. Once the Geographic Review and Art Show is over, the maps would make a wonderful display in the learning center.

Closure

Display the completed Topography, Tourists, and Products posters as suggested. Invite other classes in to preview the show. Each student will be standing by their creation to answer any questions. Finally, discuss the project in general with the class, checking what they learned in the process of completing the maps and what they would change to make the learning more worthwhile.

Books Used in This Lesson

Panzer, Nora. *Celebrate America in Poetry and Art.* Illus. by National Museum of American Art staff. New York: Hyperion, 1994.

San Souci, Robert D. *The Talking Eggs.* Illus. by Jerry Pinkney. New York: Dial, 1989.

Suggested Companion Titles

Aylesworth, Thomas, and Virginia L. Aylesworth. *The South: Alabama, Florida, Mississippi.* New York: Chelsea House, 1992.

Carson, Robert. *Mississippi.* Chicago: Children's Press, 1989.

Farris, Diane. *In Dolphin Time.* Illus. by author. New York: Four Winds Press, 1994.

Fradin, Dennis. *Georgia.* Chicago: Children's Press, 1992.

Fredeen, Charles. *South Carolina.* Minneapolis, Minn.: Lerner, 1991.

Hudson, Wade. *Pass It On: African-American Poetry for Children.* Illus. by Floyd Cooper. New York: Scholastic, 1993.

London, Jonathan. *Red Wolf Country.* Illus. by Daniel San Souci. New York: Dutton, 1996.

Martin, Rafe. *Will's Mammoth.* Illus. by Stephen Gammell. New York: Henry Holt, 1989.

Thomassie, Tynia. *Feliciana Feydra LeRoux: A Cajun Tall Tale.* Illus. by Cat Bowman Smith. Boston: Little, Brown, 1995.

Trosclair. *Cajun Night Before Christmas.* Illus. by James Rice. Gretna, La.: Pelican Publishing, 1992.

Lesson 2

Looking at the Southeastern States as a Region Through the Themes of Location, Place, and Region

Objectives

- to investigate the topography of the southeastern states
- to research and pick places of interest to include in a regional game
- to use state maps or atlases to figure mileage between locations and incorporate that information into the game
- to work as a team to create an educational and enjoyable learning experience for others
- to write coherent, sequenced instructions to the game
- to use teaching skills to instruct others in how to play the game

Materials

- paper, pens, tagboard, and other materials to create a board game
- old board games for reference and to evaluate
- *Mike Fink* by Steven Kellogg
- *Carolina Shout!* by Alan Schroeder
- atlases, tourist materials, road maps, and travel guides to discover places of interest to visit

Motivator

Read aloud the rambunctious *Mike Fink*, a tall tale told by Steven Kellogg. It is illustrated so imaginatively that it might inspire creative artwork for the game of the southeastern states that the students will be creating. Talk about the images of New Orleans that are presented through the tale. Then read *Carolina Shout!* to give students another image of the South. The text is short, the rhythm and beat are appealing, and the illustrations give listeners an idea of what the South was like at another time. Perhaps the people and their songs will work their way into the board games.

Activity

Creating a Game

Tell the students about the creative challenge ahead. Then bring out a number of board games for the students to dissect and study. The class may also bring in their own favorite board games from home. As the games are analyzed, record comments on the board. Zero in on what it is that makes these games enjoyable. Why are they challenging? How are the directions written? Is it easy to learn the game? How many can play at once? What do students like about the design of the game board? Based upon students' discussions, draw up the parameters of what elements should be a part of the regional board games they create.

Divide learners into groups based upon Lesson 1 in this chapter. Because each student will know quite a bit about one state from working on their Topography, Tourists, and Products poster, draw on that expertise by asking that each person in the group be from a different state. This way they can combine their areas of expertise and not have to start from scratch. Learning triads might be a good idea for grouping as each learner will have input in a smaller group. Use a variety of resource materials as games are created. Booklets sent from state tourism departments might have coupons that students could integrate right into their games, room rates that might be fun to use, or ideas for illustrations.

Initially, groups will meet to discuss the theme of their game. After consulting maps and other materials, they can jot down places to be included as part of the game. Topography, sites of interest, and natural disasters like floods, tornadoes, or hurricanes might be worked into the scenario. Requiring the game player to chant a verse as in *Carolina Shout!* or similar actions could be fun. Questions to be solved might include whether the game should be from one destination in one state to a final destination in another or be a round-trip. Decide as a group whether students must go through each state or just a few. Markers, spinners, dice, and other game pieces will need to be planned. When decisions are complete, the game will have to be designed. It should be sketched out on newsprint and carefully explained to the teacher before the artwork begins. The rules must be in readable rough-draft form to be perused by the teacher or parent helper. Then, the final version of both game and rules can proceed.

Closure

Have a morning or afternoon or two set aside so that students can play each other's games, cementing geography knowledge in the process. Games can be stored in a geography center and played during students' free time. Perhaps another class could come in and learn about the southeastern states via these games.

Books Used in This Lesson

Kellogg, Steven. *Mike Fink.* Illus. by author. New York: Morrow, 1992.

Schroeder, Alan. *Carolina Shout!* Illus. by Bernie Fuchs. New York: Dial, 1995.

Suggested Companion Titles

Cech, John. *Django.* Illus. by Sharon McGinley-Nally. New York: Four Winds Press, 1994.

Coles, Robert. *The Story of Ruby Bridges.* Illus. by George Ford. New York: Scholastic, 1995.

Crews, Donald. *Bigmama's.* New York: Greenwillow, 1991.

Harrell, Beatrice O. *How Thunder and Lightening Came to Be: A Choctaw Legend.* New York: Dial, 1995.

Hooks, William H. *Freedom's Fruit.* Illus. by James Ransome. New York: Alfred A. Knopf, 1996.

Hoyt-Goldsmith, Diane. *Mardi Gras: A Cajun Country Celebration.* Photographs by Laurence Migdale. New York: Holiday House, 1995.

Johnson, Delores. *Seminole Diary: Remembrances of a Slave.* Illus. by author. New York: Macmillan, 1994.

Ludwig, Warren. *Good Morning, Granny Rose: An Arkansas Folktale.* Illus. by author. New York: Putnam, 1990.

Miller, William. *The Conjure Woman.* Illus. by Teresa D. Shaffer. New York: Atheneum, 1996.

Ringgold, Faith. *Aunt Harriet's Underground Railroad in the Sky.* Illus. by author. New York: Crown, 1992.

San Souci, Robert D. *Cut from the Same Cloth: American Women of Myth, Legend, and Tall Tale.* Illus. by Brian Pinkney. New York: Philomel, 1993.

Schertle, Alice. *Down the Road.* Illus. by E. B. Lewis. San Diego, Calif.: Browndeer/Harcourt Brace, 1995.

Sneve, Virginia Driving Hawk. *The Seminoles.* Illus. by Ronald Himler. New York: Holiday House, 1994.

Weeks, Sarah. *Hurricane City.* Illus. by James Warhola. New York: HarperCollins, 1993.

Wiesner, David. *Hurricane.* Illus. by author. New York: Clarion Books, 1990.

Wright, Courtni C. *Jumping the Broom.* Illus. by Gershom Griffith. New York: Bradbury Press, 1994.

Zolotow, Charlotte. *The Seashore Book.* Illus. by Wendell Minor. New York: HarperCollins, 1992.

Lesson 3

Looking More Closely at the Wetlands in the Southeast in General and at the Everglades in Particular Through the Themes of Location, Place, and Human/Environmental Interactions

Objectives

- to locate the wetlands in the United States on students' state maps
- to devise a set of criteria defining wetlands
- to examine humans' effect on these wetlands and to look for solutions to protect this environment
- to create a mural illustrating the geography and life within the Everglades
- to share one book on the Everglades as a small group using drama or Readers' Theatre

Materials

- state maps or travel guides showing the location of wetlands
- a large piece of butcher paper for a mural of the Everglades
- art supplies
- reference materials and books on wetlands in general and the Everglades in particular
- *Everglades* by Jean Craighead George
- *Peach and Blue* by Sarah S. Kilborne

Motivator

Agree or Disagree

This activity should set the stage for thinking about the wetlands as an important region in the Southeast and in other areas of the United States. Ask for a panel of ten volunteers and have them line up in the front of the room. Each student will get to answer one question, supporting the answer that is given. The rest of the class will decide if they agree or disagree, writing their response on a piece of scratch paper. If they disagree, they must write why. After all ten questions have been asked and answered, discuss the responses. Then read the excellent book, *Everglades* by Jean Craighead George to begin study on a most unique geographic location.

Questions

1. There is only one environment like the Everglades in the whole world. *(agree)*
2. If you are careless when traveling in a swamp, you are likely to drown in quicksand. *(disagree)*
3. If it hadn't been for glaciers, many of the bogs in the United States wouldn't be here today. *(agree; glaciers gouged out basins in which bogs later formed)*
4. Along with nature, beavers, humans, and construction have helped to create some wetlands. *(agree)*
5. Three animals that are likely to be found in a wetland include ducks, crocodiles, and egrets. *(agree)*
6. The mangrove is the most abundant tree growing in the coastal saltwater swamps. *(agree)*
7. Two ways humans can damage the wetlands are by digging canals and draining the water and by allowing pesticides and fertilizers to leach into the water. *(agree)*
8. The bog turtle, alligator, whooping crane, and green pitcher all live in wetlands and are not endangered. *(disagree)*

9. Two large bodies of water where there are saltwater wetlands in the United States include the Atlantic Ocean and Gulf of Mexico. *(agree)*
10. For every one hundred birds that lived in the Everglades in the 1960s, only three to five live there today. *(agree)*

Activities

Wetlands: Where Are They?

Wetlands exist in the following states: Nebraska; the Prairie Pothole Region in parts of Iowa, Minnesota, North and South Dakota, and three provinces in Canada; Boston, Massachusetts; Chesapeake Bay, Maryland; Dismal Swamp in North Carolina; Four Holes Swamp in South Carolina; Georgia's Okefenokee Swamp; Everglades in Florida; Atchafalaya in Louisiana; Big Thicket in Texas; Pine Barrens in New Jersey; Alakai in Hawaii; San Francisco Bay area in California; and Yukon Flats in Alaska. Using detailed state maps or tourist guides for these states, have the students locate the wetlands and put them on their United States maps.

Wetlands: What Are They?

Gather materials to describe wetlands as a region. One question to be answered is, Do they have common characteristics? Some generalizations learners can draw are that wetlands can be marshes, swamps, or bogs. It is common to have changing water levels and waterlogged soil in these areas but they are not wet all of the time. This region is an important habitat to a plethora of plants and animals, some of them now endangered.

Another question to research is, Why are wetlands beneficial? One idea is that coastal wetlands can be buffers from storms that blow in from the sea. In addition, their land and plants filter pollutants out of the water, purifying it as some is used for drinking water. Finally, they prevent dangerous flooding as the water is able to spread out over a large, low area rather than battering land, causing erosion, or flooding communities.

Are Wetlands All the Same?

Students might want to define marsh, bog, and swamp. They will learn that freshwater marshes make up about 90 percent of the wetlands in North America. Thick clumps of soft-stemmed plants like grasses, rushes, sedges, cattails, waterlilies, arrowheads, and other nonwoody types of plants grow here. Bogs are acidic freshwater wetlands with a buildup of peat, which is rich organic material made of partially decayed plant material. In some bogs this peat can be over 40 feet thick. They are found in colder regions of the world where there is very little movement of water. Black spruce, orchids, bladderworts, and pitcher plants are common in bogs. Finally, swamps might be characterized by wetlands that are filled with shrubs and trees. While they are saturated with water during the growing season, they may dry out late in summer. They may have anywhere from a foot to 4 feet of water. Water willow, inkberry, bald cypress, red maple, and cottonwood are common trees growing in swamps.

Creating a Classroom Everglades

To get the students looking at the Everglades with keen eyes, read *Peach and Blue* by Sarah S. Kilborne. It leaves the listeners with a sense of appreciation for things seen every day and taken for granted. They should apply that fresh sight to the Everglades project. Students can work in teams dividing up the task of making a large group mural of the Everglades for the classroom wall. They might elect to start from the bottom up, investigating the soil and plants under the water, then the plants and animals in the water, and finally all on the ground. Each student might research a plant and an animal that live in the Everglades and add it in appropriate places on the mural. Information can be gleaned by using the books suggested and other resources found in the school's learning cen-

ter. An articulate guest speaker knowledgeable about the wetlands would strengthen students' understanding of these areas.

As learners rebuild the Everglades on the classroom wall, they can look for reasons why the area is endangered, what is critical to the survival of this unique area, and what is being done to preserve it. Discuss that information when the mural is complete. In her book, *Everglades*, Jean Craighead George calls this unusual ecosystem "a kaleidoscope of color and beauty." The students should strive to make their mural just that.

For information about Everglades National Park, one of the students can write to:

Everglades National Park
P.O. Box 279
Homestead, FL 33030

Closure

Discuss what was learned about the Everglades during the creation of the mural. How can humans repair the damage that has been done to this fragile environment and to others like it in the United States?

Books Used in This Lesson

George, Jean Craighead. *Everglades.* Illus. by Wendell Minor. New York: HarperCollins, 1994.

Kilborne, Sarah S. *Peach and Blue.* Illus. by Steve Johnson with Lou Fancher. New York: Alfred A. Knopf, 1994.

Suggested Companion Titles

Appelt, Kathi. *Bayou Lullaby.* Illus. by Neil Waldman. New York: Morrow, 1995.

Asch, Frank. *Sawgrass Poems.* Illus. by Ted Levin. San Diego, Calif.: Harcourt Brace, 1996.

Guiberson, Brenda Z. *Spoonbill Swamp.* Illus. by Megan Lloyd. New York: Henry Holt, 1992.

Kroll, Virginia. *Sweet Magnolia.* Illus. by Laura Jacques. New York: Charlesbridge, 1995.

Lavies, Bianca. *Mangrove Wilderness: Nature's Nursery.* New York: Dutton, 1994.

Lourie, Peter. *Everglades: Buffalo Tiger and the River of Grass.* Honesdale, Pa.: Boyds Mill Press, 1994.

Luenn, Nancy. *Squish! A Wetland Walk.* Illus. by Ronald Himler. New York: Atheneum, 1994.

Patent, Dorothy Hinshaw. *Ospreys.* Photographs by William Munoz. New York: Clarion Books, 1993.

Staub, Frank. *America's Wetlands.* Minneapolis, Minn.: Carolrhoda Books, 1994.

Culminating Activity

Enjoy a sharing day where students act out, pantomine, or try a Readers' Theatre with a picture book or novel on the southeastern states. In Readers' Theatre the students write and build their own scripts, using the dialogue directly from a book with lots of dialogue and an exciting plot. A narrator sets the scene based on information taken from the story. Students do not memorize their lines, but they do need to be familiar with them so that they are able to read with expression. No sets, costumes, or staging are required. Instead, students stand in front of the class and interpret the story through their readings. Invite another class in to watch the performances and to learn about more wonderful books to read.

11

Alaska and Hawaii

The study of Alaska and Hawaii, the two youngest members of the United States, is going to take geographic investigators from one extreme to the other in a number of respects. In the process of learning about these two very different regions, students will spend time on relatively small tropical islands and traverse broad expanses of frozen tundra, intimidating mountains, and mammoth glaciers. What a contrast! They will bask in soft, balmy weather and wander along black sand beaches in Hawaii. They will then learn that it is not wise to step out-of-doors when temperatures plummet to minus fifty degrees Fahrenheit in northern Alaska, but be sure not to miss the northern lights, nature's fabulous light shows. One way to approach these two states is with a general description of each, considering the similarities and differences afterward through student activities.

If you had two cents to spare in 1867, you could have purchased an acre of land in the then Russian territory of Alaska. The vast and magnificent wilderness, once called Seward's Folly, was purchased by Secretary of State Seward in 1867 from Russia for $7.2 million amidst much ridicule and disbelief. Why would one ever want this huge chunk of snow-filled land? Today, this "last frontier" has proven its worth time and time again. In terms of the geographic theme of movement, there are changes to note over the years as adventurers and businesspeople sought out Alaska's riches.

The people who have moved to Alaska could be classified as hearty, enterprising, spirited types.

Depending on where they choose to locate, Alaskans need to adjust to nights without darkness and months when the sun rarely shines. As people have moved to the land, change has followed in their footsteps. Consider the salmon industry: First came the fishermen. When the industry began to flourish, canneries were built bringing more people to the coastal regions. Small towns sprang up and arrangements for transporting the fish were put into place. One thing seemed to lead to another and wilderness was replaced by humanity.

Men and women came to this land for other reasons, too. In the late 1800s, men dreaming of riches headed for the goldfields in Nome and Fairbanks. Loggers sought jobs near Juneau. During the Depression, Oklahoma dust bowl farmers and their families moved to the Matanuska River Valley to farm. They reveled in the nineteen-hour, sun-filled days in the summer and were immensely pleased with the mammoth vegetables that grew as a result. And Alaska had even more to offer.

When gas and oil were discovered on the North Slope in the Arctic Circle in late 1960, Prudhoe Bay became a town where the especially resilient lived. Here the temperature can reach minus one hundred degrees Fahrenheit with windchill, and winter is an enemy with whom to be reckoned. To get access to the wealth of natural gas and oil in such inhospitable land, people put their heads together. The resulting Trans-Alaska Pipeline across the almost permanently frozen land was an amazing feat. What an example of humans adapting to the physical environment! One negative impact of humans' movement to this particular area was the tragic oil spill from the grounded Exxon *Valdez* tanker. Here our effect upon the environment in Prince William Sound, Alaska, was dismal to say the least.

Such an immense land, but only 599,591 people live here. Spreading the population out across the state, it averages out to one person per square mile. Wildlife like grizzly bears, polar bears, caribou, sea otters, beluga whales, penguins, and walruses vastly outnumber human beings. The greatest concentration of people is in the southern part of the state although people are scattered at great distances from each other in tiny villages throughout the land. The best mode of travel, whether traversing perpetually frozen tundra, avoiding slowly moving glaciers, or circumventing heavily forested lands, is by airplane. In fact, one out of every fifty people in the state is licensed to fly. Perched up near the top of the earth, the "Land of the Midnight Sun" is a fascinating place.

In sharp contrast to Alaska is an archipelago, a close group of small islands, that makes up the state of Hawaii. These islands were settled by Polynesians over 1,000 years ago and have seen many changes in the population and leadership since then. This multiculturally diverse fiftieth state is really not a part of the continent of North America at all. It lies scattered for 1,523 miles from the first island to the last across an expanse of the Pacific Ocean. Of the 132 islands that make up the state, only 8 are of an appreciable size. The major islands include Hawaii, Maui, Kahoolawe, Lanai, Molokai, Oahu, Kauai, and Niihau. Growing slowly up from a hot spot in the ocean floor over millions of years, these islands were created by volcanoes. They are actually the tops of immense volcanic mountains, part of a 1,500-mile undersea mountain range.

In terms of geographic diversity, these islands have rainforests, areas almost as dry as the desert, and light snow atop the summits of peaks like Mauna Loa and Mauna Kea. There are lush forested areas where 2,500 varieties of plants grow, and grow only here and nowhere else. Parker Ranch, the largest cattle ranch in the United States, is located on the plains of Hawaii, the Big Island. In the state of Hawaii there is fertile farmland to be had and coastal beaches that draw an incredible number of tourists yearly. From the tips of the volcanic peaks to the shallows on the sparkling beaches, this temperate region is truly a tropical paradise.

Each island is distinctive in its own right. For example, Lanai is called the Pineapple Island because of the huge pineapple plantations there. It is owned by the Dole Company. Oahu is the most populated island and is where Honolulu, the state capital, is located. Popular attractions on the island are Diamond Head, a 760-foot tall volcano; Pearl Harbor and the Memorial to the USS *Arizona;* and the beaches near large hotels to attend the ever-popular luau. Kauai, the setting for the movie *South Pacific,* boasts of rolling farmlands filled with sugarcane. Mount Waialeale, the wettest spot on earth, is on this island. Rainfall here measures between 400 and 450 inches a year. Nicknamed the "Garden Island," it was discovered by British Captain James Cook in 1778. Cook's arrival here and those that followed after him reflect how movement, in the form of explorers and other adventurers, irrevocably changed the lives of the natives who lived on the islands. Newcomers arrived, inadvertently bringing diseases like cholera and measles. As a result, many natives lost their lives and those who remained lost their island paradise. Obviously, change is not always for the better. Each of the islands has its own story to tell, and the students will find them appealing.

Hawaii is the newest state geologically and it is still growing. There is even a new island on the way. Named Loihi Seamount, it is located 20 miles southeast of Hawaii and is still underwater at this point. It will surface after stretching up about a half mile more, which could take as little as 2,000 years or as many as 20,000 depending on the volcanic activity that is fueling its growth. The Aloha State—what a place! Students will enjoy ferreting out information on each unusual piece of Hawaii.

Initiating Activity

Explain to the class that they are going to be playing an imagination game. They are to close their eyes and listen as various items are described. As they listen, they are to try to paint a visual picture in their minds in reaction to the words. Start with a herd of caribou, the kind of gear used to climb an icy mountain; 20,320-foot-high Mount McKinley; the northern lights; a totem pole; a ride on a dog sled; and a musk ox. Now create an image with a beach made of black sand, tall palm trees swaying in the wind, and a volcano erupting. Tell listeners to think of tastes like juicy pineapple, fresh, sweet coconut, and crunchy macadamia nuts. Now ask the listeners to open their eyes, take out a sheet of paper, and list the things they had trouble visualizing. Discuss those items together and show pictures to support the learning by using books or magazines like *National Geographic*.

Next, have learners put images into words. Give them prompts such as to list what they would wear if they had to walk to school when it is minus twenty-five degrees Fahrenheit. What would they do if they lived in a place where the sun didn't come up in its regular pattern for six months? After a short time, ask them to switch their thinking and imagine six months of sunshine, twenty-four hours a day. What about surfing? How might that feel to skim over the tops of rolling waves? As they write, ask them to think about what they might hear during some of these experiences as well. Ask students to share some of their descriptions. Tell the students they have been reacting to bits of life in Alaska and Hawaii and testing what they know about these two states in the process. Now it is time to learn a little more about each state.

Students might enjoy the opportunity to ask their questions firsthand by writing to pen pals. This could be arranged by the teacher before the study of these two states begins. If students have access to computers and the incredible Internet options, they might be able to carry on their correspondence via electronic e-mail or a chat group.

Lesson 1

Looking at Alaska Through the Themes of Location, Place, Human/Environmental Interactions, and Movement

Objectives

- to give the relative location of Alaska
- to locate the mountain systems that traverse Alaska: Saint Elias Range, Wrangell Mountains, Aleutian Range, Alaska Range, and Brooks Range
- to locate the Aleutian Island chain, the Pacific Ocean, Bering Sea, Bering Strait, Gulf of Alaska, and Arctic Ocean

- to locate major cities including Nome, Fairbanks, Juneau, Point Barrow, Prudhoe Bay, and Valdez, and important rivers like the Yukon River, Tanana River, and Kuskokwuim River
- to investigate the climate of Alaska, noting temperature ranges, annual rainfall in three student-selected locations, and deciding where the most temperate regions of the state are
- to learn what life is like in one part of the state and compare it to life where the student lives; just how do people and place interact?

Materials

- outline maps of Alaska, student atlases
- travel guides, information from offices of tourism, fiction and nonfiction books on Alaska
- *This Place Is Cold* by Vicki Cobb
- *Go Home, River* by James Magdanz

Motivator

Read *This Place Is Cold* by Vicki Cobb. In a pleasing manner, the book gives listeners an idea of what it is like to live in Alaska. Then share *Go Home, River,* a turn-of-the-century story about a young Eskimo boy who goes on a geographic journey across the mountains to the beginning of a river. Historically accurate and appealing, both culture and geography are illuminated by reading this new book.

Activities

What Goes Where?

Initially, ask the class to write down the relative location of Alaska. Talk about their explanations before moving on to the more specific locations. Using blank outline maps of Alaska and student atlases, locate the geographic places listed in the objectives. During that process, ask the students

to study the topography of the land and notice where most of the population seems to be concentrated. While they are engaged in their initial geographic work, tell them to pick a spot they would like to learn more about. Review the locations as a group using the large classroom map before moving into individual explorations of a place of interest.

What Is It Like There?

Students are to look for information about a city or an area that intrigues them in Alaska. They are to learn about the climate, average rainfall, daily life, how people support themselves, how they travel from place to place, and what forms of recreation there are. Once everyone has gathered information about their spot, spend some time having conversations. Students might sit in groups of three or four and tell what they learned about one spot in particular. Then, staying in the same group or switching groups, direct the conversations to what they have learned about Alaska in general. The teacher can move between the clusters of children listening to their talk. If any misconceptions occur, correct them before joining another group.

Childhood Days in Alaska

Using all of the materials available to them, encourage students to learn as much as they can about being a child in Alaska. In a journal entry, have them discuss what they have learned, how life is different from where they currently reside, and speculate about what they like best about living in each place.

Partial Closure

Since the study of these two states is not concluded yet, it might be helpful to quickly review what has been completed thus far, outline what will be continued with Hawaii, and tell the learners that there are a couple of larger projects yet to come.

Books Used in This Lesson

Cobb, Vicki. *This Place Is Cold*. Illus. by Barbara Lavallee. New York: Walker, 1989.

Magdanz, James. *Go Home, River*. Illus. by Dianne Widom. Seattle, Wash.: Alaska Northwest Books, 1996.

Suggested Companion Titles

Bernhard, Emery. *Reindeer*. Illus. by Durga Bernhard. New York: Holiday House, 1994.

———. *How Snowshoe Hare Rescued the Sun: A Tale from the Arctic*. Illus. by Durga Bernhard. New York: Holiday House, 1993.

Carlstrom, Nancy White. *Northern Lullaby*. Illus. by Leo Dillon and Diane Dillon. New York: Philomel, 1992.

Conway, Diana Cohen. *Northern Lights: A Hanukkah Story*. Illus. by Shelly O. Haas. Rockville, Md.: Kar-Ben Copies, 1994.

Damjan, Mischa. *Atuk*. Illus. by Jozef Wilkon. New York: North-South Books, 1996.

Dixon, Ann. *How Raven Brought Light to People*. Illus. by Jim Watts. New York: McElderry Books, 1992.

Hoyt-Goldsmith, Diane. *Arctic Hunter*. Photographs by Lawrence Migdale. New York: Holiday House, 1992.

Jessell, Tim. *Amorak*. Illus. by author. Mankato, Minn.: Creative Education, 1994.

Joose, Barbara M. *Mama, Do You Love Me?* Illus. by Barbara Lavallee. New York: Chronicle Books, 1991.

Kendall, Russ. *Eskimo Boy: Life in an Inupiaq Eskimo Village*. New York: Scholastic, 1992.

Kroll, Virginia. *The Seasons and Someone*. Illus. by Tatsuro Kuichi. San Diego, Calif.: Harcourt Brace, 1994.

Kusugak, Michael. *Northern Lights: The Soccer Trails*. Illus. by Vladyana Krykorka. Willowdale, Ont.: Annick, 1994.

Miller, Debbie S. *A Caribou Journey*. Illus. by Jon Van Zyle. Boston: Little, Brown, 1994.

Murphy, Claire Rudolf. *A Child's Alaska*. Photographs by Charles Mason. Seattle, Wash.: Alaska Northwest Books, 1995.

Owens, Mary Beth. *A Caribou Alphabet*. Illus. by author. New York: Farrar, Straus & Giroux, 1988.

Petersen, Palle. *Inunguak: The Little Greenlander*. Illus. by Jens Rosing. New York: Lothrop, Lee & Shepard, 1993.

Philip, Neil. *Songs Are Thoughts: Poems of the Innuit*. Illus. by Mary Claire Foe. New York: Orchard Books, 1995.

Renner, Michelle. *The Girl Who Swam with the Fish: An Athabascan Legend*. Illus. by Christine Cox. Seattle, Wash.: Alaska Northwest Books, 1995.

Sloat, Teri. *The Hungry Giant of the Tundra*. Illus. by Robert Sloat and Teri Sloat. New York: Dutton, 1993.

Winslow, Barbara. *Dance on a Sealskin*. Illus. by Teri Sloat. Seattle, Wash.: Alaska Northwest Books, 1995.

Lesson 2

Looking at Hawaii Through the Themes of Location, Place, and Human/Environmental Interactions

Objectives

- to give the relative location of Hawaii in relation to North America
- to locate the eight main islands, the major cities of Honolulu, Hilo, Kailua, Kaneohe, and Waipahu, the Pacific Ocean, the Kaukonahua Stream, the Wailuku River, and the Waimea River
- to learn what it is like there using both fiction and nonfiction books
- to pick a special spot and learn about it, pinpointing it on a large map of Hawaii for others to see

Materials

- blank outline maps of Hawaii, travel guides, and student atlases

- brochures, information from offices of tourism or travel agencies
- a large outline map of Hawaii with a blue background on the bulletin board
- fiction and nonfiction books on both countries
- *Luka's Quilt* by Georgia Guback

Motivator

Introduce the students to Hawaii by reading *Luka's Quilt* to the class. The illustrations are done with collage, a technique the students might want to try in future projects. This is a delightful story of relationships and compromise, filled with the flavor of life in Hawaii.

Activities

A Brief Topography Lesson

Have the students describe the relative location of the state of Hawaii as compared to the other United States to each other. Work together to write the best location on a piece of tagboard and include

it on a bulletin board about this state. Locate the other features listed in the objectives and have students look at the topography of the state as they work. Check the points by having students locate each place on a classroom map in a quick review.

If You Could Go Anywhere

Give the class time to browse through the books and tourist materials available in the classroom. Tell them to pick one spot that strongly appeals to them. They are to learn as much as they can about it, write a summary of what they have learned on a card about the size of a 5-by-8-inch index card, and add that card to the bulletin board. Using yarn, the student can pinpoint the spot he or she has researched and attach the card to it so that other students can read about it, too. Another option is to present the information in one of the book forms suggested in Appendix III and tack the completed books to the bulletin board.

Book Used in This Lesson

Guback, Georgia. *Luka's Quilt*. Illus. by author. New York: Greenwillow, 1994.

Suggested Companion Titles

Aylesworth, Thomas G., and Virginia L. Aylesworth. *The Pacific*. New York: Chelsea House, 1992.

Coste, Marion. *Nene*. Illus. by Cissy Gray. Honolulu: University of Hawaii Press, 1993.

Fradin, Dennis Brindell. *Hawaii*. Chicago: Children's Press, 1994.

Johnston, Joyce. *Hawaii*. Minneapolis, Minn.: Lerner, 1995.

Lovett, Sarah. *Kidding Around the Hawaiian Islands*. Illus. by Michael Taylor. Santa Fe, N.Mex.: John Muir Publications, 1990.

Nunes, Susan. *To Find the Way*. Illus. by Cissy Gray. Honolulu: University of Hawaii Press, 1992.

Rattigan, Jama Kim. *Dumpling Soup*. Illus. by Lillian Hsu-Flanders. Boston: Little, Brown, 1993.

Comparing and Contrasting Alaska and Hawaii Through the Themes of Place, Human/Environmental Interactions, and Movement

Objectives

- to study the topography of each state by creating a map of salt dough, painting it topographically, and identifying each island, major bodies of water, key mountains, and major cities in both states
- to learn more about Alaska and Hawaii through comparison and contrast
- to identify and apply the geographic themes during state presentations

Materials

- *The Sleeping Lady* by Ann Dixon
- *Flight of the Golden Plover: The Amazing Migration Between Hawaii and Alaska* by Debbie Miller
- the books and materials for Lessons 1 and 2
- materials to make salt dough, lightweight boards for the maps' foundations
- paper and art supplies for creating a Quilt of Comparisons and Contrasts

Motivator

Read *The Sleeping Lady* by Ann Dixon to the students. In this pourquoi tale, it is revealed that Alaska's Mount Susitna is really a woman, one of the giant people who once resided in Alaska. She is sleeping while patiently waiting for her lover, but he was killed as he carried out a mission of peace. The illustrations are done in a native folk style to portray the people of Alaska and their land. This delightful folktale can pull students further into the study of the state as students begin to

compare and contrast Alaska and Hawaii. Then, to connect the two states, read *Flight of the Golden Plover* by Debbie Miller, which tells of a tiny shorebird that migrates between Alaska and Hawaii each year. The illustrated map and color illustrations make this nonfiction selection appealing.

Activity

Building a State

This activity will involve both Alaska and Hawaii and four groups of students. Using a favorite salt dough recipe, two groups will be building replicas of Hawaii and two will be constructing Alaska. With all of their mountains, loose pieces in the forms of islands, and interesting shapes, these two states just beg to be re-created out of salt dough. After creating the states, painting them to indicate topography, and labeling important points from their individual outline maps, students can focus on the next step.

For the next activity two of the groups will be in charge of planning dream tours, one group working on Alaska and the other on Hawaii. Cost must be explained as the tour proceeds, but just for fun it will not be a factor. Tours must include something for everyone so they should be informative and filled with play time as well. Students can plan the trip together, making an outline to guide them first. As the tour develops it would be wise to discuss it with the teacher. Each student will be responsible for a part of the tour when it comes to their presentation, so they should all be well informed. The group should practice once the tour is complete, so that the presentation goes smoothly.

On presentation day the group from Hawaii could come dressed for the trip, and bring a suitcase of collected props like suntan lotion, sunglasses, beach towel, camera, sun hats, snorkeling gear, and so forth. Some of the same items might be chosen by the group from Alaska, but wool clothing, fishing pole, boots, and thermometer would be more appropriate. Perhaps each group should have a large stack of play money, too! At the appropriate times during each tour, these items could be pulled out of the suitcase and worked into the presentation. The salt dough map can be used as students show the route of the tour.

The remaining two groups can look at the native people and what they do in each state, environmental issues, or movement of people and products. For example, one student may come to class dressed as a worker on the Alaska pipeline. He or she will have researched gas or oil as a natural resource, the work that went into building the pipeline, the conditions under which people worked, and the value of that natural resource to the rest of North America. That student would show where he or she lives as a worker and where the products can be found on the salt dough map. Both people and products exemplify movement in this case.

Several students might work on a collage of plants and animals that live in Hawaii, discuss their importance, and review any environmental concerns. Another pair of students might enjoy researching the games that Eskimo children play, like high kick. They could demonstrate and then teach the class. Before the day of the group presentations, students can decide how best to arrange themselves to teach the specifics that they have learned in an appealing fashion.

Books Used in This Lesson

Dixon, Ann. *The Sleeping Lady.* Illus. by Elizabeth Johns. Seattle, Wash.: Alaska Northwest Books, 1994.

Miller, Debbie. *Flight of the Golden Plover: The Amazing Migration Between Hawaii and Alaska.* Illus. by Daniel Van Zyle. Seattle, Wash.: Alaska Northwest Books, 1995.

Suggested Companion Titles

Ewing, Susan. *Lucky Hares and Itchy Bears.* Illus. by Evon Zerbetz. Seattle, Wash.: Alaska Northwest Books, 1996.
Griese, Arnold. *Anna's Athabaskan Summer.* Illus. by Charles Ragins. Honesdale, Pa.: Boyds Mill Press, 1995.
Heinrichs, Ann. *Alaska.* Chicago: Children's Press, 1991.
Helman, Andrea. *O Is for Orca: A Pacific Northwest Alphabet Book.* Photographs by Art Wolfe. Seattle, Wash.: Sasquatch Books, 1995.
Patent, Dorothy Hinshaw. *Humpback Whales.* Photographs by M. Ferrari and D. Glocknew-Ferrari. New York: Holiday House, 1989.
Rand, Gloria. *Aloha, Salty!* Illus. by Ted Rand. New York: Henry Holt, 1996.
Smith, Roland. *Sea Otter Rescue.* New York: Cobblehill Books, 1990.
Turbak, Gary. *Ocean Animals in Danger.* Illus. by Lawrence Ormsby. Flagstaff, Ariz.: Northland, 1994.

Culminating Activities

A Huge Venn Diagram

As a class, fill in a large, bulletin board–size Venn diagram as Alaska and Hawaii are compared and contrasted. This is an excellent way to check learning to this point and to get a sense of what else might be covered before moving on to another part of the country. (See Appendix III for an example.) The teacher could ask for volunteers, one student at a time, to discuss a similarity or difference. If the rest of the class agrees that this is an important criterion to consider, that student writes it on the Venn diagram. Climates, topography, lifestyles, earthquakes, volcanoes, tsunami, environmental issues, and foods might be some of the topics covered.

Once this review has been completed, give the students time to reflect in their journals. Give them the prompt that they have just received a wonderful opportunity to go to Alaska or Hawaii, the state of their choice. They are to write about which state that would be, what the opportunity would be, and how they would adjust to life there.

Creating a Quilt of Comparisons and Contrasts

Using squares of paper as quilt squares, students can create a quilt of Alaska and Hawaii together. The outer rings will reflect the uniqueness of place in each state, what it is that makes them different. As the squares move into the center, the similarities will be emphasized. For instance, both areas are volcanic, both have islands, both have rainforests, both have some snow, and both consider the oceans as a part of people's lives. The quilt will be based upon work previously done with Venn diagrams, as students look at similarities and differences in such things as topography and climate, jobs and leisure time, environmental issues, or what it is like for a child to live there. A neatly written explanation can accompany the finished product when it is displayed.

As a grand celebration, bring in another class and give them a dream tour of Alaska and Hawaii. Highlight the quilt if one was made. Several students might enjoy reading a favorite book from each state as well.

12

An Introduction to Our Neighbor to the North: Canada

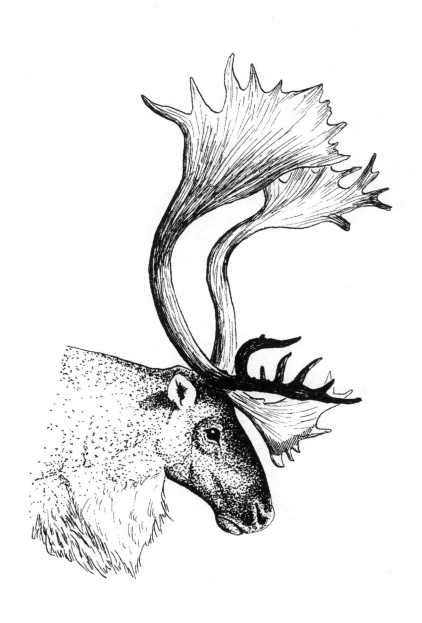

The second largest country in the world is right here in North America. It shares the border with the United States and is called Canada. This immense country is filled with a staggering number of freshwater lakes, many yet unmapped and unnamed. It is a land edged by a 150,000-mile jutting, curving, and indented coastline. Amazingly, that coastline would encircle the world six times if it was pulled and stretched out into a straight line. Here is a country shaped by glaciers that sculpted the craggy Rocky Mountains, the ragged coastlines, numerous riverbeds and lakes, and deposited rich, invaluable soil on the prairie lands of Manitoba, Saskatchewan, and Alberta. This is a region of swiftly running rivers that fuel hydroelectric power for incessant human consumption. Within the land is a wealth of minerals, oil, and natural gas. There is an extensive thickly forested wilderness where a dwindling number of grizzlies still make their homes, and a lush rainforest where Douglas firs over 600 years old dwell. Cattle ranches and golden, wheat-filled prairies roll on and on for as far as the eye can see. Canada could be likened to a kaleidoscope of different provinces, people, and products. As kaleidoscope pieces shift and reshape themselves, a vision of a country of contrasts emerges.

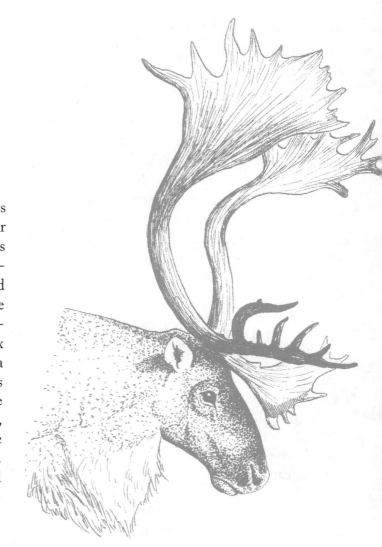

Consider the fact this is the second largest country in the world, about 3,849,954 square miles, and yet it has relatively few predominant cities. Some of the largest and busiest include Ottawa, Quebec City, Toronto, Montreal, Halifax, and Yellowknife. Despite its size, this sweeping land is sparsely populated, especially in the more northern climates where people outnumber the bears by only four to one! In fact, the entire population of Canada, approximately 27 million people could comfortably fit into the state of California, whose current population is close to 30 million A country of wide open spaces is an apt description of the neighbor to the north.

Canada is a country of one contrast after another. In the north the winters are so severe that one could get frostbite in a matter of minutes or face death in the blast of a winter blizzard if care is not taken. Yet in Alberta, it is habitually sunny and temperate. Another climate change occurs when journeying to the Pacific Coast's rainforests, which will envelop the visitor in dense, mossy greenery and moist air. Then, too, there is the bustle of traffic and milling crowds, steel and glass buildings in the metropolitan areas, as contrasted with the miles and miles of gently rolling prairie or animal-dominated wilderness. The ancient rock of the Canadian Shield where little vegetation can take root contrasts vividly with the orchards in the river valleys and fertile farms of the prairies. Solitude or city crowds, seashore or jagged, snow-covered mountain peak—the list could go on and on as one investigates Canada, just over the border, north of the United States.

Initiating Activity

As the study of the United States concludes, ask for a student volunteer to write to the Canadian Consulate General at the address below and request travel materials to be used in the study of Canada. Since it takes two to three weeks to receive most tourist information, it is wise to write well ahead of time:

Canadian Consulate General
Tourist Division
550 S. Hope Street
Los Angeles, CA 90071
(213) 346-2700

Before the study of Canada begins, prepare a colorful bulletin board to highlight new vocabulary that might be encountered as students tackle learning about this country. Top with a catchy title and scatter words across the board written in large print or script on colored slips of paper, tagboard, or index cards. Be sure there is enough room on each card to include a student-generated definition. Then, cover the bulletin board with a cloth sheet or pieces of butcher paper. On the outside of the cover print a curiosity-inducing warning not to peek. The time of the unveiling might also be listed. Some suggested words include:

archipelago
chinook
Cordilla
coulee
curling
Free Trade Pact
hoodoo
Inuit
Klondike
"Land of the Midnight Sun"
Metis
Mounties
mukluk
nomadic
Nunavut
parliament
permafrost
pingoes
province
soapstone
subarctic
tundra
voyageurs

Briefly introduce Canada to the students. Because students will probably be covering new terrain, support their knowledge base with a video overview of the country. An area travel agent or the local library might be a resource for an up-to-date video journey across Canada.

An excellent book that will continue the discovery of this wonderful country is *Selina and the Bear Paw Quilt* by Barbara Smucker. Each picture is beautifully framed by a handmade quilt square, a lovely way to enhance both the story and illustrations. Explain that the class will be moving from the United States to Canada, in a sense, just like Selina, encountering some unknowns along the way. One of those unknowns will be unique vocabulary words. At this point, unveil the bulletin board. Read through the words. Tell the class that they will come across these words in their research. The first student to "discover" a word will take the word from the bulletin board, write an understandable definition, and then return the word to the board. At a specified time each day, the teacher might announce a vocabulary break. At that point, the students will teach their words to the class and discuss them as need be.

Put a large piece of paper up entitled Cultures. Draw students' attention to it. Ask them to keep a running list of the different cultures they encounter in their reading. The list will be a starter for the next activity and will plant the idea that Canada is a country of many cultures. The teacher can add to the list as necessary before the second activity.

Lesson 1

Looking at Canada Through the Themes of Location, Place, Movement, and Human/Environmental Interactions

Objectives

- to map the provinces and territories of Canada
- to chart the topography of Canada including the Rocky Mountains, St. Lawrence Seaway, the Great Lakes, Hudson Bay, Lake Winnipeg, Canadian Shield, the Arctic, the Atlantic and Pacific Oceans, prairie lands, and rainforests
- to research an area or key topic on Canada and present that information to the class in an innovative way
- to look for similarities between Canada and the United States as far as topography, movement of people, and cultural makeup of the inhabitants
- to discuss and evaluate the interactions of people and place within Canada as compared to that of the United States, looking for similarities and differences between the two countries

Materials

- books, travel booklets, maps, road atlases, student atlases
- large outline map of Canada created by the students
- art supplies to fill in the map
- T-shirts, safety pins, note cards
- *The Cremation of Sam McGee* by Robert Service
- *O Canada* by Ted Harrison

Motivator

In your best dramatic voice, read *The Cremation of Sam McGee* written by Canadian author Robert Service and illustrated by Canadian illustrator Ted Harrison. It is a poetic, humorous introduction to the frigid winters in the Yukon during the mad rush for gold. Then, share parts of Ted Harrison's picture book, *O Canada*. Using the title of the Canadian national anthem, the book proceeds to give a brief introduction to the Canadian provinces. The text complemented with bright, full-page paintings is an excellent preview of information about this expansive country. The words and music to the anthem are included in the book and might be fun for the class to learn at some point.

Activity

Looking at Canada
from Topography to Towns
Before starting this activity, label index cards or squares of colored paper with the following

provinces, places, or things of importance in Canada. Color-code the provinces that should be grouped together in their particular region as noted below. Use colored dots in the corner of the cards or coordinate colored index cards for each grouping. Students will make their presentations based upon these coded cards.

Regions
Atlantic Region, the Canadian Shield, the Lowlands, the Interior Plains, the Cordilla, the Arctic

Atlantic Provinces
Newfoundland (including Labrador), Nova Scotia, New Brunswick, Prince Edward Island

Canada's South
Ontario, Quebec

Prairie Provinces
Manitoba, Saskatchewan, Alberta

Pacific Coast
British Columbia

Far North
Yukon, Northwest Territories

Key Cities
Ottawa, Quebec City, Toronto, Montreal, Halifax, Yellowknife

Places and Things.
Point Pelee, rainforests, St. Lawrence Seaway, Great Lakes, Hudson Bay, Transcontinental Highway, railroads

Place the prepared cards facedown on a large table and let each student pick one. Places and things to examine in Canada can be adjusted according to the number of students in the class. Using materials gathered from the school learning center, public library, and tourist bureaus, stu-

dents can pursue their topics. To organize the work, students can brainstorm a list of points to research. These can be written on a large classroom chart for all to follow. In a more teacher-directed approach, the teacher might choose to develop a "guide for knowledge" instead, and include the following:

- Name of region, province, or city
- Location and size
- General information: well organized and presented in a lively manner
- Category called "Imagine That!" to include some especially interesting pieces of information

If students are learning about one of the cities, they should investigate the history and growth and answer the question, Why here? Bodies of water might be explained in light of their uses, how people and places interact, what the water means to the area surrounding it, and what the role of pollution is. For students looking at the railroads or highways, they might focus on the history behind their development and construction, how the land has changed as a result of their existence, and what their importance is to the people of Canada.

On the days set aside to learn from each other, the students who are presenting might come to class in oversized T-shirts. On the shirts can be safety-pinned notecards with clever snippets of information shaped like the object to be discussed, thus making the student a walking and talking piece of Canada. Some of the special pieces might be removed, discussed, and then glued in an appropriate spot of the relatively blank outline map of Canada, which was created by the students and is large enough to fill a large bulletin board or a classroom wall. Filling it in as they go, the students doing regions should go first, coloring in or painting in the topography ahead of their actual presentations to save time. The order of the remaining presentations can be varied, but might be waterways, provinces, cities, and transportation. Canada as a place will be emerging right before the students' eyes.

Closure

As discussion occurs following each segment, ask students to look for similarities with the United States. For instance, review where the prairie lands are and what crops are grown there. Draw a connection to the rainforest in Washington. Discuss the size of some of the cities in the United States as compared to those in Canada, or the location and effect of the Rocky Mountains on the development of a state. Consider the role played by rivers and lakes in both countries. This activity will build important knowledge connections between the two neighboring countries.

Books Used in This Lesson

Harrison, Ted. *O Canada.* Illus. by author. New York: Ticknor & Fields, 1993.

Service, Robert. *The Cremation of Sam McGee.* Illus. by Ted Harrison. New York: Greenwillow, 1987.

Smucker, Barbara. *Selina and the Bear Paw Quilt.* Illus. by Janet Wilson. New York: Crown, 1995.

Suggested Companion Titles

Bannatyne-Cugnet, Jo. *A Prairie Year.* Illus. by Yvette Moore. Plattsburgh, N.Y.: Tundra Books, 1994.

———. *A Prairie Alphabet.* Illus. by Yvette Moore. Plattsburgh, N.Y.: Tundra Books, 1992.

Bouchard, David. *If You're Not from the Prairie …* Illus. by Henry Ripplinger. New York: Atheneum, 1995.

Butler, Geoff. *The Killick: A Newfoundland Story.* Illus. by author. Plattsburgh, N.Y.: Tundra Books, 1995.

Cooper, Michael. *Klondike Fever: The Famous Gold Rush of 1898.* New York: Clarion Books, 1989.

Deschamps, Yvon. *The Montreal of My Childhood.* Illus. by Antonio De Thomasis. Plattsburgh, N.Y.: Tundra Books, 1994.

Fox-Davies, Sarah. *Little Caribou.* Illus. by author. Cambridge, Mass.: Candlewick, 1996.

Godkin, Celia. *Wolf Island.* Illus. by author. New York: Freeman, 1993.

Hancock, Lyn. *Nunavut.* Minneapolis, Minn.: Lerner, 1995.

Harrison, Ted. *Children of the Yukon.* Illus. by author. Plattsburgh, N.Y.: Tundra Books, 1991.

Haskins, Jim. *Count Your Way Through Canada.* Illus. by Steve Michaels. Minneapolis, Minn.: Carolrhoda Books, 1989.

Hutchins, Hazel. *Tess.* Illus. by Ruth Ohi. New York: Annick Press, 1995.

Jam, Teddy. *The Year of the Fire.* Illus. by Ian Wallace. New York: McElderry Books, 1993.

Kalman, Bobbie. *Canada, the Land.* New York: Crabtree, 1993.

Kurelek, William. *A Prairie Boy's Winter.* Montreal, Que.: Tundra Books, 1996.

LeVert, Suzanne. *Let's Discover Canada: British Columbia.* New York: Chelsea House, 1991.

Lourie, Peter. *Yukon River: An Adventure to the Gold Fields of the Klondike.* Illus. by author. Honesdale, Pa.: Boyds Mill Press, 1992.

Murphy, Wendy, and Jack Murphy. *Toronto.* New York: Blackbirch Press, 1992.

Oberman, Sheldon. *The White Stone in the Castle Wall.* Illus. by Les Tait. Plattsburgh, N.Y.: Tundra Books, 1995.

Rotter, Charles. *The Prairie.* Mankato, Minn.: Creative Education, 1994.

Sateren, Shelley Swanson. *Canada, the Star of the North.* New York: Benchmark Books, 1996.

Taylor, C. J. *How We Saw the World: Nine Native Stories of the Way Things Began.* Illus. by author. Plattsburgh, N.Y.: Tundra Books, 1995.

Lesson 2

Understanding Canada Through the Themes of Place and Movement as They Relate to Cultural Diversity

Objectives

- to learn what it is like to live in Canada by examining its cultures
- to compare Canadian cultures to cultures within the United States
- to recognize that cultural diversity is inherent in Canada's population
- to reaffirm how cultural diversity can both divide and enrich life
- to prepare a Cultural Taste Fest to savor popular cultural foods

Materials

- recipes, cookbooks, cooks from different cultures if possible
- selected books and materials about the different cultures in Canada
- *The Ghost and the Lone Warrior* by C. J. Taylor

Motivator

Read *The Ghost and the Lone Warrior* by C. J. Taylor to the class. Discuss the fact that Native Americans were the first residents in Canada as they were in the United States. The Inuit or Eskimos arrived first, followed later by French explorers and trappers, the British, and then many other nationalities. This is truly a country of immigrants as less than 2 percent of the people today are descendants of the original Native Americans or Inuit. In fact, people in Canada find it difficult to describe the nature of their country in a word or two because of the diversity of its people. It has been likened to a patchwork quilt where the topography is the background and the unique faces of the people create appealing designs on each patch. After their work during this segment, ask the students if they agree with the patchwork image.

Tell the learners that they are going to get a better sense of what it is like to live in Canada from a cultural perspective. Remind them that culture includes many facets. The food one eats, the clothes worn, the stories told, and dances and music played are part of one's roots. Customs, traditions, religions, and even types of buildings are additional elements that make each culture unique. Send students on a quest to study as many facets as possible as they learn about Canada through its people.

Activity

A Closer Look at Cultures

Working in pairs, the students can investigate a culture from those the students have discovered in their work and listed on the chart mentioned earlier. The teacher can add to the list if it is not representative of the cultures of the country. Through a chart, collage, or straightforward report, pairs are to share their knowledge. The information might include when their group emigrated to Canada, why they came, where they chose to live in general, which festival or holiday they are known for, and what delicious recipe represents their culture.

Closure

Discuss the multicultural look of Canada and compare it to that of the United States. Then, plan the Taste Fest. Decorate the room with colors, symbols, and pictures representing the cultures to be celebrated. Share information about special festivals, a unique belief, and something especially interesting that students learned about the culture they researched. Ask for parents' help for creating a feast that shows the diversity of Canada. Invite another class to be guests, treat them to a bit of information about the culture, and enjoy the feast.

Book Used in This Lesson

Taylor, C. J. *The Ghost and the Lone Warrior.* Illus. by author. Plattsburgh, N.Y.: Tundra Books, 1991.

Suggested Companion Titles

Ekoomiak, Normee. *Arctic Memories.* Illus. by author. New York: Henry Holt, 1990.

Greene, Jacqueline Dembar. *Mamabozho's Gifts: Three Chippewa Tales.* Illus. by Jennifer Hewitson. Boston: Houghton Mifflin, 1994.

Greenwald, Barbara. *A Pioneer Story.* Illus. by Heather Collins. New York: Ticknor & Fields, 1995.

Harrison, Ted. *A Northern Alphabet.* Illus. by author. New York: Tundra Books, 1982.

Kalman, Bobbie. *Canada Celebrates Multiculturalism.* New York: Crabtree, 1993.

———. *Canada, the Culture.* New York: Crabtree, 1993.

Kinsey-Warnock, Natalie. *Wilderness Cat.* Illus. by Mark Graham. New York: Cobblehill Books, 1992.

Kusugak, Michael Arvaarluk. *Baseball Bats for Christmas.* Illus. by Vladyana Krykorka. Willowdale, Ont.: Annick Press, 1990.

Larry, Charles. *Peboan and Seegwun.* Illus. by author. New York: Farrar, Straus & Giroux, 1993.

Malcolm, Andrew H. *The Land and the People of Canada.* New York: HarperCollins, 1991.

Prentzas, G. S. *The Kwakuitl Indians.* New York: Chelsea House, 1993.

Reynolds, Jan. *Frozen Land: Vanishing Cultures.* San Diego, Calif.: Harcourt Brace, 1993.

Rodanas, Kristina. *Dance of the Sacred Circle: A Native American Tale.* Illus. by author. Boston: Little, Brown, 1994.

Taylor, C. J. *Bones in the Basket: Native Stories of the Origin of People.* Plattsburgh, N.Y.: Tundra Books, 1994.

Towle, Wendy. *The Real McCoy.* Illus. by Will Clay. New York: Scholastic, 1993.

Culminating Activities

Geography Game

The popular game, Trivial Pursuit®, was invented by four creative Canadians. After studying the game a group of students might like to invent a version on Canada for the classroom. Using the five basic themes of geography as the foundation, students could pull in trivia on categories including provinces, cultures, topography, vacation options, and children's authors. The game board could be patterned after the one in Trivial Pursuit. Cards might be made out of 3-by-5-inch index cards. Some of the cards could review information from presentations while others could stretch students' learning, without being too far-fetched, of course. The finished product can be tested and refined by class members and stored for continued enjoyment in the class geography center.

Students might write a poem using the diamond-shape format that follows. It enables them to look at the contrasts in Canada in a poetic way. Large 5-by-8-inch index cards cut into diamond shapes work well to display the completed poetry. The poem can be written neatly on the lined side of the card and illustrated attractively on the blank side. Four or five poems can be grouped together to form a mobile using a hanger as a base. It can then hang from the classroom ceiling.

Pattern to follow:

1. Choose a noun about Canada that has an opposite. Write the first noun down. Skip down seven lines and write the opposite noun.
2. On the second line, write two adjectives describing the first noun.

3. On the third line, write three participles (verbs ending in -ing or -ed).

4. On the fourth line, write down four nouns related to Canada. The second two nouns have opposite meanings from the first two as meanings now switch to the final noun in line seven.

5. On the fifth line, write three participles further indicating change or development of the last opposite noun. If -ing endings were used in line three, stay with them.

6. On the sixth line, write two adjectives carrying the idea of change toward the opposing noun.

7. Illustrate the blank side of the diamond.

Enjoying Canada Through Its Authors

A sampling of Canadian authors might include:

James Houston

Houston's books about survival and Inuit legends make fascinating reading about life in the frozen Canadian Arctic like *Frozen Fire, The Falcon Bow,* and *Black Diamonds: A Search for Arctic Treasure.*

Jan Hudson

This author wrote *Sweetgrass* and *Dawnrider,* two excellent novels that take the reader back in time to the Blackfoot tribe.

Jean Little

Gradually losing her sight over the years hasn't deterred this wonderful author. Enjoy her poetry in *Hey World, Here I Am!,* the more thoughtful *Mama's Going to Buy You a Mockingbird,* or her autobiography entitled *Little by Little.*

Janet Lunn

Readers can learn about Canada's history through *Shadow on the Bay,* do some time travel to the Civil War era with Rose in *The Root Cellar,* or experience Christmas in the Canadian wilderness in *One Hundred Shining Candles.*

Lucy Maud Montgomery

Written in 1908 about a young orphan girl, *Anne of Green Gables* continues to be a book that is much loved by many readers. It may just be the most famous of Canadian children's books. Anne has been brought to life on the stage in Canada's longest-running musical, for thirty-plus years and continuing. Students can read this and Montgomery's seven sequels, learn about life on Prince Edward Island through the books and an additional bit of research, and present the author and the heroine to the class. Students can write for a visitor's guide to Prince Edward Island at this address:

Visitor Services
P.O. Box 940
Charlottetown, Prince Edward Island
Canada C1A7M5

Another way to bring any of these books to life is by acting out a bit of the story through Readers' Theatre.

Robert Munsch

Author of a number of books including *Love You Forever, Millicent and the Wool, The Paper Bag Princess, Show and Tell,* and *Thomas' Snowsuit.* A brief introduction from *Something About the Author,* usually found at the local library, might precede a play. *The Paper Bag Princess* is great fun acted out through Readers' Theatre.

See Appendix II for other talented authors who will shed light on Canada through their novels.

ABC Book

Prepare an ABC book about Canada patterned after *A Prairie Alphabet* or *A Northern Alphabet* by Ted Harrison. Students will pull together all they have learned together in the process. Each student could take a letter or work in pairs on the project, depending on the size of the class and look at multiculturalism, the land itself, or plants and animals of Canada to complete the book. Share the books in class and with other classes.

13

An Introduction to
Our Neighbor to the South:
Mexico

In the 1970s, the Mexican Tourism Department used the slogan "So near, and yet so far" to promote tourism to its country. What a thought-provoking slogan. Tourists have no trouble finding Mexico and many leave a part of their hearts behind when they return home. Countless inhabitants of the country's crowded cities are so eager to leave, they are willing to be smuggled into the United States. They are looking for a better life for themselves and their families. Mexico is a beautiful country that has a long way to go to solve some monumental problems. "So near, and yet so far." It might be interesting to have students respond to that slogan after taking a closer look at a country of promise.

The total longitude distance from north to south, border to border in Mexico is 1,250 miles. From its greatest distance east to west, the unusually shaped country measures 1,900 miles. If one decided to walk those miles the traveler would cross mountains, deserts, rolling hills, broad expanses of plains, and flourishing rainforests. Beneath the land is a wealth of natural resources like silver, oil, coal, iron, forests (which are dwindling at an alarming rate), and seafood. A long, somewhat horn-shaped country, this neighbor to the south of the United States draws an endless stream of tourists to its temperate climate to visit ancient ruins, bask in the sun, and unwind in popular resorts like Acapulco and Cancun. Mexico is a country of contrasts, beauty, and history that continues to intrigue and puzzle people even today.

To paint a word-picture that gives a sense of what it is like there, one might start with visions of ancient Indians. Mexico is a country with a fascinating history where ancient civilizations like the Olmecs, Zapotecs, Mayans, and Aztecs grew to power, prospered for a time, and then disappeared. They left amazing stone structures and innumerable questions about their legacy. Next, one might add color to the picture. The people of Mexico fill their immediate worlds with color. Whether one is rich or poor, containers brimming with flowers adorn a house, decorate a yard, or add beauty to a neighborhood park. In some communities even the houses are painted in pretty, soft hues. Fiestas are popular and they fairly shout with color permeating ornate costumes, floats in parades, whimsical piñatas, special religious decorations, and sprays of fireworks bursting in the night sky. The crowded marketplaces are alive with folk art, jewelry, pottery, baskets, weaving, and piles of luscious fruits and vegetables—a riot of different colors. A picture of this unique country should be taking shape and will become more distinct with textures added.

Adding texture when creating a visual image of Mexico makes sense because of its varied topography. If you closed your eyes and ran your fingers across the northern part of the country from west to east, the fingers would dip in at sea level into the Gulf of California, then skim along the lonely seashore, and move quickly up a range of the Sierra Madras Occidental, touching snow-covered peaks along the way. Fingers would continue to travel across the high, dry, rocky plateaus before bumping into additional mountains, the Sierra Madras Oriental. Finally, they would slip down again to the coastline to dabble in the surf of the Gulf of Mexico. During the tactile investigation, those fingers would experience reasonably temperate weather due to the higher altitude of the plateaus, find it cooler in the mountains, and balmy along the coasts. Moving down toward the south, the texture depicts the volcanic Cordillero range. As the travel continues to the southeastern coastal areas, the humidity rises. One is soon enveloped in steaming rainforest and jungles near Central America. Topography and climate have been added to the picture of Mexico, but there is more to see.

Looking closer, one could fill in the picture with men, women, and children. It would include faces of varying hues. The people who make up the population of our southern neighbor are of different ethnic backgrounds. Mestizos, the largest group, are descendants of ancient Indians; mulattos are of mixed Native and African heritage; criollos are European or American; and there are numerous Indian groups. As a people they represent a country of deep religious beliefs, primarily Roman Catholic. In addition, the Mexican people have impressive family values and appreciate having their extended family living close by and often under one roof. Mexican children have been praised as being well behaved, respectful children. An astonishing statistic is that this is a country of young people where at least one-third of the population is fifteen years old or less. The details in the picture of Mexico continue to emerge.

Beneath the earth's crust is something that cannot be seen but surely must be recognized. This is a land of volcanoes, most of them extinct. However, there still seems to be quite a bit of activity underground as evidenced by the two earthquakes in 1985, which killed 10,000 people and destroyed many large buildings in Mexico City. Again in 1989, another major earthquake rocked the country. This one measured 7.0 on the Richter scale and injured hundreds. There is a reason for Mexico's propensity for earthquakes. The country is located where four crustal plates meet. These plates are constantly shifting and jostling each other. The resulting impacts cause tremors, earthquakes, and even volcanoes. City planners are learning from the devastation created by recent earthquakes and are rebuilding with stronger, sturdier materials to try to prevent further loss of life. From topography to people to action under the earth's crust, the picture one paints of Mexico is compelling, indeed.

Nature presents problems aside from earthquakes and occasional volcanic eruptions. Calamities in the form of weather affect the people of the country, too. Drought often makes eking sustenance out of the soil a major challenge for farmers. Occasionally, severe storms like Hurricane Gilbert head toward land. (Gilbert battered the Yucatan Peninsula in 1988, destroying approximately 30,000 homes.) Despite its appeal to tourists as they relax in Puerto Vallarta or Cozumel, and the love it holds in the hearts of many, Mexico does not always seem to be a hospitable land.

As with the United States and Canada, Mexico can be described in terms of contrasts. Consider, for example, the modern hospital in Mexico City where people can receive free treatment if necessary. Yet, in the shantytowns and slums in the shadow of the hospital, many people first consult a *curandera*, a curer in whom they place greater trust. The curandera charges a fee for her services. Born out of tradition, people first turn to this ancient form of medicine instead of to modern medicine, or at least for a valued second opinion. Tall contemporary skyscrapers become the mountains of the city skyline while at their feet are the humblest of dwellings pieced together with scraps of wood, tin, and cardboard. This is a disheartening contrast as it seems the cities cannot keep up with the demands of an ever-growing population.

Another sharp contrast is between wealth and poverty. There are wealthy people in this country, to be sure, but there are even more who are poor. Poverty could be said to be rooted in the land. Because of the lack of rainfall and poor rocky soil, single family farming, or collective farming in *ejidos,* is very difficult. In fact, many farmers or their older children are heading to the cities to find better work, only to be disappointed. There is no affordable housing, so people erect temporary houses in shantytowns or slum areas. Sadly, 1.5 million destitute children live on the streets of Mexico's cities. The picture of life in the cities for the majority of people is a difficult one. Other people choose to live in tiny fishing villages along the coasts, but that is not an easy life, either. The majority of people in Mexico, whether they are farmers, live in villages or the city, or fish the shores, work diligently to provide for themselves and their families and often have little to show for their earnest efforts.

Mexico is a country striving to solve its problems. A rising debt, poor soil, lack of rainfall to sustain crops, tremendously overcrowded cities shrouded by clouds of severe pollution, and too few jobs present sometimes overwhelming problems. In a effort to help their families, desperate Mexicans turn to the United States for help. Illegal immigrants are a growing problem despite a heavily patrolled border between Mexico and the United States. The flow of illegal entries is a source of conflict between the two countries. Yet it is also a country with an interesting history, whose beaches and climate attract tourist dollars, of colorful festivals and masses of flowers, of the natural beauty in the desert, mountains, and jungle. This remarkable country is the southern neighbor to the United States.

Initiating Activity

Go to the local community and enlist the help of people who have traveled to Mexico and would be willing to share a short slide show and impressions of their visit. Another resource might be to ask the high school, junior college, or college Spanish teacher to come in and talk to the class. They may have traveled throughout the country as part of their studies. Talk to local restaurant owners who may volunteer their mariachi players and some authentic tortillas and enchiladas for tasting. Parents may have additional information to give to the class and might be excellent resources for an explanation of the religious celebrations so important to the lives of these people. Begin the unit with as much of a cultural immersion as is possible. If all else fails, show a quality video on the country. This kind of activity will build a common base for further learning for all of the students. One student should write for materials on this country at the following address:

Mexican Government Tourist Office
10100 Santa Monica Boulevard
Los Angeles, CA 90067
(310) 203-8191

Lesson 1

Looking at Mexico Through the Themes of Location, Place, and Human/Environmental Interactions

Objectives

- to fill in the topography of Mexico on outline maps of the country including both Sierra Madres Mountain Ranges, Yucatan Peninsula, Sea of Cortez, Rio Grande River, Atlantic and Pacific Oceans, Gulf of Mexico, Gulf of California, Valley of Mexico, Mexico City, Guadalajara, and Monterrey
- to distinguish the following regions on student maps: central highlands, northwest deserts, central plateau, tropical lowlands, mountainous south, and Yucatan Peninsula
- to study the climate and topography together to support advantages or disadvantages for living in certain locations in the country
- to research the ancient Indian cultures of Mexico and look for remnants in the lives of people today
- to use folktales to learn about the emotional feel of the country and its culture
- to form and then confirm growing geographic generalizations about Mexico as a place

Materials

- atlases, maps, and tourist guides to the country
- nonfiction books on Mexico, its history, and its culture including the August 1996 issue of *National Geographic* magazine
- a collection of Mexican folktales
- *Pablo and Pimienta* by Ruth M. Covault
- *The Legend of Food Mountain* by Harriet Rohmer

- *When Jaguars Ate the Moon and Other Stories About Animals and Plants of the Americas* by Maria Christina Brusca and Tona Wilson

Motivator

Read the appealing picture book, *Pablo and Pimienta* by Ruth M. Covault. This story of courage and family love is written in both English and Spanish. If the classroom teacher is not fluent in Spanish, try to find someone else to read the Spanish text. Discuss Pablo's life briefly. Give students some quiet time to reflect on Pablo's life, compare it to their own, and write their thoughts in their journals.

Look at the classroom map and locate Mexico. Students can use their student atlases, too. Have them study the topography of the land, which they should be able to "read" quite well by now. On a sheet of scratch paper, have them list the occupations they think people might be involved in, what the climate of the country seems to be like, what leisure time activities might be popular, and a general comment about what it seems to be like to live there. Impressions and information from the initiating activity will probably help with the accuracy of some of the observations. Then share impressions, correct any that are too far afield, and invite the students to learn more about a country proud of its family ties, arts, and culture.

Activities

Topographic Finds

First, ask students to locate Mexico using latitude and longitude. Compare their coordinates and agree upon the most accurate set. Complete the topographic outline map and ask the students for their impressions of the lay of the land in this country. During a class discussion analyze what could be problematic in earning a living here. What is a strong reason for choosing to live here? What solutions are there to any problems that the students think might exist? Tell them to continue to analyze problems and think of solutions throughout the study of Mexico.

A Temperature and Rain Gauge

Using precipitation maps and information from assorted books and materials, construct a graph of the rainfall for a region in Mexico by the month for a year. Do the same for the area in which the students live. Compare the graphs and write an analysis of the information as it affects the people in both areas.

Time Line of Civilizations Past

On the chalkboard or overhead write the names of the four ancient civilizations who once made this area their home. These would include the Olmecs (1400 B.C.–400 B.C.), Zapotecs (500 B.C.–A.D. 800), Mayans (400 B.C.–A.D. 800), and the Aztecs (A.D. 1300–A.D. 1550). Give a few enticing tidbits about each group. Then let groups of students choose a civilization to study. Their assignment includes placing the civilization on a time line displayed in a designated part of the room. Working together, students can write short, informative blocks of text to set along the time line, and illustrate their segment with "authentic" designs. When the work is completed, groups can give an overview of their work and suggest interesting books for the rest of the class to read.

Using Folktales as a Source of Information

Model the way in which students can use a folktale to learn more about a country. Explain that most folktales came from the oral tradition as elders taught values and lessons to the young through

stories. Such stories are excellent sources for others to learn from, too, whether it is a sound lesson in behavior or cultural values.

On the board or overhead write important points to watch for as students read. They can learn from both the story and the illustrations as they look at architecture, relationships between characters, color and design, foods, dress, festivities, music, and ancient beliefs that may have been passed down to present generations. Another question to answer is, What might be a lesson that the book is teaching? The point here is not to overanalyze the book, but to be aware of what can be learned.

Briefly introduce the selection of folktales that have been assembled with the help of the school and public librarians. Read one aloud that is newly discovered or is a personal favorite. One idea is to

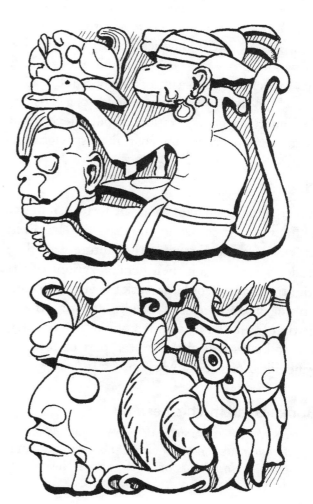

read "Corn and Chocolate" from the delightful picture book, *When Jaguars Ate the Moon and Other Stories About Animals and Plants of the Americas* by Maria Christina Brusca and Tona Wilson. It is a short tale about how ancient Indians were given food. The same tale, a little different version, is brightly illustrated in *The Legend of Food Mountain* by Harriet Rohmer. Read that one, too, and discuss similarities and differences between the two. Talk about what the students might have learned about the Mexican culture from the stories. On their own notebook paper have the students list any information they gleaned from topographic study to ancient civilizations to folktales. They can add to this information or confirm it as they continue reading.

Divide the learners into groups. They are to select a book, read and learn from the tale together, and then share observations with the class. Does one group's observations support something another group has surmised? Have learners try tying the information into some major generalizations. Next, they may choose to consult a nonfiction title, read it, and add to their previous categories. As a class, refine emerging generalizations about Mexico and write them on a classroom chart for easy reference.

Closure

As geographic generalizations are formed, it might be fun to invite someone into class who has lived in Mexico or understands the culture well. The students can explain their generalizations of the country and its people, and ask the visitor to confirm or expand on their learning thus far. Information from history, topography of the country, and folktales will all become a part of forming generalizations about Mexico.

Books Used in This Lesson

Brusca, Maria Christina, and Tona Wilson. *When Jaguars Ate the Moon and Other Stories About Animals and Plants of the Americas.* New York: Henry Holt, 1995.

Covault, Ruth M. *Pablo and Pimienta.* Illus. by Francisco X. Mora. Flagstaff, Ariz.: Northland, 1994.

Rohmer, Harriet. *The Legend of Food Mountain.* Illus. by Graciela Carrillo. San Francisco: Children's Press, 1988.

Suggested Companion Titles

Aardema, Verna. *Borreguita and the Coyote: A Tale from Ayuita, Mexico.* Illus. by Petra Mathers. New York: Alfred A. Knopf, 1991.

Arnold, Caroline. *City of the Gods: Mexico's Ancient City of Teotihuacan.* Photographs by Richard Hewett. New York: Clarion Books, 1994.

Climo, Shirley. *The Little Red Ant and the Great Big Crumb: A Mexican Fable.* Illus. by Francisco X. Mora. New York: Clarion Books, 1995.

Czernecki, Stefan, and Timothy Rhodes. *The Hummingbirds' Gift.* New York: Hyperion, 1994.

———. *Pancho's Pinata.* New York: Hyperion, 1992.

dePaola, Tomie. *The Legend of the Poinsettia.* Illus. by author. New York: Putnam, 1994.

Dupre, Judith. *The Mouse Bride: A Mayan Folk Tale.* Illus. by Fabricio Vanden Broeck. New York: Alfred A. Knopf, 1993.

Fisher, Leonard Everett. *Pyramid of the Sun, Pyramid of the Moon.* Illus. by author. New York: Macmillan, 1988.

Gerson, Mary-Joan. *People of Corn: A Mayan Story.* Illus. by Carla Golembe. Boston: Little, Brown, 1995.

Gollub, Matthew. *The Moon Was at a Fiesta.* Illus. by Leovigildo Martinez. New York: Tambourine, 1994.

Greger, C. Shana. *The Fifth and Final Sun: An Ancient Aztec Myth of the Sun's Origins.* Illus. by author. Boston: Houghton Mifflin, 1994.

Grifalconi, Ann. *The Bravest Flute: A Story of Courage in the Mayan Tradition.* Illus. by author. Boston: Little, Brown, 1994.

Johnston, Tony. *The Iguana Brothers: A Tale of Two Lizards.* Illus. by Mark Teague. New York: Blue Sky/Scholastic, 1995.

Kalman, Bobbie. *Mexico, the Culture.* New York: Crabtree, 1993.

Kimmel, Eric A. *The Witch's Face: A Mexican Tale.* Illus. by Fabricio Vanden Broeck. New York: Holiday House, 1993.

Lewis, Richard. *All of You Was Singing.* Illus. by Ed Young. New York: Atheneum, 1991.

Ober, Hal. *How Music Came to the World: An Ancient Mexican Myth.* Illus. by Carol Ober. Boston: Houghton Mifflin, 1994.

Patent, Dorothy Henshaw. *Quetzal: Sacred Bird of the Cloud Forest.* Illus. by Neil Waldman. New York: Morrow, 1996.

Stein, R. Conrad. *The Aztec Empire.* New York: Benchmark Books, 1996.

Wisniewski, David. *Rain Player.* Illus. by author. New York: Clarion Books, 1991.

Wolf, Bernard. *Beneath the Stone: A Mexican Zapotec Tale.* Photographs by Bernard Wolf. New York: Orchard Books, 1994.

Wood, Tim. *The Aztecs.* New York: Viking, 1992.

Zubizarreta, Rosalma, Harriet Rohmer, and David Schecter. *The Woman Who Outshone the Sun: The Legend of Lucia Zenteno.* Illus. by Fernando Olivera. San Francisco: Children's Book Press, 1992.

Lesson 2

Looking at Mexico as a Region

Objectives

- to answer the geographic question, How and why is one area of Mexico similar or different to another?
- to demonstrate an understanding of how it would feel to live in Mexico through poetry, art, or drama
- to write a geo (geography) poem based upon the country as a whole, its history, or one of its cities
- to illustrate accumulated geographic knowledge by painting a class mural
- to celebrate the country and its people with a fiesta, a play based upon one of the folktales, or a poetry reading

Materials

- use the materials gathered for Lesson 1 plus additional nonfiction suggestions
- butcher paper and paints or markers for the mural work
- used file folders or tagboard for poetry "billboards"
- instructions for writing an autobiographical poem and transitioning to a geo or geographic poem

- *My Mexico-Mexico Mio* by Tony Johnston
- *Diego* by Jeanette Winter
- *The Tree Is Older than You Are* by Naomi S. Nye

Motivator

For younger learners read selected poems from *My Mexico-Mexico Mio* by Tony Johnston. *The Tree Is Older Than You Are* by Naomi S. Nye has beautifully descriptive poetry and tales, some quite thought-provoking. It is probably more appropriate to read aloud for upper grades. Both books will be popular for later reading and reflection. Students will have the background to enjoy the poetry and form accurate images in their minds based upon the study they have done to this point. Ask the students if the poems support what they have learned thus far.

Activities

Writing an Autobiographical Poem

Give the students a sheet of directions for writing a poem about themselves. Read one that you have written, sharing the rough drafts, to model the process and the product. Then practice by writing a poem as a class. The subject might be someone most people in the class know. After this practice, learners are to write their own poem, polish it, and read it to the class on a poetry sharing day. For display purposes, the poems might be put on one side of a used file folder with the tab edges trimmed off neatly. Poems can be illustrated with something that reflects the student. The folder will stand up like a billboard to show off the student's writing.

Following the same directions as for the autobiographical poem, add a twist and adapt it to describing a place in Mexico. The class could practice by writing about their school, drafting a poem on the board or overhead. Then they can work on their own. The students are to write their own geo poem about Mexico, the country, its roots, the people, or a specific city that has been researched. This poem goes on the other side of the file folder. Illustrations on this polished product should reflect the country. Set up the poetry billboards around the room or on a counter in the learning center or library.

Pattern for an Autobiographical Poem.

Line 1: First and last name
Line 2: Describe yourself in three interesting, powerful words
Line 3: Name four things you like to do
Line 4: Name three things you love
Line 5: Repeat name

Students in upper grades with more developed writing abilities may want to use short descriptive phrases in place of single words.

Diego and a Mural

One of the most famous Mexican painters is Diego Rivera. Read the picture book *Diego* by Jeanette Winter to the class to give the students some background on the dedicated, sometimes controversial artist. Then ask the students to depict what they have learned about Mexico by painting a mural of Mexico past and present. They will be echoing the work of ancient Mayan and Aztec artists who depicted scenes from their lives on murals as well.

Pairs of students can be divided to cover different periods of history or topics that represent the culture. Students will be responsible for a specific area of a long piece of butcher paper according to an agreed-upon time line. As they look at the overall plan, they will need to work together to transition from one piece of the mural to another. Sketches of subject matter should be done first, a larger version of the final sketch might come next, and then students could transfer their carefully planned segment to the paper. If the students draw a pencil grid over their polished sketch, and draw a larger grid on their piece of the mural, they can transfer the design square by square before painting it. The finished product can decorate the wall in the hallway outside of the classroom so that more people can enjoy it.

Closure

When the mural is completed, let the students talk their way through it, each group of artists explaining what they have done and why they chose to depict the scene as they did. In the process, the history and evolution of Mexico and its people will be reviewed. This would also be a good time to celebrate the poetry created by the class members.

Books Used in This Lesson

Johnston, Tony. *My Mexico-Mexico Mio*. Illus. by F. John Sierra. New York: Putnam, 1996.

Nye, Naomi S. *The Tree Is Older than You Are: A Bilingual Gathering of Poems and Stories from Mexico with Paintings by Mexican Artists*. New York: Simon & Schuster, 1995.

Winter, Jeanette. *Deigo*. Illus. by author. New York: Alfred A. Knopf, 1991.

Suggested Companion Titles

Ancona, George. *The Pinata Maker*. Photographs by author. San Diego, Calif.: Harcourt Brace, 1994.

————. *Pablo Remembers: The Fiesta of the Day of the Dead.* Photographs by author. New York: Lothrop, Lee & Shepard, 1993.

Anzaldua, Gloria. *Friends from the Other Side.* Illus. by Consuelo Mendez. San Francisco: Children's Press, 1993.

Ciavonne, Jean. *Carlos, Light the Farolito.* Illus. by Donna Clair. New York: Clarion Books, 1995.

Flora, James. *The Fabulous Firework Family.* Illus. by author. Riverside, N.Y.: Macmillan/McElderry, 1994.

Grossman, Patricia. *Saturday Market.* Illus. by Enrique O. Sanchez. New York: Lothrop, Lee & Shepard, 1994.

Haskins, Jim. *Count Your Way Through Mexico.* Illus. by Helen Byers. Minneapolis, Minn.: Lerner, 1989.

Kalman, Bobbie. *Mexico, the Land.* New York: Crabtree, 1993.

————. *Mexico, the People.* New York: Crabtree, 1993.

Kent, Deborah. *Mexico: Rich in Spirit and Tradition.* Tarrytown, N.Y.: Benchmark Books, 1996.

Krull, Virginia. *Maria Molina and the Days of the Dead.* Illus. by Enrique O. Sanchez. New York: Macmillan, 1994.

Madrigal, Antonio Hernández. *The Eagle and the Rainbow: Timeless Tales from México.* Illus. by Tomie dePaola. Golden, Colo.: Fulcrum Publishing, 1997.

Morrison, Marion. *Mexico and Central America.* New York: Franklin Watts, 1995.

Parkison, Jami. *Pequena the Burro.* Illus. by Itoko Maeno. Kansas City, Mo.: MarshMedia, 1994.

Silverthorne, Elizabeth. *Fiesta! Mexico's Great Celebrations.* Illus. by Jan Davey Ellis. Brookfield, Conn.: Millbrook Press, 1992.

Spurr, Elizabeth. *Lupe and Me.* Illus. by Enrique O. Sanchez. New York: Gulliver, 1995.

Stein, R. Conrad. *Mexico.* Chicago: Children's Press, 1994.

Van Rose, Susanna. *Volcano and Earthquake.* New York: Dorling Kindersley/Random House, 1992.

Culminating Activity

Showing the artwork off and explaining why it was done might be a part of a festival involving parents and family one evening or another classroom during the day. One of the students' favorite folktales could be acted out. After the play, the significance of the tale might be explained to the audience. Bring those mariachi players back! Because most festivals center around food, authentic foods should be served because they so reflect the culture. In addition, music, a game, or a Mexican folk dance taught by the P.E. teacher or a dance teacher might be a part of the celebration. Several festivals might be explained to the audience, including their important religious significance. This could be a repeat performance of the initial cultural immersion, but this time students will get more out of it because of their newly acquired knowledge about Mexico.

Appendix I

Teacher Resources

General Information

For a tremendous wealth of information including topographic maps of individual states, contact:

United States Geologic
Survey Information Service
Box 25286
Denver Federal Center
Denver, CO 80225
(303) 202-4700

For specific information on maps, call (800) USA-MAPS (872-6277).

For a colorful map showing the Tribes of the Indian Nation, write to:

American Eagle Distributors
610 E. Bell Road, #2295
Phoenix, AZ 85022

For a free catalog of carefully reviewed videos and films, including a selection on the geography of the United States:

The American Film and Video Review
The American Educational
Film and Video Center
Eastern College
10 Fairview Drive
St. Davids, PA 19087-3696

Titles Related to Geography

Chapman, Gillian, and Pam Robson. *Maps and Mazes: A First Guide to Mapmaking.* Brookfield, Conn.: Millbrook Press, 1993.

Fromboluti, Carol Sue. *Helping Your Child Learn Geography.* Washington, D.C.: Office of Educational Research and Improvement, 1990.

Jouris, David. *All Over the Map: An Extraordinary Atlas of the United States.* Berkeley, Calif.: Ten Speed Press, 1995.

Lasky, Katherine. *The Librarian Who Measured the Earth.* Illus. by Kevin Hawkes. Boston: Little, Brown, 1994.

Van Rose, Susanna. *The Earth Atlas.* Illus. by Richard Bronson. New York: Dorling Kindersley, 1994.

Weiss, Harvey. *Maps: Getting from Here to There.* Boston: Houghton Mifflin, 1991.

Other Titles

Barchers, Suzanne I., and Patricia C. Marden. *Cooking Up U.S. History: Recipes and Research to Share with Children.* Illus. by Leann Millineaux. Englewood, Colo.: Teacher Ideas Press, 1991.

Caduto, Michael J. *All One Earth: Songs for the Generations.* Golden, Colo.: Fulcrum Publishing, 1994.

Caduto, Michael J., and Joseph Bruchac. *Keepers of the Animals: Native American Stories and Wildlife Activities for Children.* Illus. by John Kahionhes Fadden. Golden, Colo.: Fulcrum Publishing, 1991.

———. *Keepers of the Earth: Native American Stories and Environmental Activities for Children.* Illus. by John Kahionhes Fadden and Carol Wood. Golden, Colo.: Fulcrum Publishing, 1988.

Cahill, Marie, and W. J. Yenne, eds. *The Pictorial Atlas of North America's National Parks.* Greenwich, Conn.: Brompton Books, 1993.

Cohn, Amy L., comp. *From Sea to Shining Sea: A Treasury of American Folklore and Folk Songs.* New York: Scholastic, 1993.

Van Laan, Nancy. *In a Circle Long Ago: A Treasury of Native Lore from North America.* Illus. by Lisa Desimini. New York: Apple Soup Books/ Alfred A. Knopf, 1995.

Whipple, Laura. *Celebrating America: A Collection of Poems and Images of the American Spirit.* Art provided by the Art Institute of Chicago. New York: Philomel, 1994.

Computer Programs/CD ROMs Related to Geography

The following materials can be ordered from Broderbund Software at the following address:

Broderbund Software
P.O. Box 6125
Novato, CA 94948-6125
(800) 521-6263

Maps and Facts: A comprehensive world atlas and excellent resource for use in the classroom.

Where in the U.S.A. Is Carmen Sandiego? This popular software draws learners into geographic investigations.

MacGlobe/PC Globe: Included in this program is valuable demographic, political, and cultural information useful in comparing and contrasting statistics. Detailed maps are included as well.

MacUSA/PC USA: Here is a useful program that gives learners quick access to maps and data on the United States.

National Geographic Society materials can be ordered from a catalog of superb learning materials. Phone (800) 447-0647 for a catalog.

Zip Zap Map! (Macintosh and Windows): A version can be ordered for the World, USA, and Canada. Students earn points for refining their maps skills.

GeoBee Software (Macintosh and Windows): This simulates the National Geographic Geography Bee with 3,000 geographic questions to stump and stimulate students.

Picture Atlas of the World: This CD-ROM Atlas includes maps, spoken language, country calendars, video clips, and more.

2
The Pacific Coast States: Washington, Oregon, and California

Offices of Tourism

Washington Tourism Development Division
Box 42500
Olympia, WA 98504
(800) 544-1800 or (360) 586-2088

Oregon Tourism Division
595 Cottage Street NE
Salem, OR 97310
(800) 547-7842
(Monday through Friday unless you want voice mail)
Be sure to ask for a copy of the map entitled "The Oregon Trail 1843–1993: A Self-Guiding Tour of the Oregon Trail Across Oregon."

California Division of Tourism
801 K Street
Sacramento, CA 95814
(800) 862-2543 or (916) 322-1397.

Other Sources

Visit aquariums or oceanariums if they are available locally; contact college or university departments of oceanography or marine science; visit maritime museums; write to state departments of marine resources. Write for titles that pertain to the ocean:

U.S. Government Printing Office
Superintendent of Documents
Washington, DC 20402
Look for the posters showing oceans and ocean life.

Life in the Oceans is a two-part tutorial and game that covers scientific, geographic, and historic information about oceans. Materials include a teacher's guide and reproducible activity sheets. Write for a catalog from:

RightOn Programs
755 New York Avenue
Huntington, NY 11743

Project WILD Aquatic Education Activity Guide (1987) by Western Regional Environmental Education Council available from:

Project WILD
Salina Star Route
Boulder, CO 80302
Materials include a number of ocean and water-related activities for learners of all ages.

For information on lumbering practices or reforestation contact:

American Forestry Association
P.O. Box 2000
Washington, DC 20010

Internet Address for information on the Oregon Trail:
http://www.pbs.org/oregontrail/

Other Titles

Bell, Neill. *The Book of Where or How to Be Naturally Geographic.* Illus. by Richard Wilson. Boston: Little, Brown, 1982.

Hatch, Lynda. *Pathways of America: The Oregon Trail.* Carthage, Ill.: Good Apple, 1994.

Hill, William E. *The Oregon Trail—Yesterday and Today.* Caldwell, Idaho: The Caxton Printers, 1986.

Kavasch, Barrie. *Earthmaker's Lodge: Native American Folklore, Activities, and Food.* Peterborough, N.H.: Cobblestone Publishing, 1995.

Miller, Brandon Marie. *Buffalo Gals: Women of the Old West.* Minneapolis, Minn.: Lerner, 1995.

Schlissel, Lillian. *Women's Diaries of the Westward Journey.* New York: Schocken Books, 1982.

Steves, Rick. *Kidding Around Seattle: A Young Person's Guide to the City.* Illus. by Mellissa Meier. Santa Fe, N.Mex.: John Muir Publishers, 1991.

3
The Mountain States: Idaho, Colorado, Montana, Nevada, Utah, and Wyoming

Offices of Tourism

Idaho Travel Council
700 W. State Street
Boise, ID 83720
(800) 635-7820 or (208) 334-2470

Colorado Tourism Board
1625 Broadway
Denver, CO 80202
(800) 433-2656 or (303) 592-5510

Travel Montana
1424 9th Avenue
Helena, MT 59620
(800) 541-1447 or (406) 444-2654

Nevada Division of Travel and Tourism
Capitol Complex
Carson City, NV 89710
(702) 687-4322

Utah Travel Council
Council Hall, Capital Hill
Salt Lake City, UT 84114
(801) 538-1030

Wyoming Division of Tourism
I-25 at College Drive
Cheyenne, WY 82002
(307) 777-7777

4
The Southwestern States: Texas, Oklahoma, New Mexico, and Arizona

Offices of Tourism

Texas Department of Commerce
Tourism Division
P.O. Box 12728
Austin, TX 78711-2728
(800) 888-8TEX

Oklahoma Tourism and Recreation Department
Travel and Tourism Division
500 Will Rogers Building, DA92
Oklahoma City, OK 73105-4492
(800) 652-6552

New Mexico Department of Tourism
491 Old Santa Fe Trail
Santa Fe, NM 87503
(800) 545-2040

Arizona Department of Tourism
1100 W. Washington
Phoenix, AZ 85007
(800) 842-8257

Other Sources

For further information about the views of the earth from space, the teacher can obtain information on space photos from the U.S. Geologic Surveys that might coordinate with this book. They have a wide variety of educational materials, so a phone call ahead of time will be of great use.

U.S. Geologic Survey
Earth Science Information Center
Box 25046, MS 504
Denver, CO 80225
(303) 202-4200
Fax: (303) 202-4188

For a catalog of intriguing books on the West that would provide wonderful background, write:

Fulcrum Publishing
350 Indiana Street, Suite 350
Golden, CO 80401-5093
(800) 992-2908

Mountain Press Publishing Company
P.O. Box 2399
Missoula, MT 59806
(800) 234-5308

National Park Services Regional Offices are excellent resources for maps and information about parks in the area. Ask for the National Park System Map and Guide as well.

Southwest Region–National Park Service
P.O. Box 728
Santa Fe, NM 87504-0728
(505) 988-6012

If students want more information about desert life and ways to preserve this intriguing ecosystem, they may write to:

The Arizona-Sonora Desert Museum
2021 N. Kinney Road
Tucson, AZ 85743

Other Titles

Hafford, William. *Arizona Mileposts: Travel Guide.* Phoenix, Ariz.: *Arizona Highways Magazine* and the Arizona Department of Transportation, 1993.

Hartley, Nancy. *Quick Facts About the U.S.A.* New York: Scholastic, 1994.

Sierra, J. *Fantastic Theater: Puppets and Plays for Young Performers and Young Audiences.* Bronx, N.Y.: H. W. Wilson, 1991.

Tweet, Susan J. *Meet the Wild Southwest: Land of Hoodoos and Gila Monsters.* Illus. by Joyce Bergen. Seattle, Wash.: Alaska Northwest Books, 1995.

Walker, Judy. *Simple Southwestern Cooking.* Illus. by Monte Varah. Flagstaff, Ariz.: Northland, 1995.

5
The Heartland: North Dakota, South Dakota, Nebraska, Kansas, Minnesota, Iowa, and Missouri

Offices of Tourism

North Dakota Tourism Department
604 E. Boulevard
Bismarck, ND 58505
(800) 435-5663

South Dakota Department of Tourism
Capital Lake Plaza
711 E. Well Avenue
Pierre, SD 57501-3369
(605) 773-3301

Nebraska Division of Travel and Tourism
Box 94666
Lincoln, NE 68509
(800) 228-4307

Kansas Travel and Tourism Division
700 S.W. Harrison Street
Topeka, KS 66603
(800) 252-6727 or (913) 296-2009

Minnesota Office of Tourism
100 Metro Square
121 7th Place E.
St. Paul, MN 55101
(612) 296-5029

Iowa Division of Tourism
200 E. Grand Avenue
Des Moines, IA 50309
(515) 242-4705

Missouri Division of Tourism
Truman State Office Building
P.O. Box 1055
Jefferson City, MO 65102
(800) 877-1234 or (314) 751-4133

Other Titles

Tanner, Helen Hornbeck. *The Ojibwa: Indians of North America Series.* New York: Chelsea House, 1992.

Tester, John R. *Minnesota's Natural Heritage: An Ecological Perspective.* Minneapolis: University of Minnesota Press, 1995.

6
The Great Lakes States: Illinois, Indiana, Michigan, Wisconsin, and Ohio

Offices of Tourism

Illinois Bureau of Tourism
310 S. Michigan Avenue
Chicago, IL 60604
(800) 223-0121

Indiana Division of Tourism
1 N. Capital, Suite 700
Indianapolis, IN 46204-2288
(800) 289-6646 or (317) 232-8860

Michigan Travel Bureau
Box 30226
Lansing, MI 48909
(800) 543-2937

Wisconsin Tourism Development
Box 7606
Madison, WI 53707
(800) 432-8747 or (608) 226-2161

Ohio Division of Travel and Tourism
Box 1001
Columbus, OH 43266
(800) 282-5393

Other Sources

Write for a copy of the forty-four-page book entitled *The Great Lakes: An Environmental Atlas and Resource Book* (ISBN 0-662-15189-5) published in 1987. It details many aspects of the Great Lakes, looking at the people, settlements, natural processes, management, and other concerns.

Great Lakes National Program Office
Environmental Protection Agency
230 Dearborn Avenue
Chicago, IL 60604

Other Titles

Anderson, William. *Laura Ingalls Wilder Country: The People and Places in Laura Ingalls Wilder's Life and Books*. Illus. by Leslie A. Kelly. New York: HarperCollins, 1990.

Field, Ellyce. *Detroit Kids Catalog: Complete Guide to Michigan Sites*. Detroit: Wayne State University Press, 1990.

Good, Phyllis Pellman. *Amish Cooking for Kids*. Intercourse, Pa.: Good Books, 1995.

Hartman, Sheryl. *Indian Clothing of the Great Lakes: 1740–1840*. Ogden, Utah: Eagle's View Publishing, 1991.

McCall, Edith. *Biography of a River: The Living Mississippi*. New York: Walker, 1990.

Pellman, Rachel, and Kenneth Pellman. *The World of Amish Quilts*. Intercourse, Pa.: Good Books, 1984.

Walker, Barbara. *The Little House Cookbook: Frontier Foods from Laura Ingalls Wilder's Classic Stories*. Illus. by Garth Williams. New York: HarperCollins, 1989.

Zimmerman, George. *Ohio, Off the Beaten Path*. Chester, Conn.: Globe-Pequot Press, 1991.

7

The New England States: Vermont, Massachusetts, New Hampshire, Connecticut, Maine, and Rhode Island

Offices of Tourism

Vermont Department of Travel and Tourism
134 State Street
Montpelier, VT 05603
(802) 828-3236

Massachusetts Office of Travel and Tourism
100 Cambridge Street
Boston, MA 02202
(800) 447-6277 or (617) 727-3201

New Hampshire Office of Travel and Tourist
   Development
Box 856
Concord, NH 03302
(800) 944-1117 or (603) 271-2343

Connecticut Department of Economic
   Development
865 Brook Street
Rocky Hill, CT 06067
(800) 282-6863 or (203) 258-4200

Maine Office of Tourism
Department of Economic and Community
    Development
189 State Street, Station 59
Augusta, ME 04333
(800) 533-9595 or (207) 289-5710

Rhode Island Tourism Division
7 Jackson Walkway
Providence, RI 02903
(800) 556-2484 or (401) 277-2601

8
The Mid-Atlantic States: New York, New Jersey, Pennsylvania, Delaware, and Maryland

Offices of Tourism

New York State Division of Tourism
Department of Economic Development
One Commerce Plaza
Albany, NY 12245
(518) 474-4116

New Jersey Division of Travel and Tourism
Department of Commerce and Economic Development
20 W. State Street, CN 826
Trenton, NJ 08625-0826
(609) 292-6963

Pennsylvania Bureau of Travel
Department of Commerce
453 Forum Building
Harrisburg, PA 17120
(717) 787-5453

Delaware Tourism Office
99 Kings Highway, Box 1401
Dover, DE 19903
(302) 739-4271

Maryland Office of Tourism Development
Department of Economic and Employment
    Development
217 E. Redwood, 9th Floor
Baltimore, MD 21202
(410) 333-6611

9
The Appalachian Highlands: North Carolina, Virginia, West Virginia, Kentucky, and Tennessee

Offices of Tourism

North Carolina Division of Travel and Tourism
430 N. Salisbury Street
Raleigh, NC 27611
(800) 847-4862 or (919) 733-4171

Virginia Division of Tourism
1021 E. Cary Street
Richmond, VA 23219
(800) 932-5827 or (804) 786-2051

West Virginia Division of Tourism and Parks
2101 Washington Street E.
Charleston, WV 25305
(304) 348-2200 or 2286

Kentucky Department of Travel Development
2200 Capital Plaza Tower
Frankfort, KY 40601
(800) 225-8747 or (520) 564-4930

Tennessee Department of Tourist
    Development
Box 223170
Nashville, TN 37202
(615) 741-2158

Other Titles

Nichols, Margaret H. *Perfect Patchwork: The Sew-Easy Way.* New York: Sterling, 1993.

Page, Linda G., and Hilton Smith. *Foxfire Book of Appalachian Toys and Games.* Chapel Hill: University of North Carolina Press, 1993.

Rollins, Jennifer. *Quilting.* New York: Crescent Books, 1993.

Wigginton, Eliot, and His Students. *Foxfire: 25 Years: A Celebration of Our First Quarter Century.* New York: Doubleday, 1991.

10
The Southeastern States: Arkansas, Mississippi, Alabama, Georgia, South Carolina, Louisiana, and Florida

Offices of Tourism

Arkansas Department of Parks and Tourism
1 Capital Mall
Little Rock, AR 72201
(800) 872-1259 or (501) 682-7777

Mississippi Division of Tourist Development
Box 22825
Jackson, MS 39205
(800) 647-2290 or (601) 359-3297

Alabama Bureau of Tourism and Travel
401 Adams Avenue, Suite 126
P.O. Box 4309
Montgomery, AL 36103
(334) 242-4169

Georgia Department of Industry, Trade, and Tourism
285 Peachtree Center Avenue
Marquis Tower Two, 19th Floor
Atlanta, GA 30301
(404) 656-3553

South Carolina Division of Tourism
1205 Pendleton Street, Box 71
Columbia, SC 29202
(800) 346-3634 or (803) 734-0235

Louisiana Office of Tourism
Box 94291
Baton Rouge, LA 70804
(800) 334-8626

Florida Division of Tourism
126 Van Buren Street
Tallahassee, FL 32301
(904) 487-1462

Other Sources

WOW! The Wonders of Wetlands, An Educator's Guide. This is a 160-page comprehensive wetland guide including a 2-page list of resources for posters, curriculum guides, and videos. It is available from:

Environmental Concerns
P.O. Box P
St. Michaels, MD 21663

11
Alaska and Hawaii

Offices of Tourism

Alaska Division of Tourism
P.O. Box 110801
Juneau, AK 99811-0181
(907) 465-2012

Hawaii Visitors Bureau
2270 Kalakaua Avenue
Honolulu, HI 96815
(800) 923-1811

Other Sources

For the latest releases in children's books and informative nonfiction titles on Alaska, write for a catalog from:

Alaska Northwest Books
2208 N.W. Market Street, Suite 300
Seattle, WA 98107
(206) 784-5071

Life in Early Hawaii—The Ahupua'a provides information about what life was like in early Hawaii. They can also learn about the flora and fauna of the state through the full-color poster and illustrated booklet. Ask for their complete catalog of materials. Write to:

Kamehameha Schools Press
Media and Publications Department
1887 Makuakane Street
Honolulu, HI 96817

Stacey Kaopuiki's *Peter Panini's Children's Guide to the Hawaiian Islands* is available from:

Hawaiian Island Concepts
P.O. Box 6280
Kahului, HI 96732

Other Sources

Canadian publishers from across the country have selected wonderful books to reflect the latest and best books available in children's and young adult publishing. The catalog is available from:

Canadian Book Marketing Centre
2 Gloucester Street, Suite 301
Toronto, Ontario M4Y 1L5
Canada
(416) 413-4930

For a colorful, informative catalog of popular Canadian books by Annick Press, Bungalow Books, Firefly Books, Owl Books, Black Moss Press, and Warwick, write to:

Phoenix Learning Resources
2349 Chaffee Drive
St. Louis, MO 63146
(800) 221-1274

Other Titles

Lunn, Janet, and Christopher Moore. *The Story of Canada.* Illus. by Alan Daniel. Lanham, Md.: Key Porter Books, 1992.
MacDonald, Kate. *The Anne of Green Gables Cookbook.* Illus. by Barbara DiLella. Toronto, Ont.: McClelland-Bantam, 1985.

12
An Introduction to Our Neighbor to the North: Canada

Office of Tourism

Canadian Consulate General
Tourist Division
550 S. Hope Street
Los Angeles, CA 90071
(213) 346-2700

13
An Introduction to Our Neighbor to the South: Mexico

Office of Tourism

Mexican Government Tourist Office
10100 Santa Monica Boulevard
Los Angeles, CA 90067
(310) 203-8191

Other Sources

The following materials on Mexico are available through:

Social Studies School Service
10200 Jefferson Boulevard, Room 1321
P.O. Box 802
Culver City, CA 90232-0802
(800) 421-4246
Fax: (800) 944-5432

Maricela: Wonderworks Video. (1992). Maricela and her mother escape the violence in El Salvador and begin new lives in Los Angeles. Their story raises issues of discrimination, tolerance, and assimilation. Order #FLM261V-16 ($29.95)

Mexican People and Their Culture. (1992). This VHS videocassette explores Mexican geography, historical development, and the role of Mexican Americans in today's society. Order #VX106V-16 ($59.95)

Mexico City: Metropolis in the Mountains. (1994). This VHS videocassette stresses the role of ancient traditions in conflict with growing modernization in the world's most populated city. Order #VX137V-16 ($29.95)

Other Titles

Coronado, Rosa. *Cooking the Mexican Way.* Minneapolis, Minn.: Lerner, 1982.

Shalant, Phyllis. *Look What We've Brought You from Mexico: Crafts, Games, Recipes, Stories and Other Cultural Activities from Mexican-Americans.* New York: Julian Messner, 1992.

Appendix II

Annotated List of Chapter Books

2
The Pacific Coast States: Washington, Oregon, and California

Avi. *The Barn.* New York: Orchard Books, 1995.

Determined to survive in the Oregon Territory in 1855, Ben, his sister, and brother build a barn on their farm, shouldering tremendous responsibility to help their ill father. The bravery, endurance, and hope displayed by these children will inspire readers of all ages.

Ayer, Eleanor H. *The Anasazi.* New York: Walker, 1993.

An excellent nonfiction account of the Anasazi, where they came from, how these pueblo dwellers lived, and what might have happened to them.

Baron, T. A. *The Ancient One.* New York: Tom Doherty Associates, 1992.

Set in a dying logging town called Blade, Oregon, this time travel tale sets young Kate and her Aunt Melanie against a group of loggers bent on destroying an ancient grove of redwood trees recently discovered in a nearby crater. Wrapped in Indian lore, magic, and reverence for nature, this riveting book takes the reader on an adventure of a lifetime while convincing readers that some things should never be destroyed.

Bloch, Louis M. *Overland to California in 1859: A Guide for Wagon Train Travelers.* Cleveland, Ohio: Boch and Company, 1990.

Students in upper grades will enjoy being personally involved in organizing their own wagon train based upon activities in this book. Descriptions of the land, maps, and prints will aid students in making wise decisions.

Blumberg, Rhoda. *The Great American Gold Rush.* Illus. with historical prints, photographs, and maps. New York: Bradbury Press, 1989.

James Marshall's chance discovery of gold in California in 1848 unleashed a series of events that brought people across the seas and across the land in search of wealth. The book relates experiences of women and minorities, especially Native Americans and Chinese immigrants, in an outstanding example of historical nonfiction.

Carkeet, David. *Quiver River.* New York: HarperCollins, 1991.

Ricky experiences more than he expected working at a summer resort in the Sierra Mountains. He becomes involved with the ghost of a Miwok Indian boy who is trying to reach manhood through his initiation rites. The Indian and Ricky are on somewhat the same quests.

Climo, Shirley. *T.J.'s Ghost.* New York: Crowell, 1989.

T.J.'s two-week stay with elderly relatives is anything but boring. A foghorn that calls her name, a strange Australian boy whom she meets on the beach, and a riveting newspaper story of a 120-year-old shipwreck make an unforgettable vacation combination. This believable fantasy filled with mystery and unique characters is based upon actual historical events that readers may want to research after reading the information in the Author's Note.

Cottonwood, Joe. *Quake! A Novel.* New York: Scholastic, 1995.

Tuesday, October 17, 1989, an earthquake measuring 7.1 on the Richter scale hit northern California. Known as the World Series Earthquake, it wreaked havoc on cities and communities for miles around the epicenter located in the hills around Loma Prieta, near San Francisco. This is an exciting fictional account of what it might have been like to be living in the hills when this quake hit.

Coville, Bruce. *Fortune's Journey.* New York: BridgeWater Books, 1995.

In an amusing, interesting twist on going west, sixteen-year-old Fortune Plunkett faces numerous challenges as she heads to California in 1853 with the acting company she inherited from her father. Many times she wishes she were back enjoying the comforts of Charleston.

Crew, Linda. *Fire on the Wind.* New York: Delacorte, 1995.

August 1933 is one of the driest months in years and it creates havoc in the forests of Oregon. Fourteen-year-old Storie has lived in a logging camp all of her life and she worries about the threat of forest fire. Her father tells her the forests will last forever but Storie is skeptical. The phenomenal destruction caused by the Tillamook Burn, an actual event in Oregon history, stays with her for the rest of her life.

George, Jean Craighead. *There's an Owl in the Shower.* Illus. by Christine Herman Merrill. New York: HarperCollins, 1995.

Bordon Watson heads into the forest to shoot any spotted owl in sight because they have cost his father his job. When he finds a helpless owlet, his compassion rises to the surface and he brings it home to raise. Anger flies between the loggers and environmentalists as the Watson family, including Bordon's father, bonds with the young owl. The message that one must care for the fragile environment is nicely conveyed through a warm, believable story.

Goldin, Barbara D. *Red Means Good Fortune: A Story of San Francisco's Chinatown.* Illus. by Wenhai Ma. New York: Viking, 1994.

Jin Mun leaves China in 1868 to join his father in San Francisco where he has a laundry business. Jin Mun delivers laundry by day and studies English at night. Jin faces a dilemma when he meets Wai Hing, a young girl who was stolen from her family in China and sold as a slave to a Chinese family in San Francisco. Instead of losing hope in gaining her freedom, Jin Mun uses a new skill that results in good fortune.

Greenwood, Barbara. *A Pioneer Sampler: The Daily Life of a Pioneer Family in 1840.* Illus. by Heather Collins. New York: Ticknor & Fields, 1995.

Page after page of sketches, vignettes of family life, recipes, games, and facts about pioneer life make this book a must for the classroom library.

Van Leeuwen, Jean. *Bound for Oregon.* New York: Dial, 1994.

This novel is based upon the experiences of Mary Ellen Todd who traveled from Arkansas to the Oregon Territory when she was only nine years old. Because it is based upon real experiences, the novel gives a realistic account of the hardships that were a part of daily life as families traveled 2,000 miles through the wilderness to a new home.

Yee, Paul. *Tales from Gold Mountain: Stories of the Chinese in the New World.* Illus. by Simon Ng. New York: Macmillan, 1990.

Eight original stories about the difficult times Chinese immigrants faced in the New World combine with traditional folklore to provide insight into a heritage that includes the building of transcontinental railroads, the gold rush, and the settling of the West Coast.

Yep, Laurence. *Dragon's Gate.* New York: HarperCollins, 1993.

Young Otter's dreams of life in America are cruelly destroyed when he joins his father and the uncle who has always been his hero. Inhumane conditions while working on laying track for the transcontinental railroad, a death, and disillusionment push Otter to desperate measures.

3
The Mountain States: Idaho, Colorado, Montana, Nevada, Utah, and Wyoming

Beatty, Patricia. *Bonanza Girl.* New York: Morrow, 1993.

Katharine Scott is determined to make a life for herself and her two adolescent children. Recently widowed, she leaves Oregon and heads for Idaho's goldfields where she hopes to teach. Her thirteen-year-old daughter relates this story, informing readers that her mother opens a restaurant instead, intent upon surviving in a wild and woolly environment. The tale is woven around true events.

Fox, Mary Virginia. *Chief Joseph of the Nez Perce Indians: Champion of Liberty.* Chicago: Children's Press, 1992.

The author tells the carefully researched story of Chief Joseph who led his people on a long journey to escape the injustices of the U.S. government.

Gregory, Kristiana. *The Legend of Jimmy Spoon.* New York: Harcourt Brace Jovanovich, 1990.

Twelve-year-old Jimmy Spoon is lured away from home to live among the Shoshoni Indians for three years. His adventure began because he was discontented with his life in a 1850s pioneer Utah town, so he moved with the Indians to southern Idaho and Montana.

———. *Jenny of the Tetons.* New York: Harcourt Brace Jovanovich, 1989.

Fifteen-year-old Jenny is befriended by a trapper when her parents are killed during an Indian raid while traveling west by wagon train. She lives with the trapper, his Indian wife, and their five children in the Teton Valley. Highlighted with actual journal entries, the story is based upon the life of the first white settler in Teton Valley.

Hobbs, Will. *Beardance.* New York: Avon/Camelot Books, 1993.

When Cloyd saw a trophy hunter kill the grizzly, an endangered species, he should have told the authorities. The outfitter told officials that the bear had attacked him, a bold-faced lie. Later, he sees a mother grizzly buried in an avalanche and he knows what he has to do. He sets out to save the cubs in what proves to be an adventure in survival. An ALA Best Book.

Lawlor, Laurie. *Gold in the Hills.* New York: Walker, 1995.

Author of *Addie Across the Prairie,* Lawlor again brings the past to life as she recounts how Hattie and Pheme must survive under harsh conditions when their father leaves them with a relative while he goes off to strike it rich in the Colorado gold mines. Readers get a sense of the times and a lesson in the realities of the life of miners in this well-written tale.

Meyer, C. *Where the Broken Heart Still Beats*. San Diego, Calif.: Harcourt Brace, 1992.

In this piece of historical fiction a twelve-year-old girl is kidnapped and raised by the Comanches. She lives with them for twenty-five years before being "rescued" by Texas Rangers.

Meyers, Walter Dean. *The Righteous Revenge of Artemis Bonner*. New York: HarperCollins, 1992.

Fifteen-year-old Artemis Bonner leaves New York City in the late 1800s to find his uncle's murderer. His is also looking for the gold mine his uncle had sketched from memory on a map as he faces many adventures in the Old West.

Mikaelsen, Ben. *Rescue Josh McGuire*. New York: Hyperion, 1991.

Careless because he has been drinking, Josh's father accidentally kills a mother bear while he and his son are hunting. Thirteen-year-old Josh undertakes an arduous journey to the mountainous Yellowstone area to try to save the cub. A cruel summer snowstorm endangers his life and makes rescue attempts difficult.

Nixon, Joan Lowery. *A Deadly Promise*. New York: Bantam, 1992.

Against an authentic historical setting, this sequel to *High Trail to Danger* pits Sarah against dangerous opponents in Leadville, Colorado, as she tries to clear her father's name.

————. *High Trail to Danger*. New York: Bantam, 1991.

After her mother's death in 1879, Sarah leaves Chicago for Leadville, Colorado, in search of her father. Her life is threatened in this lawless town when her father's reputation alienates her from local people who might otherwise have helped her.

O'Dell, Scott, and Elizabeth Hall. *Thunder Rolling down the Mountain*. New York: Dell, 1993.

The daughter of Chief Joseph, Sound of Running Feet, relates the story of the Nez Perce Wars of 1988. Completed by O'Dell's wife after the author's death, the story reveals a daughter's respect for her father; the strong love for the warrior, Swan Necklace; and the grief over the changing lives of her people.

Paulson, Gary. *The Haymeadow*. New York: Delacorte, 1992.

Tending his father's herd of sheep on his own proves to be quite a growing-up experience for fourteen-year-old John as he battles the elements and animals in the Wyoming mountains.

Ruckman, Ivy. *Spell It M-U-R-D-E-R*. New York: Bantam, 1994.

In a fast-paced tale set on the rural high plains of Colorado, two girls run away from an unpleasant camp experience right into bigger trouble when they see two men dumping body bags into the lake one foggy night.

Taylor, Theodore. *Walking up a Rainbow*. New York: Harcourt Brace, 1994.

Set in 1852, Susan, a gutsy orphaned teenage girl, travels from Iowa to California with a herd of 2,000 sheep. The reader gets a strong sense of time and place as Susan experiences gunfights, gamblers, and shady ladies during this memorable journey.

Thomasma, Ken. *Naya Nuki: Shoshoni Girl Who Ran.* Charlotte, N.C.: Baker & Taylor, 1992.

Naya Nuki is kidnapped by a rival tribe and must walk alone through the wilderness for over a month in an effort to return to her people. This story of courage and survival is a winner of the Wyoming Children's Book Award.

———. *Pathki Nana: Kootenai Girl Solves a Mystery.* Charlotte, N.C.: Baker & Taylor, 1992.

A shy Kootenai girl goes into the mountains to seek a guardian spirit as is the tribal custom. Her visit results in an exciting life-and-death struggle. Winner of the Wyoming Children's Book Award.

Woodruff, Elvira. *Dear Levi: Letters from the Overland Trail.* Illus. by Beth Peck. New York: Alfred A. Knopf, 1995.

An orphan heading west in 1851, young Austin writes letters to his brother Levi whom he hopes can also travel the West someday. The letters relate the hardship, fears, and friendships that are a part of the journey.

Wyss, Thelma Hatch. *A Stranger Here.* New York: HarperCollins, 1993.

Jada Sinclair has no idea how interesting her summer is going to be as she takes care of her ailing aunt in a small Idaho town. Meeting Starr Freeman, a spirit from the past, helps her to get priorities straight in her life.

4
The Southwestern States: Texas, Oklahoma, New Mexico, and Arizona

Anaya, Rudolfo. *The Farolitos of Christmas.* Illus. by Edward Gonzales. New York: Hyperion, 1995.

Ingenuity is needed when Abuelo cannot cut the wood for the traditional Christmas luminarias. Luz creates small lanterns of her own by placing candles in paper bags, which are weighted down with sand. Set in New Mexico during World War II, the warm story explains the tradition of farolitos.

Antle, Nancy. *Beautiful Land: A Story of the Oklahoma Land Rush.* Illus. by John Gampert. New York: Viking, 1994.

Annie Mae and her family have traveled from Missouri to Kansas but aren't settled yet. They are lined up on the border with hundreds of other settlers to rush across the line and claim land of their own in the newly opened Oklahoma Territory.

Dewey, Jennifer Owens. *Cowgirl Dreams: A Western Childhood.* Honesdale, Pa.: Boyds Mill Press, 1995.

In this honest biography, Dewey tells of her childhood growing up on a ranch in New Mexico. She enjoyed the freedom to roam but had to deal with the high expectations of a father who was often away from home. She shares her love of nature, animals, and the adventures that prompted her to become a writer.

Ellison, Suzanne Pierson. *The Last Warrior.* Flagstaff, Ariz.: Northland, 1997.

Solito, a teenage Apache brave, is unable to complete his warrior training before his band is captured by the U.S. Army. Forced to adapt to the white man's ways and stripped of his culture, he eventually finds himself at odds with the new world into which he has been thrust and the old world to which he tries to return. This coming-of-age story is based on the true story of Geronimo's Chiricahua Apaches.

Hobbs, Will. *Kokopelli's Flute.* New York: Atheneum, 1995.

Thirteen-year-old Tepary Jones finds an ancient flute made of eagle bone in the ruins of an Anasazi cliff dwelling during a summer eclipse. Unable to resist blowing on it, he becomes a changeling: adolescent by day, wood rat by night. When it appears his mother has contracted a deadly virus, a mysterious stranger offers help.

———. *Downriver.* New York: Atheneum, 1992.

A group of seven unruly teenagers enrolled in a wilderness education program decide that they can run the Colorado River through the Grand Canyon on their own. They steal the gear from the river guide and are off on the adventure of their lives. It proves to be a growing-up experience for fifteen-year-old Jessie, the teller of the tale.

Lasky, Katherine. *A Voice in the Wind: A Starbuck Family Adventure.* San Diego, Calif.: Harcourt Brace, 1993.

The telepathic Starbuck twins discover an Anasazi ghost in New Mexico and eventually free her to join her family in the spirit world. They also become entangled with a dangerous group that steals Native American artifacts in this suspense-filled adventure.

Lightfoot, D. J. *Trail Fever: The Life of a Texas Cowboy.* New York: Lothrop, Lee & Shepard, 1992.

This is the biography of George Saunders, a cowboy who endured cattle drives, stampedes, and skirmishes with Indians on the wild and unruly Texas frontier around the period of the Civil War.

McComb, David G. *Texas, An Illustrated History.* New York: Oxford University Press, 1995.

Visually appealing and filled with information, this book is interesting to browse through or to use for research. Chapters include Native Americans and the Land, Texas and Spain, The Lone Star: Nation and State, The Last Frontier, and Museums and Historical Sites.

MacGregor, Rob. *Prophecy Rock.* New York: Simon & Schuster, 1995.

Spending a summer with his father, a police chief on a Hopi reservation, helps Will to better appreciate his Native American heritage. While there, he becomes involved in solving a mystery of a killer who is obsessed with an ancient prophecy.

Meyer, Carolyn. *White Lilacs.* New York: Gulliver, 1993.

This story is based upon actual events that occurred in Quakertown, Texas, in the 1920s. An entire African-American community known as Freedomtown is forced to relocate so that a park can be built.

Moore, Martha. *Under the Mermaid Angel.* New York: Delacorte, 1995.

When Roxanne, a grown woman, moves into the trailer next door, thirteen-year-old Jesse finds a close friend in whom she can confide. An amusing story with appealing characters!

Myers, Anna. *Rosie's Tiger.* New York: Walker, 1994.

Rosie, a sixth grader, lives in a small Oklahoma town. She has a difficult adjustment to make when her brother returns from the Korean War with a Korean wife and her son. Her true feelings emerge during a crisis when her nephew, Yong So, falls into a cistern.

Paulson, Gary. *Canyons.* New York: Bantam Doubleday Dell, 1990.

A mystical link across time joins fifteen-year-old Brennan Cole and Coyote Runs, an Apache boy on the brink of adulthood. A skull with a bullet hole and the search for an ancient sacred place change Brennan's life.

Roessel, Monty. *Songs from the Loom: A Navajo Girl Learns to Weave.* Minneapolis, Minn.: Lerner, 1995.

Jaclyn's grandmother teaches her the art of Navajo rug weaving and in the process, the ten-year-old learns the songs and stories that fill the rug with meaning. She is taught to use the proper tools and techniques as well. The photographs and text are both excellent.

Russell, Sharman Apt. *The Humpbacked Fluteplayer.* New York: Alfred A. Knopf, 1994.

May has recently arrived in Phoenix and is homesick. When she gently touches a cave drawing of a humpbacked flute player, she and a classmate are transported into a parallel world where they become slaves of a harsh, magical desert tribe.

Vick, Helen Hughes. *Walker's Journey Home.* Tucson, Ariz.: Harbinger House, 1995.

In this fast-paced sequel to *Walker of Time,* Walker must lead the Sinagua out of Walnut Canyon to the Hopi Mesas, a journey filled with danger. Tag has traveled forward in time so Walker is on his own as the Indians battle distance, enemies, drought, and superstition. In the final book in the trilogy, *Tag Against Time,* released in 1996, twelve-year-old Tag starts a journey that will return him to his own time. When he is faced with the destruction of the abandoned cliff dwellings he knows so well, he wonders what he can do to affect a history that is already written.

——. *Walker of Time.* Tucson, Ariz.: Harbinger House, 1993.

Voted as a Best Book for Young Adults by the American Library Association, this time-travel tale takes the reader back to A.D. 1250 to live with the Singagua in Walnut Canyon. This is an engrossing story as Walker, a fifteen-year-old Hopi, and his amusing companion, Tag, learn what threatens this clan of Walker's ancestors and their role in helping them to survive.

Wisler, G. Clifton. *Jericho's Journey.* New York: Lodestar Books, 1993.

In this adventure story, eleven-year-old Jericho has difficulties facing the realities of Texas after moving from Tennessee. The romantic tales that had filled his head with Davey Crockett and Sam Houston are not enough, but the help of an older brother makes all the difference in the world.

5

The Heartland: North Dakota, South Dakota, Nebraska, Kansas, Minnesota, Iowa, and Missouri

Andrews, Elaine. *Indians of the Plains.* New York: Facts on File, 1992.

Part of an eight-part series that presents many Native American tribes within the appropriate geographic location. Chapters include Roots, Living, Rituals and Religion, and Change. Excellent resources for upper elementary grades and for teachers to use as well.

Armstrong, Jennifer. *Black-Eyed Susan.* Illus. by Emily Martindale. New York: Crown, 1995.

Ten-year-old Susie and her father love living on the South Dakota prairie with its endless uninterrupted views of the land and sky, but Susie's mother greatly misses their old life in Ohio. The emptiness and open space weigh heavily on her mind as she reflects that "it's too big here."

Beatty, Patricia. *Jayhawker*. New York: Morrow, 1991.

Set just before the Civil War, this story tells of the troubles faced by Lije Tulley and his father who are Jayhawkers or abolitionists. After his father's death during a raid on a Missouri plantation, Lije joins a group of Confederates working undercover to inform Kansans of raids on the Kansas Territory.

Bunting, Eve. *Train to Somewhere*. Illus. by Ronald Himler. New York: Clarion Books, 1996.

In this longer picture book, Marianne tells of her travel westward in the 1800s on the Orphan Train as she looks for her mother.

Conrad, Pam. *My Daniel*. New York: HarperCollins, 1989.

Ellie and Stevie listen to their grandmother tell how her brother Daniel discovered a brontosaurus on the family farm in Nebraska. As the story moves from the present to the past, and forward again, the children learn of the love shared between their grandmother and her brother.

Freedman, Russell. *An Indian Winter*. Illus. by Karl Bodmer. New York: Holiday House, 1992.

This book gives a detailed description of the Mandan and Hidasta tribes based upon accounts of two European explorers who were befriended by the two tribes. The two men learned of their rich traditions after wintering with the tribes, which were gradually eroded by a smallpox epidemic, the slaughter of buffalo, and the loss of lands to the white man.

Holland, Isabelle. *The Journey Home*. New York: Scholastic, 1990.

Maggie Lavin is an Irish Catholic immigrant who was orphaned at the age of twelve. She escapes poverty in New York City by traveling with her younger sister to Kansas on an Orphan Train. There she finds a home with a kindly couple but has many adjustments to make in this unfamiliar rural environment. Not being able to read, having poor skills when working with animals, and maintaining her Catholic beliefs are added burdens with which she must cope.

MacLachlan, Patricia. *Sarah, Plain and Tall*. New York: HarperTrophy, 1985.

Life is extremely difficult when mother dies. When their father decides to invite a mail-order bride to come to live in their prairie home, Caleb and Anna grow to like her and hope that she will stay.

Paulsen, Gary. *Father Water, Mother Woods: Essays on Fishing and Hunting in the North Woods*. Illus. by Ruth Wright Paulsen. New York: Delacorte, 1994.

Older readers will enjoy the memories Paulsen shares of hunting and fishing in the Minnesota woods when he was younger. Very realistic, the essays give the reader a sense of place.

Rossiter, Phyllis. *Moxie*. New York: Four Winds Press, 1990.

Thirteen-year-old Drew works diligently to help his family survive a hard life on a Kansas farm through dust storms, poverty, and hoboes in the 1930s during the Great Depression.

Ruby, Lois. *Steal Away Home*. New York: Macmillan, 1994.

Two parallel stories told in alternating chapters introduce twelve-year-old Dana Shannon (who finds a skeleton in a secret room of her house) and James Weaver (who lived in the house back in the 1850s). Dana's story involves a diary that is overlooked when the skeleton is removed while James relates events that occur when his home becomes a stop on the Underground Railway.

Turcotte, Mark. *Songs of Our Ancestors: Poems About Native Americans.* Illus. by Kathleen S. Presnell. Chicago: Children's Press, 1995.

This is a collection of more than twenty poems focusing on famous North American Indians and memorable events in their history. Poetry about the Trail of Tears, Sitting Bull, the Code Talkers of World War II, and Buffy Sainte-Marie are included.

Turner, Ann. *Grasshopper Summer.* New York: Macmillan, 1989.

Is it an adventure to leave Kentucky in post–Civil War years and establish a home in the unknown Dakota Territory? Young Billy thinks so, but his older brother Sam White is quite skeptical. The story is related through the eyes of the boys as the family makes the arduous trek across the country leaving family and friends behind. After the hard work of rebuilding their lives, grasshoppers devour every green thing in sight.

Twain, Mark. *The Adventures of Huckleberry Finn.* Illus. by Steven Kellogg. New York: Morrow, 1994.

This classic is enhanced by seventeen full-color illustrations as the exploits of Huck Finn and the runaway slave, Jim, are shared. Rafting down the Mississippi River they encounter some knotty problems.

Welch, Catherine A. *Clouds of Terror.* Illus. by Laurie K. Johnson. Minneapolis, Minn.: Carolrhoda Books, 1994.

A gripping and realistic fictional account of an 1870s invasion of Rocky Mountain locusts on a Swedish American family's farm in Minnesota. The book gives readers insight into life on the prairie, economic hardship, a family's ability to cope, and children's roles on the farm.

Wilder, Laura Ingalls. *Little House on the Prairie.* New York: HarperCollins, 1935.

Beginning with this timeless classic and reading all of the others in the series as well, students will get an understanding of life on the prairie including the joys and sorrows inherent in pioneer life.

6
The Great Lakes States: Illinois, Indiana, Michigan, Wisconsin, and Ohio

Anderson, William. *Laura Ingalls Wilder: A Biography.* New York: HarperCollins, 1992.

Two of the chapters in this book pertain to Laura's life in Wisconsin. This is a carefully researched, readable book that reveals Laura's ninety years as daughter, sister, teacher, wife, mother, and author.

Bauer, Marion Dane. *On My Honor.* Boston: Houghton Mifflin, 1986.

This Newbery Honor winner makes engrossing reading. Twelve-year-old Joel promises his father never to go near the dangerous Vermillion River, polluted and filled with undertows. His daredevil friend Tony convinces him to swim instead of finishing a bike ride to Starved Rock State Park. When Tony drowns, Joel has difficulty telling both sets of parents and then dealing with the death.

Blos, Joan. *Brothers of the Heart: A Story of the Old Northwest, 1837–1838.* New York: Aladdin, 1987.

In this realistically told story, a dying Native American woman teaches a fourteen-year-old physically handicapped boy how to survive in the Michigan wilderness.

Brink, Carol Ryrie. *Magical Melons.* Illus. by Marguerite Davis. New York: Macmillan, 1990.

The fourteen stories about Caddie Woodlawn and her family paint a picture of life in a small Wisconsin farming community in the 1860s. Native American stereotypes might be discussed; otherwise, this is an entertaining peek at Wisconsin history.

Cavan, Seamus. *Daniel Boone and the Opening of the Ohio Country.* New York: Chelsea House, 1991.

Daniel Boone played an important role in the exploration of the Ohio River Territory, which became Ohio, Indiana, and Illinois. Interesting photographs and maps add to the text.

Collier, James Lincoln. *The Jazz Kid.* New York: Henry Holt, 1994.

Set against a background of Chicago in 1927, a young boy obsessed with jazz tries to break into the music world. Steeped in the real world of jazz and a carefully researched picture of life in Chicago at the time, this is an excellent read.

De Angeli, Marguerite. *Copper-Toed Boots.* New York: Doubleday, 1992.

Country living in the nineteenth century is illustrated through Shad's teasing, his friends, the relationships with his family, and his efforts to get a longed-for dog. The book is based upon childhood stories told to her by her father.

DeFelice, Cynthia. *Weasel.* New York: Macmillan, 1990.

A fast-paced adventure story set in 1839 Ohio that relates the struggle to survive torment by a cruel Indian hunter named Weasel. Courageous Nathan and Molly have the help of a mute frontiersman as they work to save their father's life after he has been left to die in one of Weasel's traps.

Fleischman, Paul. *The Borning Room.* New York: HarperCollins, 1991.

In a sensitively written tale, Georgina shares scenes from the borning room where she lies dying. This seldom-used room has seen the births and deaths of this frontier Ohio family, each one leaving its mark on the family history.

Freedman, Russell. *The Wright Brothers: How They Invented the Airplane.* New York: Holiday House, 1991.

This photobiography describes the lives of the Wright brothers and explains how they developed the first airplane. An added attraction are the original photos taken by the brothers.

———. *Lincoln: A Photobiography.* New York: Clarion Books, 1987.

This intriguing presentation of Lincoln's life won the Newbery Award. It covers Lincoln's early childhood, early work in law, his political career, and his presidency during the Civil War. A nice touch is the appendix containing a sampling of his notable quotes.

Grove, Vicki. *Rimwalkers.* New York: Putnam, 1995.

Living in the shadow of her popular younger sister is difficult for fourteen-year-old Tory. A summer on her grandparents' farm getting reacquainted with her cousin Elijah is welcomed.

When troubled Rennie arrives, the peace of the summer appears to be destroyed. The ghostly apparition of a little boy waving from the window of an abandoned house is another ingredient that makes this a wonderful read.

Henry, Joanne Landers. *A Clearing in the Forest: A Story About a Real Settler Boy.* Illus. by Charles Robinson. New York: Four Winds Press, 1992.

This is a biographical novel about Elijah who grew up in Indianapolis in the 1830s. The characters are lively and the text is based upon Elijah's unpublished manuscript and his father's diaries.

Herman, Charlotte. *A Summer on Thirteenth Street.* New York: Dutton, 1991.

Shirley Cohen finds growing up in a Chicago neighborhood during World War II a challenge. Being eleven and in love certainly complicates things but having Morton as a good friend helps.

Holling, Holling Clancy. *Paddle-to-the-Sea.* Boston: Houghton Mifflin, 1969.

This classic tells the tale of a toy canoe carved by an Indian boy and sent on a four-year journey through the Great Lakes and down the St. Lawrence River to the Atlantic Ocean.

Howard, Ellen. *The Chickenhouse House.* Illus. by Nancy Oleksa. New York: Atheneum, 1991.

Based upon a great-aunt's memories this story tells of Alean's dismay when she learns that her first winter home on the prairie is a chicken house. In the spring, family and neighbors build a new home but it takes some adjusting to as well. An easily read book for younger readers.

Levine, Ellen. *Ready, Aim, Fire! The Real Adventures of Annie Oakley.* New York: Scholastic, 1989.

Annie was born in a cabin on the Ohio frontier and became the world's most famous female sharpshooter. Photos include some of Annie, her husband, and posters from the Wild West Show.

McKissack, Patricia, and Frederick McKissack. *A Long Hard Journey: The Story of the Pullman Porter.* New York: Walker, 1989.

George Pullman tried out his first sleeping car on a run between Bloomington, Indiana, and Chicago. Thousands of African-American porters who served on those Pullman sleepers struggled for fair treatment, forming the first African-American union in the process. The photos and quality writing make this an excellent resource for research or just general information.

Weinberb, Larry. *The Story of Abraham Lincoln, President for the People.* Illus. by Tom LaPadula. New York: Dell, 1991.

Well-written text and full-page sketches combine to present an appealing biography of Abraham Lincoln. The book begins with his grandfather selling the farm in Virginia then discusses life in Kentucky, including the Gettysburg Address, and ends with a thorough time line highlighting Lincoln's life.

Willis, Patricia. *A Place to Claim as Home.* New York: Clarion Books, 1991.

Henry, a thirteen-year-old orphan, is hired for the summer by Miss Morrison, a rather unfriendly woman. It is 1943 when many of the men are gone to war, a time when two people find that they need each other.

Woodyard, Chris. *Haunted Ohio: Ghostly Tales from the Buckeye State.* Beavercreek, Ohio: Kestral, 1991.

Ohio ghost stories and lore ranging from Native American tales to contemporary haunted houses have been carefully documented in this appealing book.

Zeier, Joan T. *The Elderberry Thicket*. New York: Atheneum, 1990.

When Mr. Parsons must leave to look for a new job, he and his rural Wisconsin family face difficult times. The Depression has already caused problems for them but they work together to get through the summer of 1938 with the help of their neighbors.

7

The New England States: Vermont, Massachusetts, New Hampshire, Connecticut, Maine, and Rhode Island

Bruchac, Joseph. *Dog People: Native Dog Stories*. Golden, Colo.: Fulcrum Publishing, 1995.

Readers slip back in time to experience a number of outdoor adventures and learn how to survive along with Abenaki children and their dogs.

Coleman, Penny. *Mother Jones and the March of the Mill Children*. New York: Millbrook Press, 1995.

This book is a biography of Mary Harris "Mother" Jones. Through text, news articles, informative photographs, and graphics, the story of the woman's efforts to defend the rights of underage mill workers is told.

Davol, Marguerite W. *Papa Alonzo Leatherby: A Collection of Tall Tales from the Best Storyteller in Carroll County*. New York: Simon & Schuster, 1995.

During one terribly cold New England winter, every one of Papa's stories freezes. His wife preserves some of them to be retold throughout the year and they are enjoyable indeed.

Freedman, Russell. *Kids at Work: Lewis Hine and the Crusade Against Child Labor*. Photographs by Lewis Hine. New York: Clarion Books, 1994.

This readable and informative photo-essay tells about Lewis Hine's work to end child labor as he entered shops, mills, and homes to record and expose the miserable working conditions children endured.

Gaeddert, LouAnn. *Hope*. New York: Atheneum, 1995.

When their mother dies, two children go to live in Massachusetts in a Shaker village. Hope dislikes the rules and wishes for her father's return from California. John, her brother, finds life with the Shakers to be quiet and healing.

Guiderson, Brenda Z. *Lighthouses: Watchers at Sea*. New York: Henry Holt, 1995.

This is a comprehensive introduction to the history and lore surrounding lighthouses. Well-written narrative, diagrams, photos, and drawings make this an enjoyable, informative book.

Hall, Donald. *Old Home Day*. Illus. by Emily Arnold McCully. San Diego, Calif.: Browndeer Press, 1996.

This book is a must in the geography curriculum as it shows the movement of people and the growth of a fictional town in New Hampshire from prehistoric times through its bicentennial.

Hall, Elizabeth, and Scott O'Dell. *Venus Among the Fishes*. New York: Houghton Mifflin, 1995.

In this fantasy, Coral, a dolphin, is sent in search of her older brother for help in saving her pod from deadly killer whales.

Hansen, Joyce. *The Captive.* New York: Scholastic, 1994.

This riveting first-person tale is modeled after an actual slave narrative. It follows twelve-year-old Kofi from his kidnapping in West Africa to his cruel enslavement in Massachusetts, then on to freedom and his career as a sailor.

Hermes, Patricia. *On Winter's Wind: A Novel.* Boston: Little, Brown, 1995.

Fearing her father is lost at sea, Gen struggles to keep their family together. When she learns that she can turn in a runaway slave for a $100 reward, she faces a moral dilemma. She learns that her Quaker friends are part of the Underground Railway and has serious decisions ahead of her. An excellent novel about believable people.

Kinsey-Warnock, Natalie. *The Canada Geese Quilt.* Illus. by Leslie W. Bowman. New York: Yearling, 1989.

Ten-year-old Ariel learns about the circle of life as news of a new baby in the family makes her feel left out and then Grandma suffers a stroke. This small book is filled with the warmth of close family relationships and the joys a quilt can bring.

Kraus, Scott, and Kenneth Mallory. *The Search for the Right Whale.* New York: Crown, 1993.

This is a scientific detective story in which researchers from Boston's New England Aquarium study and record information about the endangered North Atlantic right whale. Excellent maps and photos are included.

MacLachlan, Patricia. *Skylark.* New York: HarperCollins, 1994.

A drought threatens the family's stability in this sequel to *Sarah, Plain and Tall.* Sarah takes the two children to Maine to visit her aunts until just before school is to start. The book ends on an upbeat with the promise of a baby in the spring.

Manitonquat. *The Children of the Morning Light.* Illus. by Mary F. Arquette. New York: Macmillan, 1994.

Stories from oral tradition of the mainland Wampanoag Indians in southeastern Massachusetts are set down here. The author worries that something happens to a tale when it is put in words versus taking on a special life when related by a storyteller, but also wants these stories of creation and migration to be preserved.

Mead, Alice. *Walking the Edge.* New York: Albert Whitman, 1995.

Scott gets satisfaction as he works on his 4H project restocking the mud flats near his Maine village with clams. It is a reprieve from his cruel father and a life of poverty. When the project is threatened, Scott fights to save it.

———. *Crossing the Starlight Bridge.* New York: Bradbury Press, 1994.

Abandoned by her father, nine-year-old Rayanne cannot begin to understand why she must leave their Two Rivers Island home and travel west. When she and her mother must also leave the Penobscot-owned town and move in with her grandmother, there are more adjustments to make. Authentic Penobscot designs decorate the text.

Paterson, Katherine. *Lyddie.* New York: Lodestar Books, 1991.

Lyddie Worthen journeys to Lowell, Massachusetts, to become a mill girl in an effort to earn enough money to gather her scattered family. The horrendous working conditions and the need to help her abused younger sister bring out the best in this determined young heroine.

Ray, Mary Lyn. *Shaker Boy.* Illus. by Jeanette Winter. San Diego, Calif.: Browndeer Press, 1994.

When his father was killed in the Civil War, Caleb's mother left him with the Shakers. In a well-told story, Caleb matures, accepting responsibility as he is positively influenced by the Shaker's beliefs.

Robinson, Jane W. *The Whale in Lowell's Cove.* Camden, Me.: Down East Books, 1992.

The main character in this story is a real humpback whale who spent a month in a cove in Harpswell, Maine. This fact-filled book includes delicate colored-pencil illustrations and excellent maps.

Sewell, Marcia. *Thunder from the Clear Sky.* New York: Atheneum, 1995.

Told in alternating accounts, a Pilgrim and a Wampanoag Indian relate their first encounters. Chief Massasoit welcomed the Pilgrims and made treaties with them. As more immigrants arrived, tensions developed between the two groups, ending in a war where many lives were lost. The presentation of the same events from two viewpoints makes thought-provoking reading.

Stone, Bruce. *Autumn of the Royal Tar.* New York: HarperCollins, 1995.

Nora and her mother have trouble dealing with their feelings over the loss of Nora's brother until a shipwreck near their home involves them with the survivors, including a boy left motherless by the wreck and a captive elephant.

8

The Mid-Atlantic States: New York, New Jersey, Pennsylvania, Delaware, and Maryland

Avi. *Encounter at Easton.* New York: Morrow, 1994.

In the sequel to *Night Journeys,* two runaway indentured servants, Robert and Elizabeth, try to find sanctuary. It is presented in an interesting format, that of the court testimony of Robert and three others, which contributes to the suspense of the story.

———. *Night Journeys.* New York: Morrow, 1994.

A suspenseful story set in colonial Pennsylvania involving Peter, an orphan who is unhappy with his guardian, and two runaway indentured servants. Part of the search party, Peter mistakenly helps one of the runaways, then shoots her when she tries to escape. When he realizes they are in similar situations, he must make a choice about whose side he is on.

———. *Captain Grey.* New York: Morrow, 1993.

Set in post–Revolutionary War America, this adventure story is about a boy captured by pirates. The leader believes it is more honest to fight for one's own personal gain than to serve any country's government, a belief that others throughout history have shared.

Bruchac, Joseph. *The Boy Who Lived with the Bears and Other Iroquois Stories.* Illus. by Murv Jacob. New York: HarperCollins, 1995.

This is an appealing collection of traditional Iroquois tales that would have been presented around the campfires by the elders as lessons to remember. A beautiful book to read and enjoy.

Clay, Rebecca. *Kidding Around Philadelphia: A Young Person's Guide to the City.* Illus. by Kim W. Iversz. Santa Fe, N.Mex.: John Muir Publications, 1991.

A lively, useful introduction to the City of Brotherly Love.

Conrad, Pam. *Our House: The Stories of Levittown.* Illus. by Brian Selznick. New York: Scholastic, 1995.

Levittown's history as a perfect Long Island suburb shortly after World War II is the organizational thread that ties these well-written stories together. The children who live in the community over the years tell their stories across the decades in a rather personal approach to history. The pen-and-ink drawings at the beginning of each story show the gradual changes in the community.

Gaeddert, LouAnn. *Breaking Free.* New York: Atheneum, 1994.

At the turn of the nineteenth century, orphaned Richard Baldwin goes to his uncle's farm in upstate New York to live. The rugged rural setting and the presence of slaves are major adjustments to a sensitive boy accustomed to city life and who believes that slavery is evil.

Girion, Barbara. *Indian Summer.* New York: Scholastic, 1990.

Jodi McCord and her family are spending the summer on the Iroquois Woodland Reservation in New York. Jodi goes with a chip on her shoulder and Sarah Birdsong knows it. It's touch and go as these two try to establish a friendship, overcoming their differences in the process.

Herda, D. J. *Ethnic American: The Northeastern States.* Brookfield, Conn.: Millbrook Press, 1991.

The ethnic makeup of the northeastern states is related through text and numerous illustrations. The accomplishments of people of diverse backgrounds are also shared.

Herold, Maggie Rugg. *A Very Important Day.* Illus. by Catherine Stock. New York: Morrow, 1995.

Individuals and families from around the globe are not deterred by the snow as they make their way to the city courthouse for their naturalization as United States citizens.

Kenna, Kathleen. *A People Apart.* Photographs by Andrew Stawicki. San Diego, Calif.: Houghton Mifflin, 1995.

The Old Order Mennonites described in this excellent photo-essay live a very different life from that of some of the more modern families in Pennsylvania. Like the Amish, they don't use modern machinery, electricity, or conveniences like zippers as they perpetuate the old ways of living and thinking. A respectfully written and interesting glimpse into the lives of these good people.

Levy, Elizabeth. *The Drowned.* New York: Hyperion, 1995.

During her summer's stay in Atlantic City, Lily researches and conducts tours of the city's haunted spots. She nearly drowns before she discovers that the boy who so intrigues her is really a ghost.

Moore, Robin. *When the Moon Is Full: Supernatural Stories from the Old Pennsylvania Mountains.* New York: Alfred A. Knopf, 1994.

Six haunting tales inspired by folk legends from central Pennsylvania include relationships between animals and people, making a fuzzy distinction between the two. For example, a hunter becomes bearlike when he lives with his former prey.

Morris, Ann. *Dancing to America.* Photographs by Paul Kolnik. New York: Dutton, 1994.

In search of freedom, opportunity, and a better way of life, the Pankevich family left the former Soviet Union. Sixteen-year-old Anton, a dancer, faces similar concerns that immigrants a century earlier faced: language, customs, and acceptance. He succeeds because of strong dreams and unfailing determination.

Nirgiotis, Nicholas. *Erie Canal: Gateway to the West.* New York: Franklin Watts, 1993.

The story of the construction of the amazing superstructure of canals dreamed about and supervised by DeWitt Clinton is told as Lake Erie and the Hudson River are eventually joined.

Press, Petra. *A Multicultural Portrait of Immigration.* New York: Benchmark Books, 1996.

Starting with the earliest immigrants, the Indians, and moving through current immigrants this informative volume relates the history of immigration to the United States.

Rose, Deborah Lee. *The Rose Horse.* Illus. by Greg Shed. San Diego, Calif.: Harcourt Brace, 1995.

Lily's father carves carousel animals at Coney Island where a clinic for "preemies" is paid for by spectators' admission fees. Lily's baby sister needs those services. Set in 1909, this story captures the era and shows how Eastern European immigrants lovingly pass on their Jewish heritage.

Sawyer, Ruth. *Roller Skates.* Illus. by Valenti Angelo. New York: Viking, 1995.

A reissue of a lively story of Lucinda's "orphan" year when she is free to explore New York on roller skates, making numerous friends in this Newbery Award–winning picture of a piece of the author's childhood.

Service, Pamela. *Phantom Victory.* New York: Charles Scribner's Sons, 1994.

In 1908, a treasure was hidden near a lovely Lake Erie island hotel but catastrophes including a drowning and a fire erased all traces of it. Overcoming their mutual dislike for each other, Terri and Brian work together with ghostly apparitions in a dangerous effort to solve the mystery that appears to link their families and the hotel.

9
The Appalachian Highlands: North Carolina, Virginia, West Virginia, Kentucky, and Tennessee

Brooks, Barbara. *The Twin in the Tavern.* New York: Aladdin, 1993.

In a story full of unexpected twists a young orphan boy finds himself in the hands of a sinister tavern owner in Alexandria, Virginia. He is not prepared for what awaits him, especially when he meets a boy who looks just like he does.

Carter, Forrest. *The Education of Little Tree.* Albuquerque: University of New Mexico Press, 1990.

A reissue of a coming-of-age story of a young Cherokee boy living with his grandparents in Appalachia in the 1930s.

Cole, Norma. *The Final Tide.* New York: McElderry/ Macmillan, 1990.

Set in 1948 in a Kentucky valley community, fourteen-year-old Geneva Haws has her hands full as a TVA project threatens to flood out the town. While most people grudgingly decide to move to higher ground, Geneva's granny refuses to move, willing to die in "the final tide."

Conly, Jane Leslie. *Trout Summer.* New York: Henry Holt, 1995.

Forced to move to the city from their rural Virginia home, Shana and Cody have some trouble adjusting. They welcome the opportunity to spend the summer in a cabin in the woods where they meet Old Henry, a self-appointed forest ranger. Time in the woods seems to help both children work out their problems with a broken family in a very well written survival story.

Creech, Sharon. *Walk Two Moons.* New York: HarperCollins, 1994.

Salamanca Tree Hiddle has lived in Virginia all of her thirteen years. She is distraught when her father moves to Ohio to start life anew after her mother leaves home. She travels with her eccentric grandparents to see her mother in time for her birthday in Idaho, hoping to bring her home. Along the way she provides an entertaining tale about her new friend, Phoebe Winterbottom.

Donahue, John. *An Island Far from Home.* Minneapolis, Minn.: Carolrhoda Books, 1994.

Joshua Loring has lost his father in the Battle of Fredericksburg. When he is asked by his uncle, stationed at George's Island, to write to a fourteen-year-old Confederate prisoner at the fort, he unhappily agrees. In the process, he learns that there are no easy answers to issues involving war.

Feelings, Tom. *The Middle Passage: White Ships/ Black Cargo.* Illus. by author. New York: Dial/ Penguin, 1995.

This is an incredibly difficult book to "read" as one relives the horrors of slavery as slaves are shipped from Africa to America. A wordless book,

each double-page spread has a story to tell in itself. Often only a third of the people survived the nightmare passage only to face degradation on the slave block upon their arrival. A powerful book for upper grade students.

Forrester, Sandra. *Sound the Jubilee.* New York: Lodestar Books, 1995.

Set in 1861, the story introduces the reader to strong-willed Maddie, an eleven-year-old slave. After being freed from slavery, she and her family struggle to earn economic security over a four-year period on Roanoke Island.

Green, Connie Jordan. *Emmy* . New York: McElderry/Macmillan, 1992.

Emmy assumes even more responsibility after Pa is injured in a mining accident as she and the rest of the family try to help keep the family together. Unfortunately, that means her oldest brother must start working in the mines so that the family can remain in their home.

Houston, Gloria. *Mountain Valor.* New York: Philomel, 1994.

Set during the Civil War and based upon a real incident, young Valor disguises herself as a boy. She joins the war with the goal of revenging a wrong that has been done to her North Carolina family.

———. *Littlejim.* New York: Philomel, 1990.

Twelve-year-old Littlejim loves to learn. He hopes to win an essay contest and win the respect of his stern father in the process.

Kraft, Betsy Harvey. *Mother Jones: One Woman's Fight for Labor.* New York: Clarion Books, 1995.

A well-written biography about a courageous union organizer who helped the coal miners. Photographs and documents enrich the text.

Myers, Anna. *Graveyard Girl.* New York: Walker, 1995.

Eli distances himself from people as he tries to adjust to losing his family in the 1878 Memphis yellow fever epidemic. He learns that by caring for others he can work through his grief. The author's careful research of a seldom written-about topic will be appreciated by fans of historical fiction.

Naylor, Phyllis Reynolds. *Shiloh.* New York: Bantam, 1991.

Set in Friendly, West Virginia, this Newbery winner relates the tale of Marty and his strong love for a runaway dog, an abused beagle he will do anything to keep.

Osborne, Mary Pope. *American Tall Tales.* Illus. by Michael McCurdy. New York: Alfred A. Knopf, 1991.

This collection of tales recounts the adventures of Davy Crockett, Sally Ann Thunder, Ann Whirlwind, Johnny Appleseed, Stormalong, Mose, Febold Feboldson, Pecos Bill, John Henry, and Paul Bunyan. Brief background notes for each character and a map showing sites of their adventures are included.

Oughton, Jerrie. *Music from a Place Called Half Moon.* San Diego, Calif.: Houghton Mifflin, 1995.

Edie Jo Houp's father suggests that they open their church's Vacation Bible School to the Indian children in the area. White residents in Half Moon, North Carolina, don't take kindly to integration, a difficult lesson for thirteen-year-old Edie Jo to learn about her community.

Paterson, Katherine. *Flip-Flop Girl.* New York: Lodestar Books, 1994.

After her father dies, Lupe's family moves to Virginia where Lupe becomes the misunderstood

rival in school. Grief and healing, jealousy and forgiveness are carefully dealt with in a memorable book.

Reaver, Chap. *Bill.* New York: Delacorte, 1994.

Life with her alcoholic, moonshiner father is difficult to endure but Jessica's much-loved dog, Bill, helps her survive. This warmly told story takes an interesting turn when her father is arrested and Jessica has to learn to trust again.

Reeder, Carolyn. *Grandpa's Mountain.* New York: Macmillan, 1991.

Carrie watches the reactions of her grandparents when they learn that the state of Virginia wants to buy their Blue Ridge home and store to create a national park. Which one, she wonders, is the most courageous? Grandpa vows to fight to save their home while Grandma plans for the inevitable changes.

———. *Shades of Gray.* New York: Macmillan, 1989.

At twelve, Will has lost everything he loved—his family, his city home in Winchester, and his lifestyle. At the close of the Civil War he travels to the Virginia Piedmont to live with Aunt Ella and Uncle Jed whom he calls a traitor because he refused to fight in the Civil War.

Rosen, Michael J. *A School for Pompey Walker.* Illus. by Aminah Brenda Lynn Robinson. San Diego, Calif.: Harcourt Brace, 1995.

Pompey Walker is an incredible human being. Even though he has escaped his brutal slave existence, he returns to the auction block thirty-nine times. Each time, his white friend poses as an auctioneer, sells Pompey, then helps him escape. The money from these numerous sales is used to open a school for African Americans. An intriguing story based upon fact.

Rylant, Cynthia. *Best Wishes*. Photographs by Carlo Ontal. Katonah, N.Y.: Richard C. Owen, 1992.

Cynthia Rylant describes her writing process and how it is intertwined with the experiences of her life. Lovely photographs show the West Virginia countryside, where she was raised as part of a coal-mining family, and her current home in Ohio.

————. *Missing May*. New York: Orchard Books, 1992.

In this 1993 Newbery winner, Uncle Ob and twelve-year-old Summer try to face the loss of Aunt May's death. They learn that love comes in many different forms as they resettle into a new way of life in the West Virginia countryside.

Yep, Laurence. *The Star Fisher*. New York: Morrow, 1991.

In West Virginia in 1927, it is difficult for outsiders to be accepted. Joan Lee's family moves from Ohio and they have a struggle ahead to gain acceptance in the face of the town's backward views and firmly set opinions.

10
The Southeastern States: Arkansas, Mississippi, Alabama, Georgia, South Carolina, Louisiana, and Florida

Andryszewski, Tricia. *Marjory Stoneman Douglas, Friend of the Everglades*. Brookfield, Conn.: Millbrook Press, 1994.

Not only is this an informative biography of the woman who worked diligently to save the Everglades, but it is packed to the brim with information about this wonderful ecosystem.

Burch, Robert. *Renfroe's Christmas*. Athens: University of Georgia Press, 1993.

Told in simple prose, this book tells how the Madison brothers discover the importance of unselfishness as the picture of old-fashioned country life and warm, caring family members emerge. Set in Georgia in the 1930s.

Curtis, Christopher. *The Watsons Go to Birmingham—1963*. New York: Delacorte, 1995.

This book is garnering its share of awards and attention. It begins in a lighthearted vein as the "Weird Watsons" head from Flint, Michigan, south to vacation in Birmingham where they are witnesses to the tragic events of the civil rights movement. It is an attitude-altering experience.

DeFelice, Cynthia. *Lostman's River*. New York: Macmillan, 1994.

This well-written, fast-paced story is set in 1906 when Tyler, working as a guide in the Everglades, is forced to be an unwilling participant in the destruction of a rookery. A subplot reveals why Ty's family is living in the swamp in the first place, leading to a conflict between ethics and survival.

George, Jean Craighead. *'Gator of Gumbo Limbo*. New York: HarperCollins, 1992.

Lisa works to save a great alligator named Dajun and to protect the environment in this tale set in the Everglades.

Hamilton, Virginia. *Her Stories: African American Folktales, Fairy Tales, and True Tales*. Illus. by Leo and Diane Dillon. New York: Scholastic, 1995.

A beautifully illustrated book that contains a wonderful collection of tales rooted in the African-American world that are instructive as well as inspirational.

————. *The People Could Fly: American Black Folktales.* Illus. by Leo and Diane Dillon. New York: Scholastic, 1985.

In this award-winning book are tales that allowed an oppressed people to share their joys and sorrows. Besides being good reading, these tales give the reader insight into part of our American past. The author describes them as a celebration of the American spirit.

Henderson, Aileen Kilgore. *The Summer of the Bonepile Monster.* Minneapolis, Minn.: Milkweed, 1995.

Set somewhere in the rural South, Hillis and his older sister spent the summer with their wily great-grandmother while their parents try to patch up their marriage. A genuine good read about mystery, friendship, and family love.

Lauber, Patricia. *Alligators: A Success Story.* Illus. by Lou Silva. New York: Henry Holt, 1993.

Quality work as always is shared as the author writes of her experiences while observing alligators in the Everglades, telling about the reptile, its habits, how it lives, and its role in the ecosystem.

Pringle, Laurence. *Dolphin Man: Exploring the World of Dolphins.* Photographs by Randall S. Wells and the Dolphin Biology Research Institute. New York: Atheneum, 1995.

Well written and filled with fabulous color photos, this book will intrigue anyone who wants to explore dolphin life.

Ralph, Judy, and Ray Gompf. *The Peanut Butter Cookbook for Kids.* Illus. by Craig Terlson. New York: Hyperion, 1995.

Illustrated with light hearted cartoon drawings, this book shows step-by-step instructions for integrating peanut butter into snacks, desserts, and main dishes. It also includes the history of the versatile peanut and explains its nutritional value.

Rorby, Ginny. *Dolphin Sky.* New York: Putnam, 1996.

When she is around her father, twelve-year-old Buddy would dearly love to do well in school and to do things right but it just doesn't seem possible. She befriends two dolphins that are being held captive and mistreated at Stevens Everglades Eden near her home in the Everglades. A warm, wonderful first novel in which readers learn about life in and around the Florida Everglades.

Smothers, Ethel Footman. *Moriah's Pond.* New York: Alfred A. Knopf, 1995.

Set in rural Georgia in the 1950s, this quiet story filled with regional dialect relates lively Moriah's life including shelling peas, getting her hair straightened, and wading in the pond. Hurt by racism, she finds it difficult to hold her peace around white folks as her grandmother advises.

Taylor, Mildred. *The Well: David's Story.* New York: Dial, 1995.

A thought-provoking novel about a hard-working African-American family in Mississippi and how they are willing to share their bounty with neighbors, black or white.

Young, Ronder Thomas. *Learning by Heart.* New York: Houghton Mifflin, 1993.

Set in the South in the 1960s this warm story describes the friendship between Rachel, a white girl, and Isabella, a young, black Mennonite housekeeper. Rachel has lessons to learn as she adjusts to the birth of a sibling, faces changing relationships at school, and learns about the underlying racial prejudices in her town.

11
Alaska and Hawaii

Fay, Stanley. *The Last Princess: The Story of Princess Ka'iulani of Hawaii.* Illus. by Diane Stanley. New York: Four Winds Press, 1991.

This is an account of a brave princess who fought to preserve the freedom of her people and of the annexation of the Hawaiin Islands to the United States.

George, Jean Craighead. *Julie.* New York: HarperCollins, 1994.

This is the long-awaited sequel to *Julie of the Wolves.* Tension develops when Julie decides to return to her father and stepmother, still worrying that he will kill the rest of her wolf pack as he did its leader.

Hill, Kirkpatrick. *Winter Camp.* New York: McElderry Books, 1993.

In this sequel to *Toughboy and Sister,* the two orphaned children are living with an elderly neighbor, Natasha. She takes them to her old winter camp to learn techniques for trapping and surviving in the bitterly cold weather. Once again the children's ability to survive is strongly tested.

————. *Toughboy and Sister.* New York: McElderry Books, 1990.

When Mama dies in October, eleven-year-old John (Toughboy) and his younger sister, Laurie, are left with their father. Daddy takes them to their fishing camp as usual. After drinking too much, he accidentally dies and the children are on their own. This is a great survival story.

Hoshino, Michio. *The Grizzly Bear Family Book.* New York: North-South Books, 1994.

Warmly presented, these fierce bears are shown protecting their cubs and searching for just the right fish in their Alaskan habitat.

Kiehm, Eve Begley. *Plantation Child and Other Stories.* Illus. by Christine Joy Pratt. Honolulu: University of Hawaii, 1995.

Told from the viewpoints of different members of a Korean family, this book examines the immigrant experience in the early 1900s in Hawaii.

London, Jack. *The Call of the Wild.* Illus. by Barry Moser. New York: Macmillan, 1994.

This classic has been nicely updated as it tells the story of a dog stolen from his California home to work as a sled dog during the Alaskan gold rush.

Salisbury, Graham. *Under the Blood-Red Sun.* New York: Delacorte, 1994.

Tomikazu Nakaji's life changes dramatically when the Japanese bomb Pearl Harbor. Gone are the days of fishing, playing baseball, and enjoying school on Ohau. His father and grandfather are arrested. He and his mother must try to retain the pride and dignity of their family name.

————. *Blue Skin of the Sea: A Novel in Stories.* New York: Delacorte, 1992.

After his mother dies, seven-year-old Sonny goes to live with his aunt. When he moves to the Big Island to live with his father, he is afraid of the sea despite the fact that he comes from a family of fishermen. In eleven different stories highlighting a thirteen-year period, Sonny grows up and faces his fears.

Walker, Sally M. *Volcanoes: Earth's Inner Fire.* Minneapolis, Minn.: Carolrhoda Books, 1994.

This is a fascinating book filled with excellent color photographs that show a variety of volcanic action. The book explores the geographic distribution of volcanoes and their impact on the world around them.

12
An Introduction to Our Neighbor to the North: Canada

Bouchard, Dave. *The Elders Are Watching*. Illus. by Roy Henry Vickers. Vancouver, B.C.: Eagle Dance/Raincoast Books, 1990.

This book addresses revival, culture, heritage, environment, and the importance of instilling such values in today's children. A young boy is sent to live with his grandfather to learn his heritage and how to care for the environment. Beautiful illustrations show the West Coast, past and present.

Canadian Childhoods: A Tundra Anthology. New York: Tundra Books, 1989.

The multicultural nature of Canada is reflected in the authors and illustrators who have contributed to this book. It will appeal to children of all backgrounds in all parts of this diverse country.

Cooper, Susan. *The Boggart*. New York: McElderry Books, 1993.

An ancient, mischievous sprite is accidentally shipped to Toronto in the drawer of an antique desk. The boggart creates a great deal of trouble before a way to ship him back to his home in Scotland is discovered.

Dramer, Kim. *The Chipewyan*. New York: Chelsea House, 1996.

This book examines the culture and history of a tribe that has adjusted to the subarctic environ-

ment and shares daily preparations, precautions, traditions, and rituals.

Ellis, Sarah. *Next-Door Neighbors*. New York: Macmillan, 1990.

Shy Peggy has trouble adjusting to the family's move to Vancouver. She learns some memorable lessons about friendship, prejudice, and tolerance as she settles into sixth grade and her new home.

Hausherr, Rosmarie. *The City Girl Who Went to Sea*. New York: Four Winds Press, 1989.

Life in a Newfoundland fishing village as experienced by a ten-year-old American girl is presented in a warm and informative story. The book includes an author's note and an illustrated salvage fishing glossary.

Hudson, Jan. *Dawn Rider*. New York: Philomel, 1990.

Kit Fox, a sixteen-year-old Blackfoot Indian girl, dreams of being the first in her tribe to own a horse. Life in the tribe is revealed through Kit as preparations are made for a buffalo run, the upcoming marriage of her older sister, battles with the enemy Snake Indians, and her romance with Found Arrow. The book is based upon information in records from the Blackfeet Nation.

———. *Sweetgrass*. New York: Philomel, 1989.

Sweetgrass proves her capability and maturity to her father when she saves her family from a devastating smallpox epidemic. The story is filled to the brim with information about the Blackfeet Indians' way of life.

Pang, Guek-Cheng. *Cultures of the World: Canada*. New York: Marshall Cavendish, 1994.

In an attractively presented manner, this book for older readers discusses the history, government, economy, and cultures of Canada.

Pearson, Kit. *The Lights Go On Again.* New York: Viking, 1994.

This is the last of the three books about Gavin and his sister Norah who were sent to Canada for safety during World War II. When the children learn that their parents were killed by a bomb in England, young Gavin struggles with some major decisions on what to do from this point on.

———. *The Sky Is Falling.* New York: Viking/Kestrel, 1990.

It is the summer of 1940 and ten-year-old Norah and her little brother are sent to Canada for safety during the war years. Placed with two wealthy women, young Gavin settles in quickly but Nora finds life lonely. Things are no better at school and it takes time for her to adjust to her new life in Canada.

Robinson, Margaret A. *A Woman of Her Tribe.* New York: Charles Scribner's Sons, 1990.

Accepting a scholarship to St. John's Academy in Victoria, British Columbia, means leaving her Nootka village, a frightening thought to fifteen-year-old Annette. She also must deal with her dual cultural heritage, a difficult process. This book is for more mature readers.

Yee, Paul. *Tales of Gold Mountain: Stories of the Chinese in the New World.* Illus. by Simon Ng. New York: Macmillan, 1990.

This collection of eight original tales was inspired by the brave history of the Chinese who immigrated to Canada in the nineteenth century. Some are funny, others are sad as they relate the adventures of frontier life and the traditions of the people.

13
An Introduction to Our Neighbor to the South: Mexico

Braun, Barbara. *A Weekend with Diego Rivera.* New York: Rizzoli International Publications, 1994.

Illustrated with reproductions of the artist's work, the life and work of this great Mexican painter and muralist are explained. Insight into the history and traditions of Mexico can be gleaned in this book.

Buss, Fran Leeper (with Daisy Cubias). *Journey of the Sparrows.* New York: Lodestar Books, 1991.

In order to escape murder in El Salvador, fifteen-year-old Maria, two siblings, and another teenager are smuggled into the United States. They suffer starvation and terrible working conditions in Chicago. Maria's courage and determination offer hope in a bleak situation. This award-winning book is for more mature readers.

Carlstrom, Nancy White. *Light: Stories of a Small Kindness.* Illus. by Lisa Desimini. Boston: Little, Brown, 1990.

Seven original short stories are set in a variety of settings including Mexico, Guatemala, Haiti, and New York City. Each story includes a "small kindness," an event that almost seems miraculous and illuminates the triumph of the human spirit.

George, Jean Craighead. *The Shark Beneath the Reef.* New York: Harper & Row, 1989.

Tomas Torres lives with his grandfather and uncle on the shores of the Sea of Cortez. He wants to follow in their footsteps and be a fisherman but also longs for a degree in marine biology. When the government tries to promote tourism over supporting the fishing industry, Tomas can more readily make his decision.

Lasky, Kathryn. *Days of the Dead.* Photographs by Christopher G. Knight. New York: Hyperion, 1994.

In this photo-essay a family is captured in their celebration of the Days of the Dead. Food preparations, decorating the family altars, and visits to the village market are explained through informative text and colored photos.

Mathews, Sally Schofer. *The Sad Night: The Story of an Aztec Victory and a Spanish Loss.* New York: Clarion Books, 1994.

Aztec codices frame the text in this story told from the Aztec perspective. Connecting past and present, it reveals how the Aztecs won a battle over their Spanish conquerors.

Paulsen, Gary. *The Crossing.* New York: Orchard Books, 1987.

Manuel Bustos battles to survive on the dangerous streets of Juarez. His dream is to escape across the Rio Grande to a better life in the United States. A chance meeting with Sgt. Robert Locke who is trying to escape the nightmares of the Vietnam War begins a relationship that bodes trouble for one and a better life for the other.

Peck, Richard. *The Unfinished Portrait of Jessica.* New York: Delacorte, 1991.

Fourteen-year-old Jessica idolizes her father and blames her mother for driving him away. An exciting trip to Acapulco to visit him shatters her illusions and helps her to rebuild her relationship with her mother.

Poynter, Margaret. *The Uncertain Journey: Stories of Illegal Aliens in El Norte.* New York: Atheneum, 1992.

Detailed, moving stories of twelve illegal aliens are told including several pages of complementary photographs. The countries included are Mexico, Central America, South America, and the Caribbean.

Putnam, James. *Pyramid.* Photographs by Geoff Brightling. New York: Alfred A. Knopf, 1994.

Filled with fascinating information, this book discusses the cultures in ancient Mexico, China, Africa, and Central America.

Stray, P. J. *Secrets in the Mayan Ruins.* Englewood Cliffs, N.J.: Silver Burdett Press, 1995.

While on vacation in Mexico, Ray and Rachel and they friend Andrew accidentally unravel the mystery of ancient Mayan artifacts that keep disappearing from the archeological site at Chichen Itza.

Appendix III

Ideas for Projects

While the activities described in Appendix III are targeted for specific states or regions in North America, they can be used interchangeably throughout the book to make geography come alive for students. Adjust them to the abilities of children in different grade levels. Add a twist of your own to make an idea work better for your particular learners. It is hoped that these ideas will be catalysts for creativity across ages and grade levels to make geographic concepts tantalizing and memorable as students become actively involved in their learning.

2

The Pacific Coast States: Washington, Oregon, and California

The Trifold Book

Directions

Fold an 8½-by-11 sheet of paper into thirds. The basic book approximately 3½ inches wide is ready to use. It can be used horizontally or vertically. Students may wish to conform to the topic they are working with to shape the book but they must leave an adequate amount of the fold intact so that the book will open and close in three segments.

If used for a report:
1. Title on the front page of the book.
2. Something about the author and a sketch or photograph on the back page of the book.
3. Pertinent vocabulary words or key concepts on the inside bottom flap.
4. Beginning, middle, and ending report on the inside.

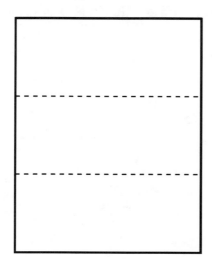

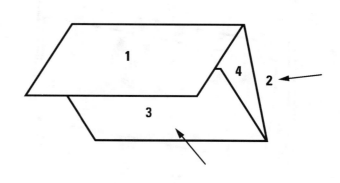

Layered-Look Book

Directions

1. Place two sheets of 8½-by-11 paper on top of each other. Slide the top sheet down about 1 inch.

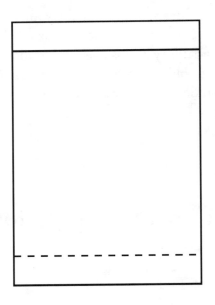

2. Bring the bottoms of both sheets up toward you and align the edges so that all of the layers are the same distance apart. Fold the papers, creasing well.

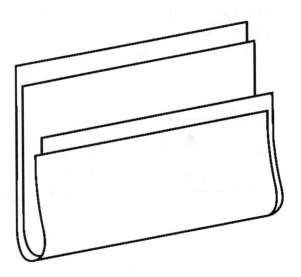

3. Open the papers and glue them together using glue in the creases sparingly.

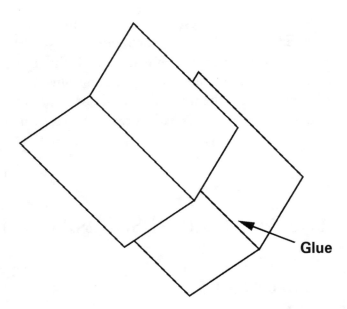

Extra sheets can be added to make six- or eight-page books. Larger paper can be used if more information is to be included or if students want more space for artwork. Books can be used sideways, or where pages flip up from top to bottom. Students may want to shape the top sheet or title page to reflect the topic of the book. Using one's imagination makes the final product creatively delightful!

3

The Mountain States: Idaho, Colorado, Montana, Nevada, Utah, and Wyoming

Looking at a Slice of Earth

Directions

Fill in the diagram below with the layers from the crust to the core making it as neat and attractive as possible.

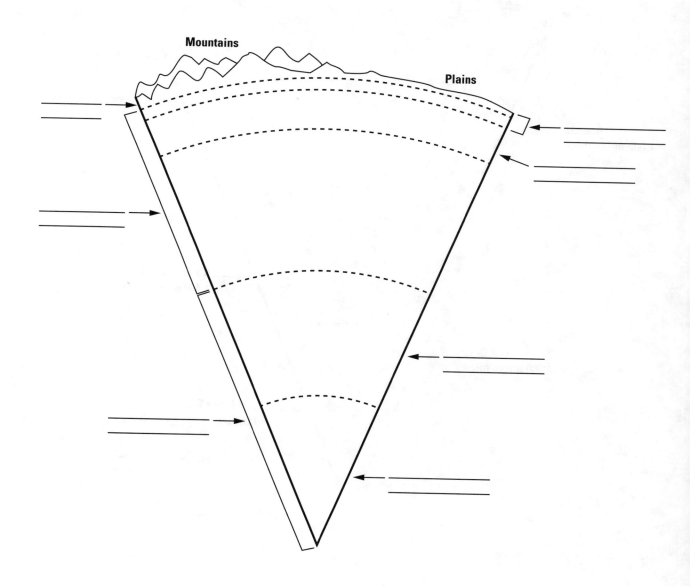

Answers to exercise on page 193.

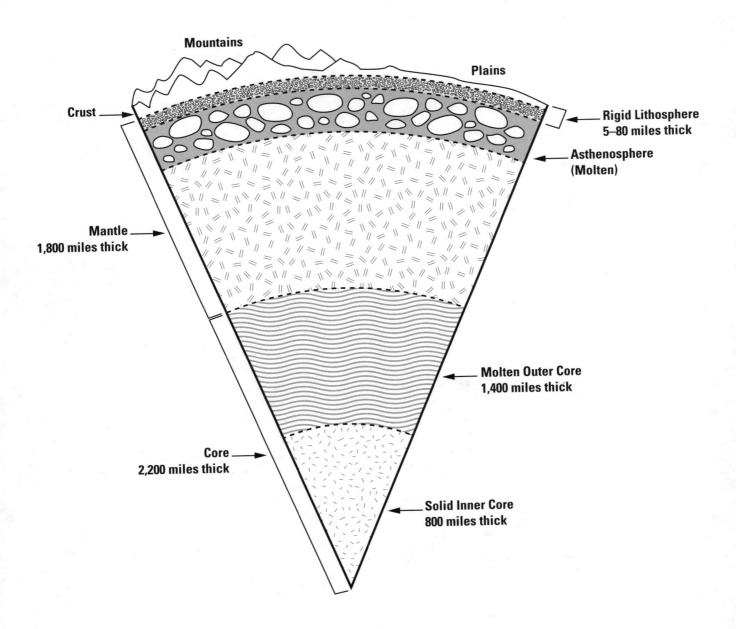

Tectonic Sandwiches

Materials

- three kinds of bread, approximately the same size. One piece should be thinly sliced white bread (which will represent the crust of the earth), and wheat and dark rye, regularly sliced, can serve as the other two lower layers of the earth. You will need enough bread for each child to make one three-layer sandwich, plus one extra slice to be used to demonstrate domes and basins.
- clean hands: Emphasize how important it is to wash hands with soap and warm water before handling food or eating
- chunky peanut butter (chunks represent rocks in the layers)
- jelly or jam
- knives for spreading and cutting
- paper plates to hold sandwiches as they are worked on
- paper towels, about six sheets per child to cover work area and to use to wipe hands on

Directions

1. Take one slice of thin white bread, a slice of rye, and one of wheat for the sandwich. The thin white bread will go on top as it represents the thin outer crust of the earth. Put a layer of jam or jelly between the white bread and the next slice, rye. Use enough jelly or jam so that the slice will slide easily but not so much that the jam oozes out between the slices. Use peanut butter between the rye and wheat slices.
2. Cut the sandwich in half into two rectangles. Set one half aside on a clean paper towel.

Fault-Block Demonstration

1. Tell the students to cut the remaining half of their sandwich into thirds.
2. Ask the students to turn the thirds of their sandwiches on their sides matching the following diagram. Now the layers are clearly visible. They can slide one section up or down to illustrate what happens when stress occurs along fault lines and one piece of the earth rises up or slides down as a result.

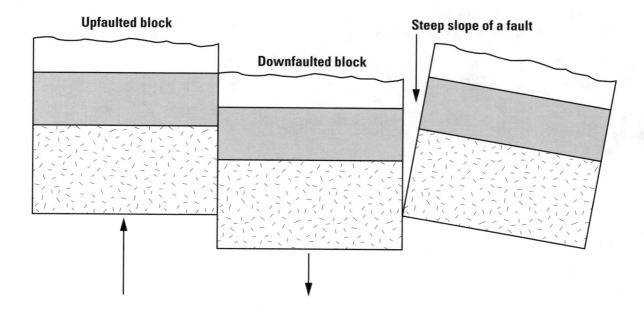

Upfaulted block   **Steep slope of a fault**

Downfaulted block

3. They can tip one-third of the sandwich away from the others at a slight angle to see how other rocks or debris could fall into the resulting opening. This is a simple illustration of how fault-block mountains are formed. Set the pieces aside.

Colliding Continents

1. Take the second half of the sandwich and cut through the thin crust only in the middle so that the top layer is divided in half.
2. Have students gently push the two top pieces, which represent continental plates, toward each other. The colliding edges will probably rise up forming a teepee shape or the beginning of a new mountain. One plate might slide under the other as well. Since the bread is not as soft as fabric material, it will not fold though, so a demonstration with a fabric placemat should follow this part. Explain to students that the Appalachian Mountains were formed in such a manner.
3. Carefully slide the top pieces of bread back into place. Cut the rectangle completely in half leaving two quarters of the sandwich.

Subduction

1. With the two quarters of the sandwich next to each other, students should gently slide one side of the top white "crust" downward and push it beneath the third layer of the other quarter. This is an example of two plates colliding, the Pacific Plate is the one sliding under the Continental Plate. They are to imagine the heat from the earth's core dissolving the Pacific Plate as it slides under the other side where the Continental Plate of the second quarter is being lifted upward. If there were holes in the Continental Plate, the lightweight molten material would ooze upward, forming volcanic mountains like Mount St. Helens or the Rocky Mountains.

Domes and Basins

1. Set the sandwiches back onto the paper plate and take one plain piece of bread.
2. Holding the bread in the left hand as firmly as possible so that it doesn't flop around, use a knuckle of the index finger of the right hand to gently push upward in the middle of the slice of bread. This simple movement shows how dome-shaped mountains like those in the Black Hills were formed. If students push downward forming a depression in the piece of bread, they can see how basins across the Midwest were created. Conclude the activity by washing sticky hands, cleaning up the area, and eating the experiment with a carton of cold milk or juice.

4

The Southwestern States: Texas, Oklahoma, New Mexico, and Arizona

The Texas Bluebonnet Activity

Reading *The Legend of the Bluebonnet* by Tomie dePaola would be a nice introduction to this activity.

Materials
- wooden shish kebab skewers
- plastic six-pack rings
- scissors
- blue and white spray paint
- newspapers to cover the painting area

(Note: If you know this is an activity that you will do, ask the students to recycle their six-pack rings in a box somewhere in the classroom starting early in the school year. They will be doing both the class and the environment a big favor.)

Directions
1. Each student needs two six-pack rings and one skewer per flower.
2. Cut the two six-pack rings to make twelve oval-shaped rings.
3. Twist an oval ring into the shape of the number 8, making certain that the center pieces are on top of each other.
4. Holding the folded ends together, carefully push them onto the pointed end of the wooden skewer. Push the ring about three-fourths of the way down the skewer.
5. Repeat steps 3 and 4, alternately turning the rings to hide the skewer and creating the look of blossoms.
6. Use about twelve rings to make one flower. Fold the last ring over the point of the skewer to form the end of the blossom.
7. Spray the bottom three-fourths of the rings with blue paint. Add white paint to the top of the flower. The paints will splatter and mix, making the final product more attractive.
8. Once the blossoms are completed and dried, display them in class or take them home to be enjoyed by the family. Encourage the students to retell *The Legend of the Bluebonnet* to their family.

5

The Heartland: North Dakota, South Dakota, Nebraska, Kansas, Minnesota, Iowa, and Missouri

Looking at Regions Group Worksheet

State:_____

Directions

Within the group, decide who will be in charge of each section of the report. Record only the basic facts on the worksheet. Each person's job is to become an "expert" on their area, make carefully organized notes so that the information can be taught to others in the group first, and then taught to the class as a whole later. Summarize what you have learned by creating a quadrarama to use as part of your class presentation.

Names of students in the group: _____

Absolute location: _____

Relative location: _____

Key geographic features (rivers, lakes, mountains, etc.): _____

_____

Key facts (general climate): _____

_____

Key facts (agriculture): _____

_____

Key facts (manufacturing): _____

_____

Places to see and things to do: _____

_____

Use the back of the sheet to note other interesting discoveries.

Looking at Regions _____

State or Territory _____

Geography	Climate	Vegetation	Wildlife	Human/Environmental Interactions

Comments and Conclusions:

The Venn Diagram

When using the Venn diagram to compare and contrast time periods, cultures, regions, or other characteristics, list the differences in the outer circles, one circle per characteristic. The similarities are to be written in the area where the two circles overlap.

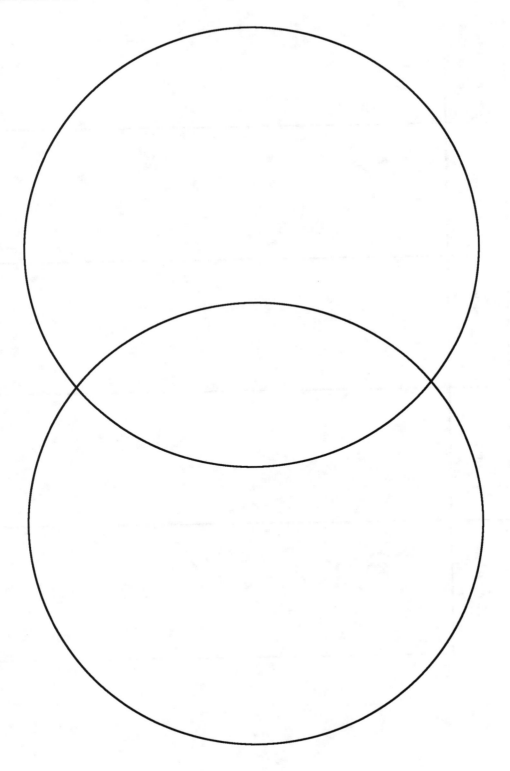

One Triarama Times Four = A Quadrarama

A triarama is a three-dimensional way for students to present what they have learned about a particular subject. If four triaramas are glued back to back, a quadrarama is formed.

Materials

- four sheets construction paper or other heavy paper cut to 9 inches by 9 inches
- construction paper scraps or other useful craft materials
- glue
- scissors
- markers, crayons, pencils

Directions

1. Using one sheet of paper, fold the top right corner down to the lower left corner. Repeat with the opposite corners.

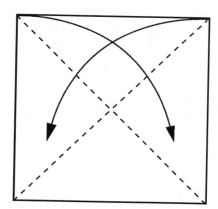

2. Open flat and cut one fold just to the center of the square.

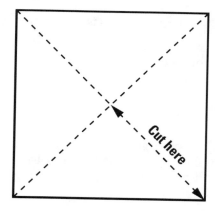

3. Draw an appropriate background scene on the upper half of the sheet in the large triangular shape.

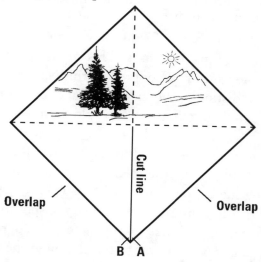

4. Overlap the two small bottom triangles and staple or glue.
5. For the quadrarama, repeat with three other sheets of paper.
6. Fill each triarama with a pop-up symbol or simple scene supported by L-shaped folded strips of paper. Glue one side of the strip to the figure and the other to the floor of the triarama.

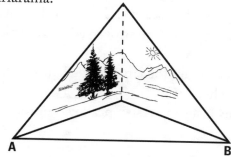

7. Write a simple, informative caption on each segment.
8. Display by hanging several together to form a mobile or on bookshelves or countertops for classmates to enjoy.

There's More to a Name than You Think: Riddles and Absolute Location

Use the riddles and the coordinates on a map of Kansas to learn more about interesting cities in this Heartland state. Note that the coordinates do not give the exact location for the answer so the students may have to look around a bit for the answer to make sense.

1. To keep a meeting moving along efficiently, prepare this ahead of time. (B 8) _____
2. They purify the air and when massed together provide a peaceful (E 8) _____ for animals and people alike: (B 7) _____, (B 6) _____, (E 12) _____, and (F 12) _____
3. No matter how difficult life was for the pioneers, (D 9) _____ kept them going.
4. Is it Georgia or Kansas? This city is found in both places. (F 9) _____
5. Immortalized by Longfellow, this Native American comes to life through poetry. (B 11) _____
6. This distinctive hound is long and low with ears that dust the ground. (E 11) _____
7. We could be talking about explorers, presidents, or popular modes of transportation, past and present. (C 12) _____, (F 5) _____, and (C 7) _____
8. A staple in the diet of many Americans and a lovely, bright color. (E 8) _____
9. You might like these fancy eggs for brunch or you could be referring to a man disliked by many during the Revolutionary War. (F 11) _____
10. On a hot summer's day, here's the spot to be for a healthy, refreshing drink. (F 8) _____
11. Speaking of drinks, do you prefer decaf or regular? They are bound to have it here. (G 11) _____
12. An inexpensive way to travel around the world, to visit places in the past and in the future, and to expand your horizons. (D 10) _____
13. Now here's a city for our fine-feathered friends. (B 2) _____
14. Native Americans who once lived in the rugged Allegheny and Great Smokey Mountains in mat-covered houses. (F 12) _____
15. Don't look for this in the Lost and Found. (D 9) _____
16. Two nouns that are at the heart of democracy. (F 11) _____ and (F 11) _____
17. Nearly hunted to extinction, this animal was highly prized by the Plains Indians. (D 6) _____ A synonym for this word is (E 11) _____.
18. In the northern regions of the United States, this is a popular item of clothing. (F 6)_____
19. A memorable skirmish locale in Boston prior to the Revolutionary War. (C 6) _____
20. This man was a controversial early explorer who put our country on the map, so to speak. (F 12) _____
21. You can roam the largest grasslands in North America and see some of Kansas' 425 species of birds if you are here. (C 12) _____
22. If this inspiring Asian peak was in Kansas, you could probably see it from border to border. (B 11) _____

Answer Key
1. Agenda 2. Haven, Burr Oak, Cedar, Lone Elm, Walnut 3. Hope 4. Atlanta 5. Hiawatha 6. Bassett 7. DeSoto, Ford, Lincoln 8. Maize 9. Benedict 10. Clearwater 11. Coffeyville 12. Reading 13. Bird City 14. Cherokee 15. Lost Springs 16. Liberty, Independence 17. Bison, Buffalo 18. Coats 19. Bunker Hill 20. Columbus 21. Countryside 22. Everest

7

The New England States: Vermont, Massachusetts, New Hampshire, Connecticut, Maine, and Rhode Island

Accordion Book Project

Materials

- one sheet of 12-by-18-inch lightweight construction paper, cut into two long strips
- scissors, paper punch
- glue, yarn or ribbon
- one small strip of paper to connect two folded pieces if students want a longer book

Note: The size of paper used will depend on the student's choice for the final product.

Directions

1. Take one strip of paper and fold it in half, bringing the short ends together and creasing firmly. Next, fold the ends backward to make a W-shaped piece.

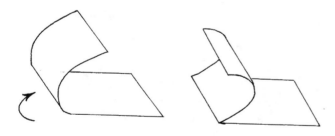

2. Take the short ends and fold them to the nearest fold. You'll be folding to the second and third folds. Now you should have a triple V-shape.

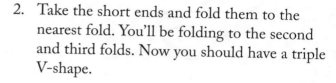

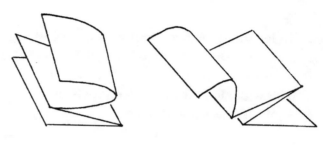

3. Take the small V-shapes and fold point A to fold B and then point C to fold B.

4. Fold the sections back on themselves at point B. You will have an accordion fold in eight equal sections or a sixteen-page book if both sides are used.

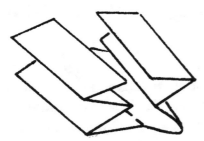

5. To lengthen the book, repeat the directions, making another eight-page book. Cut a strip of paper the same height as the book and 1 inch wide. Fold it in half lengthwise and carefully cover it with glue.

6. Attach one side of the strip to one accordion and then to the other. Be sure both pieces of the accordion meet in the center of the glued strip.

7. Once the book is folded, use a paper punch and punch holes at each end. It might be wise to measure 1 inch in from the edge and make a small pencil dot so that holes will line up. Punch each hole separately instead of trying to punch several at once.

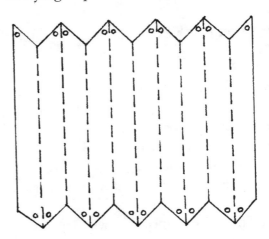

8. To bind the book, run a piece of yarn or ribbon and wrap it around the book and add one extra length. Thread yarn or ribbon through the holes when the book is folded and tie closed with a bow. To read the book, untie the bow, open carefully, and enjoy!

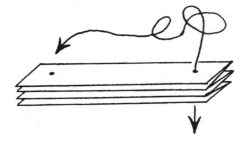

8

The Mid-Atlantic States: New York, New Jersey, Pennsylvania, Delaware, and Maryland

Geographic Investigation Sheet for the Chesapeake Bay

A good book to get you started is *Waterman's Child* by Barbara Mitchell. Look closely at the illustrations by Daniel San Sousi for clues to life in the Chesapeake Bay area. Jot down notes to be compared with at least two other books on this area.

Investigation Team Focus Questions:

1. Where is Chesapeake Bay? Give both its absolute and relative locations.

2. How was this particular region formed? Based on your investigation, when did this happen?

3. What is it like in and around Chesapeake Bay? What would it be like to live nearby and to earn your living doing something related to the bay? What kinds of jobs are connected to the bay?

4. What is the relationship between people and place as you learn about the area? Is it mutually beneficial to both humans and the bay?

5. How has the area changed since early settlers built the homes along its shores? What major cities have grown up here? Why?

6. What role does the theme of movement play when applied to Chesapeake Bay?

When the investigative work is completed, how will it be presented to the class? There are many options:

- create a mural of the area and how it has changed over the years
- read an appropriate picture book to the class and then expand on what the book describes
- read a collection of poems that pertain to life in this area and support them with further information
- pantomime some of the jobs that are done on the bay, following up with your report
- write a poem about one aspect of life on the bay and then share additional knowledge
- make up a game that would involve your classmates and teach them about the Chesapeake Bay at the same time
- make a mobile of pertinent features that relate to the bay and use it as a prop as you teach the class more about the area
- think up your own project to be discussed with the teacher

Mid-Atlantic States Scavenger Hunt

Directions

Invite the students to work on this activity in pairs, which will help build skills in cooperation and teamwork. They may search for answers to the clues in a collection of classroom books used in chapter 8. It might be fun to give each team one special pass to the library to consult an expert on a particularly elusive clue. Prepare the librarian ahead of time! Set a time limit based on the abilities of your particular class. Once a team has written down answers to all the questions, the teacher will check them to determine the winners. The winning team might win a paperback book set in this part of the country, while everyone else receives Hershey's Kisses® for their efforts.

1. Once a major gateway to America. Give its name and the state. (Ellis Island, New York)
2. Match a type of mouth-watering candy to the town in which it is created. Don't forget the state. (Hershey; Hershey, Pennsylvania)
3. Find two rivers in New Jersey that have boy's names. (Tom's River, Maurice's River)
4. Find a state sliced in two by a bay. Name both. (Maryland, Chesapeake Bay)
5. Go back in time and discover the first state to join the Union and the date. (Delaware; December 17, 1787)
6. Use your imagination and find a state shaped somewhat like a wolf with a collar. (New York)
7. Who's counting? Find the fifth largest city in the United States. (Philadelphia)
8. "There she is, Miss America." Just where is she? (Atlantic City, New Jersey)
9. Home of art galleries, theater, art museums of world acclaim, and a street called Broadway. (New York City)
10. Founder of the state of Pennsylvania. (William Penn)
11. Location of the first dinosaur skeleton discovered. What kind of dinosaur was it and in what year was it discovered? (Haddonfield, New Jersey; Hadrasaur—it has webbed toes, millions of teeth, a beak like a duck, and is 30 feet long; it was found in 1858)
12. Look in Maryland for a mountain based on anatomy. (Backbone Mountain)
13. Name and location of a group of long, narrow trenchlike bodies of water, almost skeletal in appearance. (The Finger Lakes in New York)
14. Find a school with a fine reputation where discipline and strategy go hand in hand. Earn two bonus points if you can find two schools. (West Point Military Academy in West Point, New York; U.S. Naval Academy in Annapolis, Maryland)
15. Because over sixty varieties of fruits and vegetables are grown here, this state has earned a nickname. (The Garden State is New Jersey's nickname.)
16. Where will you be if you are at the highest point in New York State? Just how high are you? (Mount Marcy at 5,344 feet)
17. Site of the signing of the Declaration of Independence, building and city. (Independence Hall, Philadelphia, Pennsylvania)
18. A sweet treat with salt in its name was created here. Name both. (saltwater taffy, Atlantic City)
19. Which state reaches from the Atlantic Ocean to the Great Lakes? (New York)
20. Name and location of the nation's first turnpike, which has turned into quite a moneymaking enterprise. (Pennsylvania Turnpike, Pennsylvania)
21. The most crowded state in the United States with nearly 1,000 people per square mile. (New Jersey)
22. While it is an area, you might mistakenly think it belongs on top of a salad. (Thousand Islands, New York)
23. A state whose nickname, Small Wonder, matches its size. (Delaware)
24. February 2 is a popular day for an animal and a town. Name both. (Punxsutawny Phil; Punxsutawny, Pennsylvania)
25. No, you're not seeing things, the blue hen chicken is this state's bird. (Delaware)
26. An ingenious human-made endeavor to link the Atlantic Ocean with the Great Lakes. (Erie Canal)
27. The birthplace of the oil industry. (Titusville, Pennsylvania)
28. A state that fits the definition of a peninsula. Explain what makes it so. (New Jersey is surrounded on three sides by water.)
29. Home of an amazing four-century-old oak called Wye Oak. (Wye Mills, Maryland)
30. Location of the ancient Cypress Swamp. Just what lives here anyway? (Trap Pond State Park near Laurel in southwest Delaware; cypress trees, rare plants and animals, numerous birds)

31. The only state to have an arc-shaped boundary. (Delaware)

BONUS: Winter home for over 3 million Canada geese. Can't you just hear them? (Maryland's wetlands in Chesapeake Bay)

9

The Appalachian Highlands: North Carolina, Virginia, West Virginia, Kentucky, and Tennessee

Dresden Quilt Graphic Organizer Worksheet

Directions

In the center circle of the quilt pattern, write down your main character. List three distinguishing characteristics about that character there as well. In the sixteen outer shapes, you are to write the geographic theme you will be touching upon, the setting of your book, a sequence of events that will move your story along, and an idea for the conclusion. This is just a planning sheet so keep thoughts simple. Identify each part on the outer edges of the pattern. You can use the back side of the sheet to elaborate on anything that will take more space.

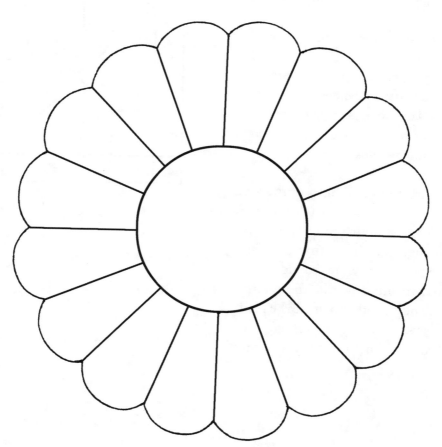

Book-Making Project

Materials

- lightweight cardboard like a file folder
- completed quilted cover with enough muslin to wrap around for the back of the book
- double-sided, iron-on adhesive like Wonder Under® or Stitch Witchery®
- white glue or rubber cement
- pencil, ruler, scissors
- paper to form the endpapers of the book (lightweight card stock works well, comes in a variety of colors, and can be purchased from copy stores; construction paper tends to tear after it has been bent by opening and closing the book frequently so it is not the best choice)
- fishing line, upholstery thread, or other heavy-duty light-colored thread for stitching the book together
- needles with large eyes for stitching the book together
- white typing paper, ditto paper, or larger paper for the pages of the book depending on the size of the book (as a guide, note that the paper will be folded in half before it is stitched into the book)

Note: Follow the directions and hints of the local quilter(s) who join your class to teach the basic steps of quilting. When planning the quilted cover, be sure to use enough muslin so that it is wide enough or long enough to wrap around a back cover of the book. In other words, the quilting will be on one half and the other half will be plain. If cotton batting is used under the quilting, run it under the entire cover so that the back is slightly padded, too.

Log Cabin Pattern

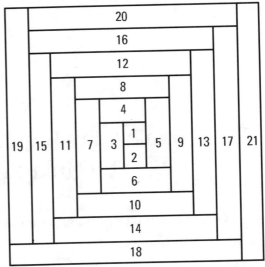

Fishtail Pattern

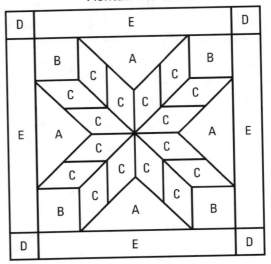

Spider Web Pattern

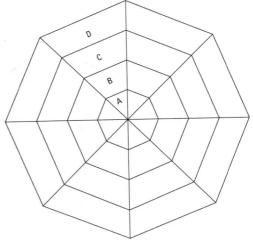

Grandmother's Fan Pattern

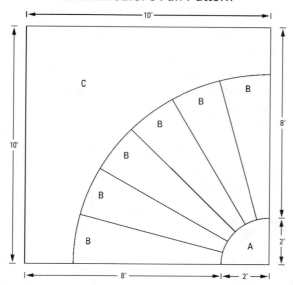

Directions

After quilting of the cover is completed, it is time to make the cover and to assemble the book. Note: The fabric cover is the largest in size, the file folder pieces fit inside of the fabric, and finally, the endpapers and book pages, stitched together, fit inside of that.

1. Measure the card stock to match the size of the pages in the book. Cut to the desired size. Eventually, it will be glued directly to the cardboard cover, holding the book in place.

2. After laying the book out in the dummy, count the number of pages that the finished book will be. Include title page, a dedication page, and a page at the end for a little information about the author.

3. Stack the inside pages on top of the card stock, which will serve as endpapers. Fold the pile in half and then open flat again. Remember that each half will count as one page.

4. With a ruler, place five dots evenly spaced down the center fold of the top piece of paper. With the help of a partner, poke holes through the pile. If $8\frac{1}{2}$-by-11 typing paper is used, the holes with be $\frac{7}{16}$ of an inch

apart. The partner will hold the pages firmly while the other person uses a large open safety pin, a small awl, or a pushpin from a bulletin board to poke the holes.

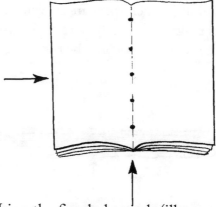

5. Using the five-hole stitch (illustrated), stitch the pages together as the partner holds them firmly together. Set this part of the book aside.

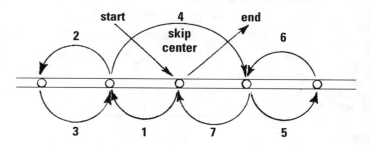

6. Cut the file folder into two pieces. The cover should be $\frac{1}{2}$ inch larger than the inside pages of the book. When the two pieces are put on top of the fabric, leave about $\frac{1}{4}$ inch space between them down the center. This will enable the book to open and close easily.

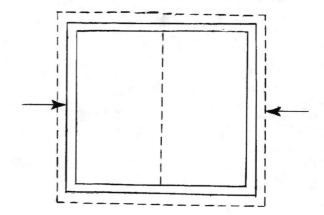

7. If double-sided, iron-on adhesive is used, cut it to the same size as the fabric, larger than the cardboard. Place it between the back side of the quilted cover and batting. Center the two pieces of cardboard on top of this, leaving that $1/4$-inch space in the center. Parents may want to help here as the ironing melts the adhesive, holding the layers together.

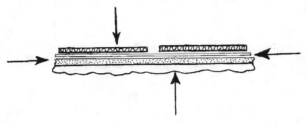

8. As the layers are ironed to the cardboard, fold the edges over the cover, not the book pages, as shown in the diagram. The corners are turned over diagonally and the edges are folded over along the sides and ironed into place.

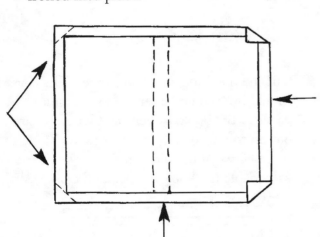

9. Open the cover so that is lies flat on the table. Put glue or rubber cement of the backs of each end page and glue the inside of the book to the back side of the cover. If ribbon is to be used to tie the book together, the ribbons should be glued in at this point. Center each piece of ribbon at the outside edge of the cover between the card stock and cover and glue firmly into place.

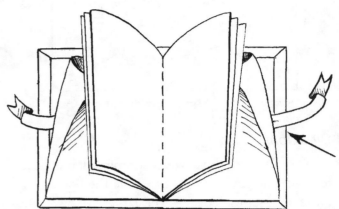

10. Once the book is dry, it is time to neatly transfer the story into it. Another option is to make the inside of the book, write the story and do the illustrations in it, and then glue it into the cover when it is done.

Checklist for Book Project

Before handing your completed book in, go through the following checklist to be certain all steps have been completed.

The option for my story is:

___ The graphic organizer has been completed and reviewed by the teacher.

___ I have included at least one of the five geographic themes in my story.

___ I have completed the necessary careful research for my story.

___ My story has been edited according to classroom procedures and polished to perfection.

___ I have completed my quilt cover as neatly and carefully as I can.

___ The dummy of my book has been completed and discussed with the teacher before working on the final copy of the book.

___ I have constructed my book.

___ On the back of the cover, I have written the name of the quilt pattern I used and several sentences about the history of the pattern.

___ I have transferred my story and illustrations into my constructed book.

___ I plan to celebrate my book and being an author by _____.

Index